ALSO BY GLENN BECK

Conform: Exposing the Truth about Common Core and Public Education

The Eye of Moloch

Control: Exposing the Truth about Guns

Agenda 21

Cowards: What Politicians, Radicals, and the Media Refuse to Say

*Being George Washington: The Indispensable Man,
as You've Never Seen Him*

The Snow Angel

*The Original Argument: The Federalists' Case for
the Constitution, Adapted for the 21st Century*

The 7: Seven Wonders That Will Change Your Life

Broke: The Plan to Restore Our Trust, Truth and Treasure

The Overton Window

Idiots Unplugged: Truth for Those Who Care to Listen (audiobook)

The Christmas Sweater: A Picture Book

Arguing with Idiots: How to Stop Small Minds and Big Government

*Glenn Beck's Common Sense: The Case Against an Out-
of-Control Government, Inspired by Thomas Paine*

*America's March to Socialism: Why We're One Step
Closer to Giant Missile Parades* (audiobook)

The Christmas Sweater

An Inconvenient Book: Real Solutions to the World's Biggest Problems

The Real America: Early Writings from the Heart and Heartland

MIRACLES AND

True and Untold Stories

WRITERS:
James Best, Jack Henderson, David Pietrusza,
Anthony J. Tata, Jason Wright

CONTRIBUTORS, RESEARCHERS & EDITORS:
Keith Malinak, Kevin Smith, Martha Weeks

WRITTEN & EDITED BY:

GLENN BECK

WITH KEVIN BALFE
AND HANNAH BECK

MASSACRES

of the Making of America

Threshold Editions

Mercury Radio Arts

New York London Toronto Sydney New Delhi

Threshold Editions / Mercury Radio Arts
A Division of Simon & Schuster, Inc.
1230 Avenue of the Americas
New York, NY 10020

First Threshold Editions/Mercury Radio Arts paperback edition August 2014

THRESHOLD EDITIONS and colophon are trademarks of Simon & Schuster, Inc.

GLENN BECK is a trademark of Mercury Radio Arts, Inc.

For information about special discounts for bulk purchases,
please contact Simon & Schuster Special Sales at 1-866-506-1949
or business@simonandschuster.com.

The Simon & Schuster Speakers Bureau can bring authors to
your live event. For more information or to book an event, contact
the Simon & Schuster Speakers Bureau at 866-248-3049 or
visit our website at www.simonspeakers.com.

Interior design by Ruth Lee-Mui

Manufactured in the United States of America

10 9 8 7 6 5 4 3 2 1

Library of Congress Cataloging-in-Publication Data
Beck, Glenn.
  Miracles and massacres : true and untold stories of the making of America / Glenn
Beck.—First Threshold Editions/Mercury Radio Arts hardcover edition.
  pages cm
1. United States—History—Anecdotes. 2. United States—Biography—Anecdotes.
  I. Title.
  E178.6.B43 2013
  973—dc23   2013034043

ISBN 978-1-4767-6474-0
ISBN 978-1-4767-7120-5 (pbk)
ISBN 978-1-4767-6475-7 (ebook)

Dedication

*To the man in Preston, Idaho, who stood and asked me when
I would start "writing history as stories to make them more interesting";*

*To the congressman who stopped himself in the middle of telling me
that the history elitists wouldn't like it if I make history entertaining;*

*And to my son, Raphe, who has curled up next to me to read
great American stories, giving me memories I will never forget.*

Contents

Author's Note

There are many great history books (and many more that are not so great) that cover American history. Some focus on just one story, one event, one decade, or one era. Others take a broader view and try to cover it all, from Christopher Columbus to President Obama.

As I began looking through some of these books, two things struck me: First, most of them are about as exciting as an Al Gore speech; and second, none of them leave readers understanding just how complex and nuanced our history really is. My goal in writing this book was to solve both of those problems.

I'm a huge history nerd, but I don't study the past so that I can memorize dates or names to pass a test; I do it because I love the stories. Ultimately, that's what history really is: an ongoing story that is far more exciting than anything a Hollywood screenwriter could ever come up with. I tried to embrace that in this book by writing history in a way that feels like you're reading a thriller novel rather than a history book. By immersing you in the action I believe you'll come to see people and events in a much more vivid and real way than you ever have before. (When you're finished, I urge you to read the section "About the Writing of This Book" so you can get a better sense for the writing and research process involved.)

The next challenge with this project was how to choose the right stories. As I searched (and reviewed the thousands of submissions that came in from fans), I adhered to a few guiding principles. I wanted to find stories that:

1. Were lesser known, or that could be told in a brand-new way;
2. Had a clear message or lesson that was relevant to today;
3. Acknowledged that our history is not all heroes—there were plenty of villains as well.

It's that last point that I want to dwell on for a moment, because I think this is where so many other books go wrong. America is *not* a bad or evil country—we truly are an exceptional nation with a miraculous past. In less than 250 years we went from being subjects of a king to being the greatest, most compassionate superpower the world has ever known.

Along the way, however, we've made plenty of mistakes. Ignoring them, or worse, covering them up, is not only ignorant, it's dangerous. A country that does not learn from its history is doomed to repeat it.

That's why stories like the Battle of Wounded Knee, the My Lai massacre, and Tokyo Rose are in this book. They are stories about times when America was not at her best. By studying them, talking about them, and, ultimately, learning from them, it's my hope that we will never make the same mistakes again.

Of course, our history is full of great accomplishments as well—people and events that have influenced and inspired us and changed America forever. The rest of the stories were chosen to remind us where we've come from and the lessons we've learned along the way. The first Barbary War, for example, gave America a glimpse at the ruthlessness and brutality of Muslim jihadists. The ensuing wars shaped our future foreign policy by teaching us that you don't negotiate with terrorists and that lasting peace can come only through strength. The Battle of Athens, Tennessee, reminds us about the importance of standing up for our rights and the rule of law—especially when it's those we've entrusted with power who are at fault.

Then there are the stories that exemplify the American spirit: the courage and selflessness of Jack Jouett; the heroism of Hugh Thompson and Jose Melendez-Perez; and the redemption sought by Al Capone's lawyer, "Easy" Eddie. Taken as a whole, the twelve stories in this book represent the full American experience: the miracles, the massacres, and all of the gray area in between.

After this book was finished, I finally sat back and had a chance to read all the stories together. It was only then that I realized that all of them can be put into one of three categories: The good guys win; the good guys win, but it takes a while; or the good guys lose because people put their trust into politicians instead of each other.

I hope that the stories in that final category—the German Saboteurs and the Battle of Wounded Knee, for example—remind people why we should rely on ourselves, our neighbors, and our God, but never on our government.

Laos Deo,

Jack Jouett:
The Ride That Saved America

Albemarle County, Virginia
June 3, 1781
10 :15 P.M.

A thin dogwood branch slashed across the rider's face like a leather whip. But the sting was no worse than any of the dozen that came before. A quarter mile earlier, a limb had cut him so deeply that blood flowed from a gash high on his cheek to the corner of his mouth.

Captain John "Jack" Jouett rode on.

With forty miles to go, the muscular twenty-six-year-old sliced through the night and gave thanks for the full moon. It could not protect his face or clothes, but it might safely deliver him and his bay mare Sallie to the green lawns of Thomas Jefferson's beloved and now-endangered Monticello estate.

It was possible, Jouett knew, that the future of the revolution might very well depend on how fast he got there.

The Cuckoo Tavern
Louisa, Virginia
One Hour Earlier

Jack Jouett had decided to live dangerously.

The British army was on the march in Virginia—even that damnable traitor Benedict Arnold had been assigned there—and Jouett had been lucky enough to capture one of Arnold's men. He might have been content to simply turn the man over to army jailers, but a daring idea had seized him. Jouett's captive was an unusually big man, roughly his own size. "Off with your clothes!" Jouett ordered him.

The prisoner's brilliant red coat festooned with equally grand gold braid fit him as though it had been tailored just for his six-foot-four-inch frame. The grand plumed hat only added to the picture. Now dressed as his enemy, Jack Jouett mounted his steed Sallie—said to be the best bred and fleetest of foot in seven counties—and hurried off to see if he might find more of the enemy. The British were up to no good, and Jouett wanted to know exactly what that might be.

Not long after riding off in his new attire, Jouett quickly stumbled across the British in the form of a fearsome detachment of Green Dragoons near the local tavern. He rode up cautiously, worried that someone might willingly or accidentally reveal his true identity. Jack Jouett was playing a very dangerous game.

A stranger wiped sweat from his unshaven face with his soiled coat sleeve as he passed Jouett outside the tavern doors. "Captain, do something about this dreadful June air, would you?" The man laughed over his shoulder and slyly shouted, "What's a soldier of the king for if not to fight for better weather?"

Jouett wasn't sure if he had been recognized but he certainly wasn't about to ask. In any case, he remained outdoors, enjoying what passed for a breeze. Sallie whinnied from her hitching post. "I know, Sallie. I know."

Jouett pretended to be absorbed in his own thoughts while he tended to his steed, but as more tavern patrons came and went, he eavesdropped on their conversations. Today, with British cavalry loitering just outside the Cuckoo, the locals were more guarded than usual. Jouett listened in to their still-energetic discussions, which became more energetic and less guarded with each draft of hard cider or flagon of rum. They soon veered toward politics. "The stubborn boys in Maryland came around," a patron shouted atop the noise. "Did you hear they finally signed the Articles?"

"I suppose every man—and colony!—has their price," belted another.

A feisty argument erupted over Maryland and Virginia's simmering land-rights feud and Maryland's long-delayed ratification of the Articles of Confederation. The Second Continental Congress had become the Confederation Congress three months earlier, but most people still didn't know quite what to call their fledgling government.

The discussion turned to Thomas Jefferson and the impending end of his tenure as Virginia's governor. "He's in mourning!" one patron loudly guffawed. Another pointed out that, for several days, there might be no governor. "Appoint me!" slurred a man hunched over the bar, his gnarled fist firmly hugging his precious pewter mug.

But none of this, of course, was Jack Jouett's real interest. He was there to hear what foes, not friends, might reveal. So far, he had heard nothing to justify risking the noose. Perhaps, he thought, it was time to call a halt to this perilous adventure and just ride away.

Suddenly, Sallie again called out and skittishly pulled her rope taut. Jouett moved to provide her with more water. As he bent down something caught his ear. He wasn't sure, but . . .

Right before him was the infamous Colonel Banastre Tarleton, commander of the Dragoons—one of the most hated of all the new nation's foes. Sallie had always been a good judge of bad character.

Jouett had difficulty making out exactly what Tarleton said. Fearing to advance any closer toward the colonel, he strained to catch whatever information he could. The words were soft and the background noise made it difficult to hear clearly, but Jouett was able to understand two words clearly: *Monticello* and *Charlottesville*.

That was all he needed to know.

Near Cuckoo Tavern
10:30 P.M.

Colonel Banastre Tarleton's uniform clung to his chest like a wet wool blanket. Like most British soldiers fighting the war, Tarleton believed the only thing worse than the insects and thick Virginia humidity was the morale of both America's people and Washington's army. The would-be nation's independence hung by a thread in the early summer days of 1781 and Tarleton lusted to sever it with his saber.

General George Washington knew that the soldiers' grievances against their officers and the Continental Congress over supply shortages and pay were legitimate. He'd experienced deplorable conditions and supply problems himself during a brutal winter in Valley Forge just three years earlier. He knew what shoeless, bleeding, frozen feet and empty stomachs did to a patriot's mind.

Tarleton and his fellow British commanders were well aware of the festering discontent that racked the Continental camp. It was their job to stir the pot and hope that discontent would boil over into chaos— and, so far, that job was going very well. The most important year of the war had begun with the New Year's Day mutiny in the ranks of the Pennsylvania Continentals.

It was no secret that many of the Pennsylvanians had been unpaid since receiving the twenty-dollar bounty bestowed for their three-year enlistments. Tired and angry, with their families facing destitution back home without them, they were ready to walk away from the front lines and return to their loved ones. Meanwhile, other colonies were enticing men with much larger sums, as high as one thousand dollars in neighboring New Jersey. General Washington and his officers did their best to prevent defections to the British, but Tarleton and his allies schemed at every turn to lure them away with fortune and impressive military appointments. With this strategy, they hoped to break the American spirit and finally deliver victory for the king and Parliament.

Washington, however, was intelligent enough to know that additional pay alone wouldn't solve the problem. What good was another twenty dollars when you had no musket balls or powder and wore the same ragged, lice-infested uniforms for weeks on end? Washington recognized what the British already knew and were capitalizing on: his men couldn't fight both the Royal Army and such insufferable conditions for much longer.

Alerted to the mutiny among the Pennsylvania Line, Washington stood with his men and demanded that additional resources be provided. After negotiations—and despite the British using the uprising to further hunt for Loyalists among the disenchanted American soldiers— the episode ended peacefully and the vast majority of soldiers were back in the fight within weeks.

Tarleton was impressed by such loyalty, even to a cause he considered disloyal. But, to his great delight, a mutiny in the New Jersey Line just a few weeks later ended quite differently.

Washington had quickly realized that the Pennsylvania Line's mutiny would only inspire other disgruntled troops to demand similar concessions. He needed to send an important, possibly war-saving message to the whole army: mutinies would not be tolerated. He quickly stamped out New Jersey's insurgency and court-martialed its ringleaders. Two were executed. All twelve members of the firing squad had also participated in the mutiny. George Washington, when he had to, could play very rough indeed.

Though he liked little about Americans in general, Tarleton secretly admired Washington's aggressive tactics to quell the insurrection. If given the chance, Tarleton would have done the same thing with his own men—though he would have liked to carry out the executions himself. Unlike some of his colleagues, he liked to get his hands dirty.

Attired in a bright white coat and high black boots polished to a shine as bright as the Virginia sun, Colonel Tarleton now watched two men stumble out of Cuckoo Tavern and exchange whiskey-weakened blows. "Such unlicked cubs," he muttered to himself.

Then, without a word, he pointed with his saber west up the road and his two hundred Dragoons fell in line behind him.

Backwoods Trails to Monticello
11:45 P.M.

Snap!

Another branch punished Jouett's forehead, but the rider knew his wounds and shredded clothing would have to wait. Plus, with Tarleton and his Green Dragoons headed west on the only main road to Monticello, Jouett knew that the mountain trails and back roads overgrown with dense thickets were his only hope for beating the British to Thomas Jefferson's front door.

Sallie stumbled to her side and Jouett hung on tight to keep his massive frame upright. His mind wandered, to images of Jefferson and members of the Virginia legislature gathered in the safety of the governor's famous retreat on the outskirts of Charlottesville. The great patriot Patrick Henry was there. So were Benjamin Harrison, Richard Henry Lee, and Thomas Nelson—each of them signers of the Declaration of Independence. They'd all fled Richmond and the red-hot pursuit of British general Charles Cornwallis as the war had moved south.

Even the most intoxicated patron at Cuckoo Tavern that night would have understood that the men atop the mountain at Monticello were in great danger. Relatively peaceful conditions in Virginia had sent the majority of its best fighting men northward. The local militia, though spirited and anxious to break free from British tyranny, were too few and without enough resources to battle the brutal Tarleton.

We have Jefferson!

Jouett's imagination heard the words burn across the hills and directly to the ears of General Cornwallis. He knew it wouldn't be long before news of Jefferson's capture—or, he shivered at the thought, *death*—would sail across the seas to the king. It would be shorter still until word spread among the colonies that the British had taken the author of their Declaration of Independence. What then? Morale and optimism were already in short supply. The capture of patriots like Jefferson, Henry, and Lee might just be more than the fragile army could handle.

More voices found audience in Jouett's mind:

We have them all!

Virginia is ours!

One signer, two signers, three signers, four! Hanging from the gallows, traitors no more!

Jouett knew the lives of important men weren't the only jewels at stake if Tarleton's infamous butchers successfully took Charlottesville and Monticello. Both the city and the mansion that overlooked it held gold, silver, and something even more valuable: information. The patriots gathered at Jefferson's estate would surely be discussing war plans and coordination with their top Virginia spies. If Tarleton and his Dragoons succeeded they could ride off with men, maps, and even letters. Perhaps, Jouett allowed himself to wonder, sensitive correspondence to General Washington himself.

He drove his heels into Sallie's sides and urged her to gallop even faster.

Plantation Near the Louisa County Courthouse
June 4, 1781
12 :15 A.M.

"The men and horses need a pause." One of Tarleton's lieutenants had approached him to deliver the news.

Unaware that Jouett was dashing ahead via the backwoods trails to Monticello, Tarleton and his men rested for several hours at a large plantation near the Louisa Court House. Tarleton sat near at his own private fire at the edge of camp, satisfied that they'd ridden that night with duty and purpose, if not breathless urgency.

Weeks earlier, General Cornwallis had been provided with an intercepted dispatch revealing that Thomas Jefferson and members of the Virginia legislature had convened in Charlottesville. Cornwallis assigned the task of tracking and capturing Jefferson to Colonel Tarleton, an officer Cornwallis admired for his athleticism, strength, and daring. For better and sometimes, Cornwallis knew, for worse, Tarleton was known for impatience in battle.

Tarleton had found great personal satisfaction and public acclaim for early-war success in raids carried out in New York, Pennsylvania, and New Jersey. When the war moved south, Tarleton added to his fearsome reputation at the battles of Cowpens, Blackstocks, Fishing Creek, Camden, Monck's Corner, and Charleston. But it was at Waxhaws, South Carolina, that his legacy had finally been sealed. There Tarleton attacked the unprepared Continental Army with a vengeance and overwhelmed them. With surrender the Americans' only option, Tarleton coldly ignored their white flag and allowed his troops to butcher as many patriot soldiers as they could. More than one hundred Continentals died and another two hundred were injured or captured.

"Sir, may I?" One of the younger British Dragoons approached Tarleton at the fire's edge as the other men rested to prepare for the rest of the ride to Monticello.

Tarleton nodded without looking up, and the two men sat in silence for a long time. "Did you know I was just twenty-three years of age when promoted to lieutenant colonel of the British Legion?" Tarleton finally asked.

"I did not," the young soldier said.

Tarleton looked at him. "But they say my legend is even older than I am." For the next half hour the leader of the Dragoons spoke in the third person, painting himself as a rare breed who was simultaneously fearless and feared by others.

"Colonel Banastre Tarleton doesn't desire acclaim from the throne for his courage alone, but also for his genius. Our gracious Royal does not always appreciate a soldier whose mind is as sharp as his sword."

After another round of silence, the young soldier finally mustered up the courage to voice the question he'd come over to ask. "So is it true? About the names they use for you?"

Tarleton smiled, knowing he'd earned his monikers honestly. "You refer to 'Butcher Man' and 'Bloody Tarleton,' I assume?"

The soldier nodded.

"I am, indeed, more hated by the traitors than most of our countrymen. Some of the things they say I've done are true. Some are not. But Colonel Banastre Tarleton does not choose to quarrel with the differences." He paused to stifle a little chuckle—one tinged more with cruelty than wit.

Tarleton poked the fire and a dozen embers raced up into the night sky. "They say that to ask you," he pointed to the soldier, "and my other Green Dragoons for surrender is futile. I hear they now call it 'Tarleton Quarter.' "

The soldier sat motionless as Tarleton described how the enemy had turned the phrase back on the Legion. When encountering surrendering British troops, the Colonials took no mercy. Hardly offended, Tarleton told the young man and several others who'd now gathered at the fire that he took pride in the enemy adopting the term and tactic. "Imitation, after all, is the greatest form of flattery."

The dragoon laughed nervously until Tarleton pulled him up short with an order, raising his thunderous shout so that all around him might hear. "Now, let us show them through action whether the words they say about Banastre Tarleton are indeed true. To Charlottesville!"

Several miles up the road from where they'd rested, Colonel Tarleton came across a caravan of twelve American supply wagons with clothing and arms headed for South Carolina. He took great pleasure in burning it.

As flames filled the Piedmont sky, Tarleton hoped the winds would move the thick smoke away from Monticello. He wondered aloud to a lieutenant whether Jefferson's servants would be taking turns throughout the night watching guard. Or perhaps Jefferson thought the grounds of his cherished Monticello provided ignorant, blissful security. "Let them sleep," he said, watching another supply wagon smolder.

Soon after daybreak, Tarleton and his soldiers stopped at Castle Hill, home of Dr. Thomas Walker, who had once been guardian to the young, orphaned Thomas Jefferson. Tarleton arrested two legislators in their nightshirts and grinned at the thought that the day's successes had only just begun. Before leaving Walker's large estate, Tarleton ordered Dr. Walker and his wife to prepare a breakfast for the hungry British Legion. With full stomachs and renewed vigor, Tarleton and his Dragoons resumed their race toward Charlottesville. But his full belly came at a high price: the cost of precious time lost in the pursuit of his great prize, Thomas Jefferson.

Thomas Jefferson's Monticello Estate
4:30 A.M.

"Faster, Sallie!" Jouett flashed through the final line of trees and across the meadow in front of Monticello. "Go!" Moments later he leapt from the horse and, without bothering to hitch her, sprinted down the brick path to the front door of Jefferson's home.

"Arise! Arise!" Jouett pounded on the heavy door just before sunrise. "Bloody Tarleton and his Green Dragoons are not far behind!"

A servant appeared and rushed Jouett into the home, where Jefferson met them in the spacious front hall. "What is it?" Jefferson demanded, adjusting his silken night robe as he entered. But his concern for his own disheveled appearance vanished at the sight of the bloody and battered Jouett. "My Lord, what is it? You've escaped capture?"

"No, sir," gasped Jefferson's visitor. "I'm Captain Jack Jouett. Sixteenth regiment of the Virginia militia."

"Of course."

"Governor, a large force of British is approaching Charlottesville. They're led by Tarleton!"

"Are you sure?"

"I am."

"How many in his command?" Jefferson asked, his manner growing more grave with each syllable.

"Two hundred, maybe more. Most of them Green Dragoons."

"Have they arrived in town?" Jefferson asked as his houseguests, woken by the commotion, began arriving in the hall.

"I cannot say. I've ridden through the night from Louisa on back trails and they're moving on the main road."

Jefferson extended a hand to Jouett and took closer notice of his torn clothes and scratched, bruised face. "Well done." He turned to a servant. "When the soldiers arrive, raise the flag over the dome. Retract it only when they've left and it's safe to return." He pivoted to his houseguests and announced with authority, "Gentlemen, let us secure our belongings quickly and depart."

As the others dressed, Jefferson calmly ate breakfast, sorted through sensitive state papers crucial for the success or failure of the revolution, and gathered his wife and children to be sent twenty miles to the west. There they would take refuge at the Enniscorthy Plantation, home of his friend and business associate Colonel John Coles.

Jefferson had not a moment to spare as Tarleton's crack cavalrymen and Royal Welsh mounted infantry began to invade the grounds of his estate. But even under the intense pressure, he could not forgo his pronounced sense of southern hospitality. "A glass of madeira, Captain Jouett?" Jefferson asked.

"Yes, Governor," answered Jouett with a smile. "I think I could use one right about now."

Soon the preparations were complete.

"God bless Charlottesville," Jefferson whispered before mounting the horse that had been saddled for him. The governor looked at his home one last time before kicking the stallion and riding up nearby Carter's Mountain. As he did, enemy horsemen clattered through his front door, riding through the entire depth of his great mansion—and out the back.

And God bless Jack Jouett.

At a safe distance from the advancing Dragoons, Jefferson stopped for one last look at his beloved Monticello—and sadly watched as a flag of occupation was raised over its stately dome.

Swan Tavern
Charlottesville, Virginia
9 :00 A.M.

As Jefferson and the other legislators fled, Jouett rode furiously to his father's inn. He burst through the front door, with the sight of his crimson British uniform startling the elder Jouett, who soon recovered his senses, however, and the two embraced. Quickly, Jack warned him and the several Virginia legislators he sheltered to flee for Staunton, in Virginia's Shenandoah Valley.

He relayed the prior evening's ride and his father's eyes gleamed with pride, for John Jouett Sr. was as great a patriot as his son. He had risked his life to sign the crucial Albemarle Declaration of 1779, which supported independence; provided beef for Continental armies; had two other sons in George Washington's service; and had lost a fourth son at the 1777 Battle of Brandywine.

When the young captain finished, the elder Jouett told him, "Your work isn't done yet, son. General Edward Stevens is here and he's wounded in the thigh. He was hit at Guilford Court House in North Carolina and is still too unsteady to run. He's healing, but not yet strong enough, I fear, to survive a chase."

Jouett knew that Tarleton's potential capture of Stevens, who was also a state senator, would fuel British confidence. The general's lack of mobility was a problem, but he had a plan. With his father's help, Jouett assembled a small militia to meet the British at the river. Then they disguised the general in a shabby cloak and helped him mount a borrowed horse.

Meanwhile, Jack Jouett dressed himself in a clean blue Continental uniform and made off in the other direction aboard Sallie. He was barely finished and mounted when the British began to close in. Tarleton and his men soon spotted Jouett, whom they correctly assumed to be an American officer, and gave frantic chase, ignoring Edwards entirely.

Jouett led the British on a winding pursuit through the woods, smiling all the way. Just as his all-night ride had allowed Jefferson to escape, this midmorning ride would do the same for General Stevens.

When the exhausted British finally gave up, Jouett stopped to let his horse drink from a creek not far from where he'd started the previous night at Cuckoo Tavern. Jouett took a long drink, too, letting the cool water run down his neck and into his uniform.

A breeze kissed the trees and his faithful horse gave a grateful whinny.

"I know, Sallie. I know."

EPILOGUE

Colonel Tarleton had arrived in Charlottesville not long after Jouett had come through to warn its citizens. Tarleton and his men destroyed goods and uniforms, along with hundreds of muskets and barrels of gunpowder. They also freed a number of prisoners and captured seven remaining assemblymen, including Daniel Boone. All were later released unharmed.

When the Virginia legislature reconvened in Staunton three days later, they voted to reward Jouett's heroics with an elegant sword and a pair of pistols. They recognized immediately what many others would not learn for days, months, years, or, perhaps, ever: Jack Jouett's courageous ride may have saved not only Jefferson and a slew of other patriots, but also the very country they were so desperately fighting to free.

Later that year, in October 1781, Lieutenant General Lord Charles Cornwallis found himself outwitted and surrounded at Yorktown. Brigadier General Edward Stevens, whose life Jouett very well may have saved, led the Third Brigade—750 men—during the battle.

Cornwallis's surrender at Yorktown effectively ended the revolution that, if not for Jack Jouett, the "Paul Revere of the South," and his incredible ride four months earlier, might have been lost.

2

Shays' Rebellion:
A Loud and Solemn Lesson

Mount Vernon
Fairfax County, Virginia
October 12, 1785

"I'll ride out to the front gate with you, James," George Washington said to his young visitor upon the end of his three-day visit.

"Oh, you don't have to do that, sir," answered thirty-four-year-old James Madison. But the look on Washington's face indicated that this offer wasn't simply a courtesy; his host had something more to say.

Madison, returning to his beloved Virginia from official business in Philadelphia and New York, had stopped at Mount Vernon to consult with Washington—and to vent his frustrations. The nation, the Confederation, was falling apart. The states could not agree on anything, be it taxes, a common defense, or trade either with foreign nations or among themselves. They were not so much a patchwork quilt of pieces sewn together, but thirteen shards of jagged glass, lying haphazardly upon the ground, ready to cut anyone foolish enough to try to reassemble them.

Before his visit, Madison had strongly suspected that Washington shared his concerns.

Now, Madison *knew* he did.

Riding out to Mount Vernon's front gate, Washington fumed once more that a stronger national government was essential to protect everything the revolution had been fought for. Madison nodded silently in agreement, his small hand firmly on his large traveling carpetbag.

The carriage reached the gate and came to a sharp halt. Washington, limber for his fifty-three years, jumped out. Rather than saying good-bye to Madison, he instead handed him a copy of Noah Webster's new pamphlet advocating a strong national government. "Read this," he counseled. "We are either a united people, or we are not. If the former, let us, in all matters of general concern, act as a nation. If we are not, let us no longer act a farce by pretending it."

George Washington's greatest fear was that these United States would fall apart. He worried that individual states would not be able to preserve their own internal order, private property rights, or the validity of their contracts. He worried about lawlessness, anarchy, and chaos taking root in one state and then spreading across the country.

As Washington bade farewell to Madison on that crisp autumn evening, he had no way of knowing that those fears were less than one year away from becoming reality.

The Hancock Manor
30 Beacon Street
Boston, Massachusetts
Nine months earlier: January 27, 1785

"Well, there you have it!" the tall, slim man exclaimed as he finished affixing his grand, sprawling signature to the official document before him.

Though that signature read "John Hancock," the document was not the Declaration of Independence, nor was the place Philadelphia, or the date July 4, 1776. Instead, it was nearly a decade later, and the Honorable John Hancock, looking far older than his forty-nine years, sat at a desk in Boston's Beacon Hill and made his resignation as governor of Massachusetts official.

"That's it!" he added for emphasis, hobbling toward the door on his gout-ridden foot. "Time to rest and get well. This body is simply worn out from service to its country. And, I suppose, service to a few other things as well!"

Everyone in the commonwealth knew very well of John Hancock's pronounced taste for the finer things in life. Some suspected, however, that it wasn't really gout or illness that plagued John Hancock, but rather the events occurring in Massachusetts' rural, western areas. Farmers and townsfolk alike were angry. Personal bankruptcy cases overwhelmed the courts. Massachusetts' state government suffered from massive debt, and its legislature, the General Court, had drastically raised property and poll taxes to pay it off.

"I wish I had gout!" Lieutenant Governor Thomas Cushing retorted. But instead of gout, Cushing now had, at least temporarily, the governorship—and all of the problems that came along with it.

"Yes, I hear you, Mr. Cushing," Hancock answered. "There's an anger out there. And it's been brewing for years. Where will it end?" Hancock shook his head. *Was the revolution really fought for this mess?*

"I don't blame them. Not entirely, anyway," he continued. "The new taxes go to pay off the bonds issued during the war. But who gets the money? Not the patriots who originally bought the bonds to help secure our liberty. Or the officers and men who bled at Lexington or Concord and kept fighting on through Yorktown. No, it's the speculators who bought the paper for pennies on the dollar. They own the bonds—and now they own the citizens of this fine commonwealth as well."

Hampshire County Convention
Hatfield, Massachusetts
Nineteen months later: August 24, 1786

"Then, it's agreed!"

"Of course, it's agreed!" came the impatient retort. "We have been here for three days and we know what we want!"

This was an unruly group, with representatives from fifty towns located in western Massachusetts' Hampshire County. They had aired their grievances and now had to present a united front against the state government in Boston. But deciding on exactly what that unified front would be was proving difficult.

Many of the men at the meeting were battle-hardened veterans of the Continental Army. One of them, Colonel Benjamin Bonney, was also acting as the meeting's chair. "So it's settled, then," Bonney said. "We will send the petition to the General Court and to Governor Bowdoin."

"Governor Bowdoin!" The name was shouted by a man in the back of the room; the words spat out as if it were Lucifer's name itself. "That's a waste of good Massachusetts paper! Our esteemed new governor, as we all know, is one of the biggest bondholders in the entire commonwealth. It is for him and his kind that we are bled white with taxes—so he and his Boston friends can be paid as much and as soon as possible. Yes, by all means, send our petition to King James Bowdoin—it will be fun to watch him use the paper to tally how much our taxes will increase next."

"Tell 'em! Tell 'em!" came a rum-soaked exclamation from a young man in a threadbare coat and torn knee breeches. "Tell 'em we can't afford to pay neither debts nor taxes. We want—we *need*—paper money printed and accepted for all transactions! We want no more of our money shipped to the Continental Congress! Tell 'em loud and clear: 'To blazes with the Senate and the courts and lawyers!' "

"Yes, we will tell them all of that," Colonel Bonney reassured him. "That's what we have agreed to by the vote of all free men present."

"And, one more thing!" came a Scotch-Irish burr-tinged demand from a man seated to Bonney's right. "We want our demands dispatched to the conventions meeting at Worcester and Lenox as well. They'll be very glad to hear that we Hampshire County men stand strong for our liberties."

"Agreed, Captain Shays," answered Colonel Bonney. "Couriers will leave in the morrow."

And with that, Daniel Shays, a resident of nearby Pelham, tapped the residue from his simple clay pipe and took comfort in the thought that the common people—he among them—were finally standing up to the wealthy merchants and lawyers of Boston town.

Court of Common Pleas
Hampshire County Courthouse
Northampton, Massachusetts
August 29, 1786

Captain Daniel Shays had not originally cared much for protest. But now, as he stood before Northampton's Hampshire County Court-house and pondered the accelerating tumult around him, he quickly reconsidered that position.

Shays was approaching forty years of age and he looked every bit of it. He had been born poor, and life had not done much better by him. The little land he owned called for endless, backbreaking work and seemed to result in nothing but an increasing pocketful of debts.

Shays had earned his fine title of "captain" during the revolution, fighting at Saratoga, Bunker Hill, Lexington, and Stony Point—the last engagement under the great Marquis de Lafayette, who had bestowed upon him an elegant gold-handled sword. Shays was, by all accounts, a good soldier, but there were some things about him that rankled his fellow officers. For one thing, he had received his commission for hav-ing recruited the private soldiers who served under him, not for any actual battlefield merit. There was also the matter of that sword. Any other patriot would have treasured it, but Shays had quickly sold it to pay a twelve-dollar debt.

And there was one other thing that bothered some of the other offi-cers: in 1780, when pay had run short and morale had run low, many—too many—of George Washington's officers ingloriously departed for home.

Captain Daniel Shays was among them.

Five hundred men marched on Northampton from Daniel Shays' hometown of Pelham. Another column of men, led by Captain Joel Billings, approached from Amherst. Hundreds more swaggered north from West Springfield under the leadership of Captain Luke Day, another veteran of Lexington. Still more rough-and-ready protesters streamed in from the hill towns to the west. They sported sprigs of green hemlock in their battered hats, carried flags, and marched to the sound of fifes and the threatening beat of drums. Some came outfitted with swords and flintlock muskets; others were armed with just sticks and bludgeons. But this was a real army—at least as real as the one that had appeared in Lexington in April 1775—and look what they had accomplished.

In all, fifteen hundred men had descended upon Northampton's courthouse, where Hampshire County's Court of Common Pleas was scheduled to be in session that morning. The sheer size of the crowd made it difficult for the three bewigged, black-robed justices and their clerk to enter the courthouse. "Allow us in," Judge Eleazar Porter demanded. Derisive laughter rang through the crowd. "You might care to rethink that request, your honor," snapped Captain Luke Day. "It looks like the people have a different idea about who's meeting where and when from now on." Day liked talking as much as he liked soldiering.

The three judges nervously conferred. After agreeing that there was no way they could force their way through this jostling, threatening mob, they retreated to a nearby inn. No cases would be heard today and no debtors or tax delinquents arraigned. Soon these judges would mount their steeds and make the wisest decision possible—to ride out of town.

It wasn't until midnight that the mobbers finally departed from Northampton's courthouse. They were tired but emboldened, and their actions had ignited a spark that would lead to an explosion in Pelham and, eventually, in all of western Massachusetts.

Daniel Shays' Farmhouse
Pelham, Massachusetts
August 30, 1786

If Daniel Shays was concerned about changing his reputation, he had a funny way of doing it. The previous morning his neighbors had asked him to lead them on their march to Northampton. He refused. Fifty-year-old Deacon John Thompson took command in his place.

But, now, after a night of rest and some deep thinking, Shays was having second—and third—thoughts. Who was better suited to lead his aggrieved neighbors than he, a man as burdened by debt and Boston oppression as anyone, a patriot who had never even been paid for his wartime service?

The more he thought about it, the more he realized that he had been a fool to turn down his neighbor's request. Daniel Shays resolved to step forward and lead.

Supreme Judicial Court
Hampden County Courthouse
Springfield, Massachusetts
September 26, 1786

The virus spread, hopscotching from town to town and county to county.

An epidemic had begun.

Three hundred men shut down the state's Supreme Judicial Court when it tried to meet at Worcester. A drunken horde—men too poor to pay their debts, but not to buy rum—pulled the same trick when Middlesex County's court convened at Concord. Mob rule struck again at Great Barrington in the Berkshires and at Taunton, south of Boston, near the Rhode Island border. Soon the Massachusetts Supreme Judicial Court would indict eleven protest leaders for rioting and sedition.

Today, that court was due to convene in Springfield and, with a thousand protesters, or "Regulators," as they now called themselves, surrounding the courthouse, it looked like the pattern might repeat itself yet again.

"A fine morning for a court closing," joked Captain Luke Day to the ex-officer standing beside him.

"Indeed," answered Daniel Shays.

Day eyed Supreme Court justice William Cushing attempting to wade through the mob and called out to him: "No trying of debtors today! The road back to Boston lies yonder! I would advise you to take it, sir! Now!"

From around the corner another column of men approached.

Ah, reinforcements, thought Shays.

He could not have been more wrong.

The men now marching toward him were responding to a far different kind of call: that of the rule of law. They formed uneven ranks in the sun-drenched courthouse square, but they snapped to a quick and soldierly attention on a sudden call of "Halt!" from Major General William Shepard, the pudgy, fifty-year-old commander of the Massachusetts state militia. "Cannon!" he barked, and a brace of cannons quickly rolled into place. Crews scurried to put them in working order—their barrels aimed squarely at Luke Day's poorly armed Regulators.

With the reinforcements in place, Chief Justice Cushing and his fellow judges gingerly entered the courthouse. Their victory, however, proved hollow. No business was conducted that day as not even one juror had dared run Luke Day's gauntlet to appear for duty.

It was difficult to say who had won the day: General Shepard or Captain Day. But one thing was clear: the forces of the law had finally entered the fight—and so had Daniel Shays.

Daniel Shays' Farmstead
Pelham, Massachusetts
October 23, 1786

"What are you writing so furiously, Daniel?" Abigail Shays asked her husband.

Daniel hesitated before answering.

General Shepard's unexpected intervention at the Springfield courthouse the previous month had angered Daniel Shays. It did not frighten him, which might have made things easier since he would have simply retreated to his own little world and abandoned any contact with the Regulators. No, the show of force was an insult, and Daniel Shays did not like to be insulted.

"Abigail," said Shays, "I have already put on my uniform. I think it is time to add my name to this fight for our liberties. Listen to this, it is going out to all the counties and towns that stand with us."

Pelham, Oct. 23, 1786

Gentlemen:

By information from the General Court, they are determined to call all those who appeared to stop the Court to condign punishment. Therefore, I request you to assemble your men together, to see that they are well armed and equipped, with sixty rounds each man, and to be ready to turn out at a minute's warning; likewise to be properly organized with officers.

When he finished, he placed his signature below his call to arms. Daniel Shays knew that he might be signing his own death warrant.

Job Shattuck's Farmstead
Groton, Massachusetts
November 30, 1786

Governor James Bowdoin and his allies in the General Court had assumed the offensive. Tired of seeing their courthouses invaded and their tax collectors harassed, they had quickly passed a series of laws to quell the commonwealth's festering unrest. They suspended the writ of habeas corpus for eight months and passed "An Act to Prevent Routs, Riots and Tumultuous Assemblies and Evil Consequences Thereof," known more commonly as simply the "Riot Act." This new law held sheriffs blameless for any fatalities inflicted against insurgents, provided for the seizure of Regulators' lands and goods, and stipulated that miscreants be whipped thirty-nine stripes on their naked backs and suffer imprisonment for up to twelve months.

Now, three hundred horsemen, fully armed, thundered west out of Cambridge.

Their destination: Groton. Their assignment: Apprehend Captain Job Shattuck.

The fifty-year-old Shattuck, a veteran of both the American Revolution and the earlier French and Indian War, had taken the lead in organizing attacks on tax collectors by men armed with rough-hewn clubs. He'd also led the Regulators' drunken attack on the Concord courthouse.

But Shattuck was no Daniel Shays—at least not when it came to finances.

Shays had barely a farthing to spare. Job Shattuck, on the other hand, was the wealthiest man in Groton, the owner of five hundred acres and a fine, three-story, wood-frame mansion. But Shays and Shattuck were both leaders of the insurrection brewing in Massachusetts, and that was enough for Governor James Bowdoin.

The horsemen who were now headed for Shattuck's home were not a typical crew of besotted roughnecks. This group featured more than its share of lawyers, physicians, and merchants. Two Harvard graduates—Benjamin Hichborn and John Warren—commanded them.

They reached Shattuck's home at daybreak.

He wasn't there.

Having been warned by Shays of the massive force hunting him, Captain Shattuck had bolted from his home through the snowy fields leading toward the icy Nashua River. Unfortunately, he'd left too late. One of the lead horsemen, a man named Sampson Read, caught up with him. "I know you not," Shattuck warned Read, "but whoever you are, you are a dead man." They grappled, falling to the cold ground, tumbling toward the riverbank. Shattuck lunged to retrieve his fallen sword and make good on his threat, but Fortescue Vernon, another posse member, proved quicker. He aimed his own sword at Shattuck's arm, but missed, the sword slipping and severing a ligament near Shattuck's knee.

They bandaged the bleeding Shattuck and carted him off to a Boston prison cell. It seemed like quick and easy work to lock up such a troublemaker. But they would soon learn that there was a much higher price to be paid for the capture of Captain Job Shattuck.

Daniel Shays' Farmstead
Pelham, Massachusetts
December 3, 1786

"What sort of times have we been cursed to live in, Abigail?" Daniel Shays mused to his wife as a single tallow candle flickered at his side.

Reading in the waning light of a December day was never an easy proposition. Reading the disturbing reports before him was even more difficult.

"They say Captain Shattuck has perished in his prison cell. Terrible! Dreadful! And what these savages did during his capture was pure evil! A sword through the eye of a neighbor woman! Another woman's breast slashed. An innocent infant murdered in its cradle! The government of Massachusetts has fallen into the hands of men just as barbaric as the heathens who aligned themselves with the French against us twenty years ago! We have no choice: We must fight them!"

Abigail Shays stayed silent. She knew no words could dissuade her husband at this point. And, she thought, if these gruesome reports were true, nothing should.

But they weren't true at all.

Job Shattuck was indeed crippled, but not dead. No women had been blinded or slashed; no infant's life snuffed out.

The rumors were false, but that didn't matter. They spread like wildfire through western Massachusetts—from home to home, tavern to tavern, and church to church.

People believed the lies, and people will fight for what they believe.

Major General Benjamin Lincoln's Home
North Street
Hingham, Massachusetts
December 4, 1786

General Benjamin Lincoln hunched over his cherrywood desk in the comfortable Hingham home. His ancestors had built this house in 1637, it had seen his birth in 1733, and it was where he hoped to die—unless, of course, these "Regulators" seized it as part of the revolution they now plotted.

Lincoln had been one of George Washington's favorite generals. He had served at Boston, Long Island, White Plains, and Saratoga. Even his surrender to British forces at Charleston, South Carolina, failed to dim Washington's respect for the easygoing Lincoln. When the British themselves later surrendered at Yorktown, it was Lincoln, paroled from British captivity, whom Washington designated to accept Lord Cornwallis's sword.

Lying in front of Benjamin Lincoln today was a letter sent from Mount Vernon by Washington, dated almost a month earlier. "Are your people getting mad?" Washington had asked Lincoln, displaying uncharacteristic bluntness. "Are we to have the goodly fabric, that eight years were spent in raising, pulled over our heads? What is the cause of all these commotions? When and how will they end?"

Lincoln answered that, yes, people in Massachusetts were indeed angry. "If an attempt to annihilate our present constitution and dissolve the present government can be considered as evidence of insanity—then yes, you are accurate in your descriptions."

Lincoln paused before answering Washington's second question—whether the government would unravel. "There is, I think, great danger that it will be so unless the current system is supported by arms. Even then, a government which has no other basis than the point of the bayonet is so totally different from the one we established that if we must resort to arms then it can hardly be said that we have supported 'the goodly fabric.' This probably will be the case, for there does not appear to be virtue enough among the people to preserve a perfect republican government."

Lincoln's answers to his former commander's first two queries were pessimistic, but his third answer conveyed even worse news. "It is impossible for me to determine when and how things will end," he wrote. "I see little probability that their efforts will be brought to an end and the dignity of government supported without bloodshed. Yet, once a single drop is drawn, not even the most prophetic spirit will, in my opinion, be able to determine when it will cease flowing."

General Lincoln knew there was no easy answer. The root cause of this growing insurrection was related to state issues like debt and property rights; issues in which the federal government, operating under the Articles of Confederation, had no ability to intervene. Lincoln also knew that other states faced similar issues. If Massachusetts' citizens could sink into such a state of disillusionment as to pick up arms against their duly elected leaders, it could happen anywhere. The mob would supplant the law and trample liberty.

And that scared him to death.

Governor's Mansion
Boston, Massachusetts
January 4, 1787

"You asked to see me, Governor?"

General Benjamin Lincoln had rushed north from Hingham as soon as he'd received the governor's message that morning.

"Yes, I have requested your presence, and I think you fully comprehend why," Bowdoin said.

"The mobs?" Lincoln asked. Massachusetts' situation had deteriorated even further in the month since he had written back to Washington. Rumors had even been circulating that the Regulators intended to attack Boston itself.

"Of course," answered Bowdoin. "We require a larger, more reliable force than General Shepard's militia to crush this pox."

"That will require patriotism . . . and, of course, gold and silver," said Lincoln, well aware of the financial difficulties the commonwealth was already suffering.

"Funds will be provided, General," answered Bowdoin. "I have taken it upon myself to raise them privately from one hundred thirty-five of the commonwealth's most substantial and patriotic citizens. Men who know the value of the rule of law." What the governor did not say, but the wily Lincoln knew very well, was that these men were not merely patriotic, they also now owned the bulk of the state's debt—most of which had been acquired at a substantial, and now very profitable, discount. The money Bowdoin raised from increased taxes went to them. Their pledge of capital to fight the rioters was motivated by their desire to ensure that the current system, which supported their wealth, remained in place.

Motivations aside, this was the solution that Lincoln had already suggested to George Washington. The commonwealth's men of property would have to dig into their pockets to fund an armed force that would guarantee both their property and the rule of law.

And that was just fine with Lincoln.

"I'm at your service," he said to the governor.

Continental Arsenal
Springfield, Massachusetts
January 19, 1787

A ragtag stream of ill-clad, freezing men marched through the falling snow up a steep New England hillside. They resembled white-covered scarecrows, with rags around their heads to secure their shabby three-cornered hats in place and rags bound around their feet to stave off frostbite.

"Column halt!" the man on horseback barked. "Take shelter indoors! You've earned it, men!"

"Damn right we have!" muttered one of the scarecrows, ice forming around his beard. "We've marched a good twenty miles today!"

The men were Massachusetts militia, and the person shouting orders was none other than Major General William Shepard, the same man who had rolled out the cannons in his face-off against Daniel Shays, Luke Day, and their band of Regulators at the Springfield courthouse nearly four months earlier.

Governor Bowdoin may not have possessed much faith in the commonwealth's militia, but General Shepard still did to a degree.

A thought—no, a fear—had raced through Shepard's mind for months. Springfield possessed more than a courthouse; it also possessed a Continental Arsenal, chock-full of everything an army might need: 7,000 muskets and bayonets, 1,300 pounds of gunpowder, and 200 tons of shot. These supplies could transform a disorganized rabble into a formidable army capable of marching right to the State House in Boston.

If the mobs seized that arsenal, Shepard's men would be cut to ribbons against them. So might General Lincoln's new contingents. If they made it all the way to Boston and overtook the State House . . . well, he couldn't even bring himself to think what might happen then.

And that was why William Shepard was marching his men through snow, ice, and cold to seize and secure that arsenal before Shays and Day finally thought of it.

But Shepard was already too late.

Daniel Shays and Luke Day *had* thought of it.

Parsonage of the First Church of West Springfield
West Springfield, Massachusetts
Four months earlier: September 1786

Even the most agitated of the Regulators grappled with the question: could their rebellion really succeed? Those who thought it could were left with another question even more difficult to answer: Was this rebellion *just*?

The Regulators certainly had their grievances. Boston called the tune, and the rest of the state danced to it. Restrictive property ownership regulations kept good men from serving in public office. Squalls and storms often kept western Massachusetts representatives away from the capitol during key legislative votes. Still, this was not 1775 or 1776. There *was* representation now, imperfect as it might be.

Was it right to rebel against a lawful, elected government? Should our fight be in the State House instead of the streets?

The questions gnawed at Luke Day, and that is why he found himself seeking out the Reverend Dr. Joseph Lathrop, minister of West Springfield's First Church. Lathrop was a man Day respected and trusted. So, after finding him at the church, Day shared a secret: He and his men were going to march on the arsenal across the Connecticut River in Springfield, seize it, and kick over the whole rotten cabal in Boston.

"You're wrong, Luke," Lathrop said.

"Well . . . no . . . I . . . I'm . . . not!" Day stammered, fidgeting with the brass buttons on his uniform coat as he spoke.

"You're wrong," chided the white-haired Lathrop, jabbing a bony finger into Day's chest, "and you know it. Your very manner tells me you know it. A resort to arms for supposed grievances is wrong. *And your men know it, too.* The path down which you lead them will destroy them—and you as well. If you refuse and rebel, ye shall be devoured by the sword."

The conversation ended abruptly, there was not even a terse good-bye, but Lathrop's words had found their mark. Luke Day might never admit it, but he was having second thoughts.

Daniel Shays' Headquarters
Wilbraham, Massachusetts
January 24, 1787

Armies were on the march.

General Benjamin Lincoln had quickly assembled an army at Roxbury and was bringing it toward Springfield via Worcester. But the Regulators were marching, too. Three separate groups of them raced against time to head off Lincoln and seize the arsenal from General Shepard's militia: Luke Day's 400 men advanced from West Springfield; Captain Shays' nearly 1,200 Regulators encamped near Palmer; and 400 Berkshire County men, led by Eli Parsons, another Revolutionary War veteran, marched from Chicopee. Combined, they had a huge size advantage over Shepard's 1,100 men.

Shays hurriedly dispatched orders to Day and Parsons: rendezvous with him before the arsenal in the waning sunlight at 4:00 P.M. on Thursday, January 25.

The clock was ticking. Seize the arsenal before Benjamin Lincoln arrived to reinforce Shepard's militia or do not seize it at all.

Zenas Parsons' Tavern
Springfield, Massachusetts
January 24, 1787

The atmosphere in the normally sleepy town of Springfield was electric. From the snow-covered streets to the handful of businesses that dotted its commercial area, a sense of excitement and dread filled the town. Nowhere was this sense of foreboding greater than at Zenas Parsons' Tavern.

While some towns had flocked to the Regulators' cause, Springfield was not counted among them. Its citizenry had stubbornly held loyal to their elected government. They had no appetite for seizing courthouses or marching on arsenals.

They also, like most people across the states, carefully scrutinized strangers stopping at the local taverns, especially in times of rebellion and sedition like the one they found themselves in now.

"Who's the bumpkin that just sauntered in?" whispered a man attired in brown. It was a cold night and he was wisely sitting near the blazing fireplace.

"Can't say I know," came the answer from a bearded man in blue. "But I do reckon that he came into town on the West Springfield road."

His companion nodded wisely. Zenas Parsons' newest customer wasn't from these parts, and West Springfield was where Luke Day's "troops" were quartered. One didn't need to be Ben Franklin to figure out what that might mean.

The man in brown sauntered over to the tavern keeper to refresh his drink. While waiting, he engaged the curly-haired stranger in conversation. "Terrible day to be out," he said.

"That's why I'm in here. A little grog never hurt anyone in this weather—nor in any other sort of weather!" the stranger laughed.

"No, not at all," said the man in blue, who was now standing on the stranger's other side. "Hope you don't have much further to go. Otherwise, you'll need *two* glasses of grog!"

"No, not far. Just over to Wilbraham."

Wilbraham was where Shays was encamped.

"Say," said the man in blue, "it looks like the wind's picking up out there. I wouldn't head outside until it lets up. Maybe another ration of grog will do the trick—on me! We like to treat strangers proper here in Springfield."

Several grogs later, the stranger was . . . groggy. A few more and he slumped over unconscious.

Quickly, the locals pawed through his coat. There, inside his pocket, was an envelope sealed securely with red wax.

A peek inside might very well be worth the price of a few glasses of grog.

Boston Post Road
Five miles from Springfield
January 25, 1787

"There's a rider coming forward, sir . . . I think . . ."

"Yes, I think so, too," answered Daniel Shays, though the descending snow made seeing anything a winter's guessing game.

"Do you measure him as friend or foe, sir?"

Shays, at the head of his column of men, pulled his spyglass up to his eye. "Both."

"Both, sir? How may that be?"

"Friend once. But now, I doubt it. It's Captain Samuel Buffington. I served with him in the Massachusetts Line. I rather doubt he is here to discuss old times."

Under cover of a gust-driven white flag of truce, Buffington advanced steadily toward his erstwhile comrade. Before reaching Shays, however, another Regulator intercepted him. "You want to see General Shays, I suppose." Buffington indicated he certainly did.

"Be my guest," came the reply. "Just know that if the matter isn't settled by sunset, New England will see such a day as she never has before."

Such arrogant chatter failed to frighten Buffington. As he continued toward Shays, he wondered who had promoted the man to such an exalted rank. When he saw Shays' own greeting—a pistol in one hand, a drawn sword in the other—he got the feeling that these mobbers were taking themselves a little too seriously.

Two can play this game, he thought. Buffington's first words virtually slapped Shays across the face. "I'm here," he pronounced, "in defense of the country you are endeavoring to destroy."

"If you are in defense of the country," Shays shot back, "then we are both defending the same cause."

"I expect we have differing views on what that means," Buffington countered.

"Let me be clear, then: we are taking the arsenal and public buildings in Springfield." Shays' bravado was overflowing, but his swagger suddenly abated. "Will they fight?" he asked, his eyes narrowing with concern.

"You can count on it," said Buffington.

"That's all I want," Shays lied, as he wrapped his scarf tighter around his neck. Despite his restored bluster, he wondered whether a woolen scarf might not be the only thing wrapped round his neck in the near future.

Buffington thought the same thing. "If you advance," he warned Shays, "you will meet those men we are both accustomed to obey."

Buffington rode away, hoping for the best, but more fearful than ever that the worst was yet to come.

Continental Arsenal
Springfield, Massachusetts
January 25, 1787

William Shepard paced nervously, awaiting Buffington's return. Would he bear news of Shays' capitulation? No, that was too much to hope for. These mobbers would have to be brought to reason not by cool words but with hot lead.

A militia member approached Shepard with a piece of paper. "General, a message . . . from Captain Day."

Shepard slowly removed his kidskin gloves and unfolded the document handed him. "Headquarters," it began, "West Springfield, January 25, 1787."

"Headquarters!" Shepard snorted, "You would think that loud-mouth brigand would at least see combat before assuming such airs. I know damned well where his 'Headquarters' is—it's the 'Stebbins Tavern,' a place better suited to commanding bottles than battles."

Shepard read on:

The body of the people assembled in arms, adhering to the first principles in nature, self-preservation, do, in the most peremptory manner, demand:

1. *That the troops in Springfield lay down their arms.*
2. *That their arms be deposited in the public stores, under the care of the proper officers, to be returned to the owners at the termination of the present contest.*

3. That the troops return to their homes upon parole.

> *Your Excellency's most obedient, humble servant,*
> *Luke Day.*
> *Captain Commandant of this division.*

Shepard sighed. This game would be funny if it were not so deadly: neighbors firing on neighbors, a state torn asunder, and a braggart in a tavern issuing orders to a lawfully elected government.

We'll see soon enough, Shepard thought, *just who tenders parole to whom.*

"Company's right on time," William Shepard muttered. "Very polite of them."

He watched a small parade of men struggling through massive snowdrifts on the Boston Road growing larger and larger still.

"Captain Buffington, Colonel Lyman, will you do the honors? Ask them what they want—for posterity's record."

"My pleasure, General," said Lyman. Both Lyman and Buffington quickly ascended their mounts to meet Shays' advancing Regulator forces. If Shepard's militia could not yet see "the whites" of the mobbers' eyes from the arsenal, they could easily see their steamy breath.

Buffington posed Shepard's question to Shays, who promptly answered, "Barracks and stores."

The Regulators pushed forward and were just about a hundred yards from the arsenal's heavily guarded perimeter when Colonel Lyman warned, "Advance no further or you will be fired upon."

"That's all we want, by God!" jeered Captain Adam Wheeler, a French and Indian War veteran who stood stoutly at Shays' side. Lyman nodded to Buffington, and the two galloped as fast as they could back to their lines.

"Take the hill on which the arsenal and the Public Buildings stand!" Shays shouted to his troops, who responded with a great roar. If noise and enthusiasm could seize the arsenal, it would soon be theirs.

While Shays was marching his men up the Boston Road on one side of the arsenal, Eli Parsons' Berkshire County lads were attacking on another and Luke Day was bringing his men to bear from a third side.

They hoped that their enormous show of force would force Shepard to fold.

But something or rather *someone* was missing.

Where was Day?

Shays pondered the problem as his men inched perilously closer to Shepard's muskets.

William Shepard's prized possession on this late January afternoon was not either of his cannons—"government puppies," his men called them—but a piece of paper hidden within his red-trimmed blue great-coat. It was the letter commandeered the day before from a drunken messenger at Parsons' Tavern, a critical communication from Luke Day to Daniel Shays.

Day had been attempting to respond to Shays to inform him that he would *not* be available to assault General Shepard and the arsenal at 4:00 P.M. on January 25—this very hour—but that they would instead cordially arrive precisely twenty-four hours later.

And, so, Shepard knew—though he took the precaution of posting some men on Main Street in case Day changed his mind—that he would have to defend only *two sides* of the arsenal, not three.

Just as important, Daniel Shays did *not* know that.

"Major Stephens!" roared Shepard, "Fire o'er the rascals' heads!"

Two fuses burned, and Shepard prayed that such a warning might bring his opponents to their senses. Not merely for their sake, but for his as well. He had no way of really knowing how his own men might react to drawing the blood of their neighbors and fellow countrymen. His own army, he fretted, might dissolve at the first shot.

BOOM! . . . BOOM!

A great, deafening roar rose from the arsenal as two cannonballs sailed safely over the heads of Shays' advancing hordes.

Or *had* they sailed safely? Most of Shays' army lay prone, facefirst, on the snowy ground, as if they were a field of harvested wheat.

One by one, Shays' army arose and dusted themselves off. "March on! March on!" Shays barked.

"Major Stephens," Shepard ordered, his words catching in his throat as he uttered them, "Another volley—this time *waist height*."

BOOM! . . . BOOM! The cannons crashed again.

Stephens' cannon shot found its target, ripping through Shays' ranks, tearing through blood, sinew, and bone like a sword through a sack of flour.

Three men—Ezekiel Root and Ariel Webster, both of Gill, and Jabez Spicer of nearby Leyden—crumpled to the ground dead. A fourth, Shelburne's John Hunter, was gravely injured. The vast remainder of Shays' troops, save for a scattered handful frozen in fear, again fell prostrate to the snow-packed ground.

"Again!" cried Shepard, and more metal rocketed through the leaden sky. But above that roar, the men manning the arsenal's guns heard a scream that shocked them to their very marrow. Artillery Sergeant John Chaloner had moved away too slowly from his cannon's mouth. Its fearsome blast ripped both of his arms from their sockets and its searing flash blinded him instantly.

The sound of Chaloner's screams echoed along with the distant rumble from the cannon. The air was thick with gunpowder, and the snow where the ill-fated group of now-dead rebels once stood was red with blood.

Militiamen watched as the Regulators retreated. After they had fallen back to a safe distance, the militiamen inched down to where the army had stood facing them just a few short minutes earlier. They retrieved the mortally wounded John Hunter and what was left of Root, Webster, and Spicer, and moved them to a nearby stable, where the bodies quickly froze solid.

About an hour later, a party of Regulators advanced again, but this time under a white flag.

"Sir, we respectfully request that we may remove the bodies of our five comrades for decent Christian burial."

"Five?" snorted Shepard. "I'm afraid I've only four, but if you care to repeat your march on the arsenal, I'll be only too glad to accommodate you with a fifth!"

They were not about to take him up on that. The thought of fighting their friends and neighbors was one thing; watching them actually die was another thing entirely.

The battle was over.

Regulator Encampment
Chicopee, Massachusetts
January 26, 1787

Daniel Shays' men had run from the armory grounds and they kept on running hard for five miles until finally reaching Japhet Chapin's Tavern at Cabotville to Springfield's east. At daybreak they fled farther—to Chicopee—where they rejoined Eli Parsons' Berkshire County men. Along the way, two hundred Regulators had deserted the cause.

A roaring fire had once threatened to engulf the entire commonwealth, and, with it, perhaps the entire Confederation.

But now that fire seemed to be nothing but dying embers.

Continental Arsenal
Springfield, Massachusetts
January 27, 1787

"They're back!"

A militia sentry watched a column of men steadily advancing toward him.

Men sprang to their posts. If Shays and his mobbers were foolish enough to attempt another attack on Springfield's arsenal, they would ensure that an even bloodier price was paid.

"Hold your fire!" came another shout. "It's not Shays! It's General Lincoln and reinforcements!" Glorious in their strength and number—three companies apiece of infantry and artillery, plus a company of cavalry—Lincoln marched them steadily along.

A great cheer went up, but General Shepard cut them short. He mounted the steps of the arsenal's wooden barracks and barked out: "Make your huzzahs short, men! Prepare your kits and your mounts. We leave within the hour—north bound, on the trail of the mobbers!"

Connecticut Valley
Western Massachusetts
January 30, 1787

General Benjamin Lincoln's men crossed the Connecticut River, marching northward along its west bank. His cavalry, under Colonel Gideon Barr, advanced gingerly upon its ice-hardened surface. General Shepard's militia trudged up the Connecticut's eastern shore.

Lincoln and Shepard moved fast, but the dispirited Regulator force moved faster, bolting out of Chicopee. Those who remained plundered several houses in South Hadley and looted two barrels of rum at Amherst. More men deserted along the way. It seemed now as though only a couple hundred remained. Shays himself retreated to his ramshackle Pelham homestead. Ensconced among his fellow hardscrabble Scotch-Irish neighbors, Shays bided his time. Unsure of his next move, and burdened with an "army" more inclined to shouting than shooting, his options had grown ever more limited.

This was not at all what he had planned.

Luke Day remained in West Springfield. He'd taken the precaution of posting a guard at the ferry house, but when Lincoln's army approached, the guard, along with the bulk of his panic-stricken men, had fled, abandoning their supplies and muskets so they might run that much faster. They fled through Southampton, and then Northampton, as quickly as they could, hoping they might find refuge in the Independent Republic of Vermont before Lincoln found them.

Major General Lincoln's Headquarters
Hadley, Massachusetts
January 30, 1787

Benjamin Lincoln was encamped at Hadley, barely ten miles to Shays' west. Lincoln could have advanced on him at Pelham, but chose not to. The township was too rugged and too heavily defended—swarming with the greatest concentration of "Shaysites" known to Christendom.

Benjamin Lincoln would not attack Pelham. At least, not yet.

Instead, he sat down to compose a letter. *Perhaps,* he thought, *blessed reason might finally work to end this unfortunate episode and an offer of mercy might go further than a twelve-pound cannon shot.*

And so, in a fine hand, he wrote to Captain Shays.

Whether you are convinced or not of your error in flying to arms, I am fully persuaded that you now realize that you are not able to execute your original purposes. Your resources are few, your force inconsiderable, and hourly decreasing from the dissatisfaction of your men. You are in a post where you have neither cover nor supplies, and in a situation in which you cannot hesitate for a moment to disband your deluded followers.

If you do not disband, I must approach and apprehend your most influential men. Should you attempt to fire upon the troops of Government, the consequences must be fatal to many of your men, the least guilty. To prevent bloodshed, you will communicate to your privates, that, if they will instantly lay down their arms, surrender themselves to Government, and take and subscribe the oath of allegiance to this Commonwealth, they shall be recommended to the General Court for mercy.

If you should either withhold this information from them, or suffer your people to fire upon our approach, you must be answerable for all the ills which may exist in consequence thereof.

Well, Lincoln sighed, *let's pray that that works.*

Regulators' Headquarters
William Conkey's Tavern
Pelham, Massachusetts
January 30, 1787

Daniel Shays figured that if he had to hide out from General Lincoln's army, old William Conkey's Tavern, remote even by Pelham standards, was as good a place as any.

Particularly when the fugitive was also its most distinguished patron: Daniel Shays.

Gone were the days when Shays exhorted his "troops" with vain or glorious boasts. "My boys," he had lectured them not long before, "you are going to fight for liberty. If you wish to know what liberty is,

I will tell you: It is for every man to do what he pleases, to make other folks do as you please to have them, and to keep folks from serving the devil."

If that was the definition of liberty, then these men were experiencing the opposite. Few at Pelham were now doing what pleased them—instead they hunkered down to defend their very homes.

Shays pondered Lincoln's offer. He didn't particularly like his opponent's tone or his threats, but an offer of pardon had its charms. Except, and here Shays read very, very carefully, the offer clearly extended only to noncommissioned recruits. That didn't do much for him or for his fellow officers like Adam Wheeler. A "general pardon" would be necessary. Until then, it was best to stall for time.

Pelham, Jan. 30th, 1787

To Gen. Lincoln, commanding the Government troops at Hadley,

Sir: However unjustifiable the measures we have adopted in taking up arms against the government, we have been forced to do so. The people are willing to lay down their arms, on the condition of a general pardon, and return to their respective homes. They are unwilling to stain the land, which we, in the late war, purchased at so dear a rate, with the blood of our brethren and neighbors.

Therefore, we pray that hostilities may cease on your part, until our united prayers may be presented to the General Court, and we receive an answer. If this request may be complied with, the government shall meet with no resistance from the people, but let each army occupy the post where they are now.

Daniel Shays, Captain.

Well, Shays sighed, *let's pray that that works.*
It didn't.

Major General Lincoln's Headquarters
Hadley, Massachusetts
February 3, 1787

General Benjamin Lincoln was not about to let Daniel Shays off so easily. He didn't trust Shays to not go back on his word and attack his army. Nor did he trust that Shays would not fade away into the hills to fight a guerilla war against the government.

But, above all, Lincoln didn't trust his own army's ability to play a waiting game against these blasted Regulators.

My army is falling apart! Lincoln thought to himself as he finished reading a dispatch from Major General John Paterson, his commander in the Berkshires. The antigovernment "frenzy," Paterson reported, infested the regions bordering New York and made him fear for his safety. He was demanding reinforcements.

"General," Lincoln's cavalry commander, Colonel Burt, interrupted, "I must have a word with you. I was unable to send out patrols again tonight . . . the rate of desertions is simply too high." The normally mild-mannered Lincoln flung Patterson's letter to the floor. "Desertions! Those madmen in the Berkshires!" he screamed. "And discipline is breaking down. Looting even here in Hadley—by my own men! Damn it, this has to end!"

Both armies—the government's and the Regulators'—were quickly collapsing. Lincoln's militia enlistments would expire in late February. Victory now seemed to be a question of which side would dissolve first.

How, thought Lincoln, *am I going to explain this to Governor Bowdoin? Or to General Washington?*

"General Lincoln?" a snow-covered lieutenant interrupted.

"What do *you* want?" Lincoln snapped.

"Uh . . . we've . . . we've learned that Shays has evacuated his Pelham stronghold and has reached Petersham for the night."

"Petersham? Where in tarnation is that?"

"It's about thirty miles northeast of here, toward Gardner."

"Yes, yes, of course," said Lincoln suddenly, very softly and calmly. A plan welled inside him. "Gentlemen, alert the troops, we are headed for Petersham . . . tonight . . . now!"

"Now?" stammered Colonel Burt. "It's nearly eight o'clock. We'd have to travel through the night—and in the most hostile territory."

"All the better to march by night, then," answered Lincoln. "Our enemies will slumber peacefully and wake to some very unwelcome company."

En Route to Petersham
New Salem, Massachusetts
February 3, 1787

General Lincoln and his troops had set off late but in fair weather. At 2:00 A.M., however, and about halfway to Petersham, that changed quickly: Veritable blizzard descended upon them. Temperatures dropped, sheets of snow drifted, and the wind blew so violently that it blinded his caravan. Soon frostbite struck.

Lincoln's men wondered what sort of madman had delivered them into such disaster, but they kept marching. They had no real choice.

Regulator Encampment
Petersham, Massachusetts
February 4, 1787

The weather was equally horrid at Petersham: freezing temperatures with near zero visibility. Daniel Shays' men may have shivered, but at least they shivered with a temporary sense of security. No one would dare attack them in this weather. Only a lunatic would dispatch an army in such conditions. Plus, it was now the Sabbath—a day of peace, when armies sheathed their swords and knelt in prayer. They rested without fear and without nearly enough sentries to warn them that trouble approached.

At 9:00 A.M. it was not merely trouble that approached, it was mayhem.

The sun had long since risen, but many Regulators still slumbered, catching up on the sleep that had been so hard to come by lately. Others tarried at breakfast. Suddenly, Shepard's militia burst upon them, easily pushing past the few sentries on duty and into the rebel camp, catching its inhabitants totally by surprise.

"Militia!" came the shout, as men scrambled to retrieve their unloaded muskets.

Then, a more frightened alarm shattered the morning's bitter cold air: "Artillery!"

Somehow, Shepard and Colonel Barr's frostbitten men had dragged with them two heavy field pieces. These were now squarely aimed at the Regulators. "Cannon!" cried the surprised men. Their screams brought back visions of the bloody debacle that had visited them at the arsenal, of lead tearing through flesh, and of Ezekiel Root, Ariel Webster, Jabez Spicer, and John Hunter, all dead or dying upon the frozen Springfield ground.

Once again, the former mobbers fled without firing a shot. Panic-stricken, they simply ran for their lives, though some did not run fast enough. Lincoln took 150 of them—mostly privates—prisoner. They had little will to resist further, but Lincoln had no manpower to waste guarding them. He let most go home on parole.

Daniel Shays and Adam Wheeler *did* run fast enough, north on the Athol Road. Dreams of capturing Boston had long since left their minds; they now thought only of finding asylum in Vermont.

The Meetinghouse
Lenox, Massachusetts
December 6, 1787

"Attention!"

The guards at Lenox's Meetinghouse snapped to strict attention, and so did the 250 spectators present.

After all, they were there for serious business.

The rebellion had not formally died after Petersham, but it had been mortally wounded. Some skirmishing continued and some looting and hostage-taking here and there, primarily at Stockbridge, near the New York border. In late February, some real fighting had finally occurred in Sheffield: five men—three Regulators, a hostage they had taken, and a militiaman—were killed, and 30 others were wounded. Colonel John Ashley's local militia captured another 150 rebels.

Some in Boston thirsted for vengeance against the Shaysites. Leading the charge was one of John Hancock's oldest enemies and one of the revolution's most ardent patriots, Samuel Adams. "In monarchies," Adams argued, "the crime of treason and rebellion may admit of being pardoned or lightly punished. But the man who dares rebel against the laws of a republic ought to suffer death."

But most people simply wanted the door closed on the whole sorry episode. From Paris, Thomas Jefferson wrote to a friend, asking, "What country can preserve its liberties if their rulers are not warned from time to time that their people preserve the spirit of resistance? The tree of liberty must be refreshed from time to time with the blood of patriots and tyrants."

In the end, Shays, Day, Shattuck, all of their fellow insurgent officers, and nearly all of their men, received pardons. Their blood would not be shed.

But not everyone proved so lucky.

The drums beat a dirge, and the crowd stood bareheaded and silent as two young men stood side by side upon Lenox's rude gallows. Stout nooses were fixed upon their necks: twenty-two-year-old John Bly, a "transient" of Tyringham, and Charles Rose, a Suffolk laborer and occasional teacher in his early twenties.

They might have been tried and sentenced for treason, insurrection, or sedition, but the authorities had decided otherwise. These two rebels would instead hang for a robbery committed at Lanesboro in the waning, sputtering days of the rebellion, when armies no longer marched and the most valiant protests the rebellion mounted were burglaries.

Bly and Rose, foolishly deluding themselves into believing that Shays would invade Massachusetts from exile in Vermont, had stolen weapons and powder at Lanesboro to facilitate Shays' phantom attack. Now they stood trembling upon the gallows. John Hancock, miraculously healthy enough to return to the governorship now that the worst had past, had rejected their petitions for mercy. Stephen West, pastor of the

First Congregational Church in nearby Stockbridge, ministered to the condemned but had little good to say of them. "As you have set yourselves against the community," he scolded, "so the community now sets themselves against you."

Bly and Rose, scapegoats for a stillborn rebellion, and a deadly warning to anyone else who might still harbor similar sentiments, had one privilege left to them: a few last words. The English-born Bly, his voice choking with emotion, chose not to condemn those about to execute him, but instead those firebrands whose angry words and reckless deeds had enticed men like him into this misbegotten adventure. "Our fate," he cried, "is a loud and solemn lesson to you who have excited the people to rise against the government."

A constable placed a hood over Bly's head, and another over Rose's. Two traps sprang. A pair of bodies plummeted downward, and the necks of two very young Regulators loudly and sickeningly snapped.

Shays' Rebellion was over, now as cold and dead as the two young burglars hanging in Lenox.

Far to the south, upon the fertile banks of Virginia's Potomac River, George Washington was done with his duties of chairing a convention in Philadelphia. He continued to ponder what other lessons—besides Bly's dying testament—might be learned from this botched rebellion.

America, he knew, required a federal government strong enough to resist the kind of lawlessness that had erupted in Massachusetts. The new Constitution he had played a vital role in drafting would be necessary to protect both the government and the governed.

He hoped that James Madison, his new friend, who was now on his way to the Virginia Ratification Convention in Richmond, might be able to help him finally achieve this goal. Virginia's vote would be crucial in deciding whether the new Constitution would succeed or fail. If it failed, Washington feared that the chaos that had briefly bubbled to the surface in Massachusetts would grow into a roaring boil and scorch the entire Union.

3

The Virginia Convention:
Compromising for the Constitution

Richmond, Virginia
State House
Fourteenth and Cary Streets
June 2, 1788

Patrick Henry smelled a rat.

And his nostrils had been twitching for quite some time.

Henry, the popular former governor of Virginia, drummed his fingers on the side of his heavy oak chair as he listened to crusty old judge Edmund Pendleton cough and wheeze. The air was heavy with anticipation as they waited for the Virginia convention, called to ratify the new federal Constitution, to finally begin.

Henry sensed that everything was now hurtling down to the wire. America had won the Revolution, but it seemed that she was losing the peace. The Articles of Confederation had bound the rebellious colonies together for the last seven years, but it had created something more akin to a social club than a nation—and a poorly run club at that.

Under the Articles, the Second Continental Congress had very limited powers, and directly taxing citizens was not one of them. As a result, it could hardly pay the interest on its debts. Hat in hand, Congress was forced to beg individual states for money like a club treasurer harassing deadbeat members for back dues.

Money wasn't the only issue. An "every state for itself" mentality meant that the country as a whole could barely field an army, but eleven different states boasted their own navies. A violent uprising— "Shays' Rebellion"—had torn apart western Massachusetts just a year earlier without any national military to quell it. Many people worried that Massachusetts was just the beginning.

With the American experiment now hanging in the balance, many leaders argued that the Articles should be changed to allow for a stronger federal government before it all fell apart. A convention met at Independence Hall in Philadelphia to work out the details, but the delegates had quickly determined that the Articles *couldn't* be fixed. They were broken beyond repair. Some delegates, led by Virginia's James Madison, went rogue and drafted an entirely new document with a new set of rules that established a very different relationship between American citizens and their government.

They called it "the Constitution."

These delegates, the "Federalists," believed they had no other choice. Patrick Henry, on the other hand, thought otherwise. The man who had challenged Britain, and, indeed, the entire universe, to give him liberty or death thirteen years earlier believed the greatest crisis currently haunting America was the possible ratification of this new Constitution. He had avoided the convention in Philadelphia where the monstrosity had been born, but now it had come to him in Virginia and he could ignore it no longer.

Henry knew that the next month might very well decide everything. The Constitution had made a lot of progress since Philadelphia. Delaware, Pennsylvania, New Jersey, Georgia, Connecticut, Massachusetts, and Maryland had already ratified the document. South Carolina might do so at any moment. Only a single additional state's ratification was necessary for the two-thirds majority needed for the Constitution to take effect—a much lower bar than the Articles had been held to; they had required unanimous approval.

The Constitution's success seemed so near, but in reality, its very survival still hung in the balance. A Union without Virginia would hardly last longer than the Articles of Confederation had endured *with* Virginia on board.

That left men like Patrick Henry in the lurch. He did not want to see the Union fall apart, but he also believed that this new document was an invitation to tyranny, which he had fought before. In 1765 he'd made a passionate speech to Virginia's House of Burgesses: "Caesar had his Brutus," he'd thundered, "Charles the First his Cromwell; and George the Third, may he profit by their example. If this be treason, make the most of it!"

Now, more than twenty years later, he believed the rat he smelled in Philadelphia was pushing them steadily toward monarchy. He was resolved to do everything in his power to stop that march dead in its tracks.

Henry's fingers drummed even faster now. His eyes narrowed. He could hardly wait for the fun to begin.

Patrick Henry was ready to go in for the kill.

Richmond, Virginia
Theatre Square ("The New Academy")
Broad Street, between Twelfth and Fourteenth Streets
June 4, 1788

The kill would not be so easy.

Patrick Henry estimated that 80 percent of all Virginians stood opposed to this new Constitution, but he knew that his opponents, the Federalists, had done their homework. They had worked hard to get the right delegates in place, and now it was becoming clear that the final vote in the ratifying convention teetered on a knife's edge. Only a handful of votes would decide the issue and potentially the fate of the entire nation.

The nearly 170 delegates formed a large crowd, but all around them, and in the gallery high above, partisans from both sides—along with the merely curious—filled the hall to its brim. Though it was only early June, the sheer mass of humanity made the room too hot and stuffy for comfort.

Patrick Henry stood tall and gaunt, six feet high and just 160 pounds, his weight and strength reduced from persistent bouts of malaria, and his posture stooped. Some thought his spare appearance only increased his power. He reminded some of an avenging angel. Less friendly observers thought he resembled "a scarecrow with a wig."

Henry's deep blue eyes peered through his spectacles, surveying his fellow delegates. He felt fortunate that the great George Washington, who presided over the convention in Philadelphia that had delivered this constitutional monstrosity, had decided to sit this one out. Henry was a great orator, maybe even the greatest on the continent—even his hated rival Thomas Jefferson reluctantly conceded that. Oratory, however, had its limits when it collided with George Washington's mighty reputation. *That was the thing about Washington*, Henry thought: *He knew when and where to fight and, perhaps more important, when to duck a battle*.

Henry fixed his sight upon his fellow delegates. Not far away sat Virginia's current governor, Edmund Randolph. If ever there was a reed blowing in the wind, it was the tall, handsome Randolph. In fact, the wind seemed to be optional; oftentimes a slight breeze would do the trick. Randolph, Henry recalled, had traveled to Philadelphia and presented his "Virginia Plan" to junk the Articles in favor of a new Constitution. Then, when the Constitution was drafted, he came out *against* it because it lacked a "Bill of Rights."

Young Randolph might be a reed blown by political winds, but, at least, thought Henry, he was now *our* reed. If Randolph could not be entirely trusted to do the right thing, at least he could be trusted to do what his heavily anti-Federalist Henrico County constituents wanted him to do.

Henry continued his look around the hall until he sighted the one man who truly worried him: James Madison—all five feet, four inches of him. It wasn't Madison's oratorical skills that concerned Henry; "Jemmy" didn't really have any. Half the time people couldn't even hear the gentleman speak. But, if anyone, anywhere, knew more about this Constitution or about the arguments for and against it than did the thirty-seven-year-old Madison, Patrick Henry had never heard of them.

The moment the Constitution was formally read into the official record, Patrick Henry bolted out of his seat. His plan was to attack, attack, and then attack once more. He would concede nothing. He would even skewer the very first words of the document: "We the People . . ." How *dare* the men at Philadelphia claim to speak for all the people, he exclaimed, pointing an accusatory finger at James Madison. "The people gave them no power to use their name."

As Henry ranted, he saw that Edmund Randolph was listening intently. Henry smiled in his direction. Acquiring the wavering Randolph for the anti-Federalist team would give them a big boost. But Randolph did not smile back.

When Henry finished, Randolph stood and slowly walked to the floor to speak. As he did, he offered a barely perceptible nod to James Madison.

Patrick Henry's heart sank. This was going to be much, much harder than he thought.

Edmund Randolph spoke not to praise Patrick Henry, but to bury him. His voice shook with rage as he refuted point after point made by his anti-Federalist predecessor. "The government is for the people," he thundered. "And the misfortune was that the people had no say in the government before."

Henry's face reddened with anger. He couldn't believe it; Randolph had switched positions again! "I am," Randolph continued, drawing out his every syllable and speaking in almost musical tones, "a friend of the Union."

Patrick Henry's mood turned as black as the suit he wore. He wanted to find the highest steeple in town and yell to everyone that their governor was the damnable crowned prince of chameleons. Instead, he sat stoically, refusing to give Randolph the satisfaction of seeing his anger and sense of betrayal.

Across the room, a disheartened George Mason, Henry's greatest ally in the hall, could not even bear to look at Randolph. *A young Benedict Arnold*, he thought, *a young Arnold*. The sixty-year-old Mason roused himself from his gloom to take the floor. Struggling to gather his thoughts, he ran his bony fingers through his long white hair.

Mason was truly angry at Randolph, but he knew that personal attacks would get them nowhere right now. Instead, he aimed his fire on one of the Constitution's more controversial new powers: the ability of the federal government to directly tax the people. "This power of laying direct taxes entirely changes the confederation into a consolidated government," he said slowly and with near perfect enunciation. "Converting a confederation into a consolidated government is totally subversive of every principle which has heretofore governed us. It annihilates the state governments. Will the people submit to taxation by two different and distinct powers? The one will destroy the other: the states *must* give way to the general government."

Mason conceded that the Constitution had many fine points, but he told his fellow delegates that it required fine tuning—a Declaration of Rights, very much like the one Mason had authored for Virginia itself in June 1776. He felt these amendments were essential to the Constitution and he wanted them adopted before Virginia ratified, even if it meant risking the whole process being sent back to square one.

Freedom, thought Mason, was worth spending the time to get right.

Richmond, Virginia
The Swan
North side of Broad Street
Evening of June 4, 1788

James Madison had barely spoken during the day's session, but the excitement had left him exhausted anyway. *We are winning;* that much was clear to him. Getting Randolph as an ally—even if he was in favor for amendments after ratification—was a huge coup for the Federalists.

Madison retreated to his lodgings at the Swan, one of little Richmond's better hostelries. Quarters were close so he had to be careful. The walls had ears, and worse, so did his fellow delegates.

Some daylight remained as Madison picked up a quill pen and began drafting a letter to George Washington at Mount Vernon. He'd promised Washington that he would keep him updated on the proceedings. After a great first day, Madison was excited to relay the news. "Randolph has thrown himself fully into our scale," he wrote. "Mason and Henry take different and awkward ground, and we are in the best spirits."

James Madison went to bed that night a very tired and very happy little man.

Richmond, Virginia
Theatre Square ("The New Academy")
Broad Street, between Twelfth and Fourteenth Streets
June 5, 1788

Patrick Henry did not know about Madison's exuberant letter to Washington. If he had, he probably would have smiled, knowing that overconfidence and bravado were the anti-Federalists' best friends. Henry, to paraphrase a phrase not yet uttered, had only just begun to fight.

For now, however, it was still the Federalists' turn. Judge Pendleton, the convention's unanimously elected chairman, roused himself onto his crutches and made his way to the floor. Despite his judge's wig, Pendleton didn't look like much. Fast approaching sixty-seven, he coughed and gasped for air. But Pendleton was smart and respected, and Henry knew he was a worthy adversary.

That opinion, however, did not appear to be mutual. Pendleton, his voice dripping with sarcasm, began by addressing Henry as his "worthy friend," before curtly informing him that no natural enmity existed between constitutional government and liberty. "The former is the shield and protector of the latter," Pendleton lectured Henry and the other anti-Federalists. "The war is between government and licentiousness, faction, turbulence, and other violations of the rules of society, to preserve Liberty."

Other Federalists followed Pendleton, all making similar points, all virtually jeering at Patrick Henry.

But it is a dangerous thing to taunt a lion.

Later that morning, the lion rose from his chair and surveyed his fellow delegates. Moving slowly for effect, he looked skyward and perused the throng in the gallery above. A profound, awesome silence enveloped the crowd. Love him or hate him, audiences hung on Henry's every word.

The Federalists had spent a great deal of time emphasizing the financial stability that they claimed a central government would bring. Henry, however, thought finances were inconsequential compared to the issue that revolutionary patriots had shed their precious blood for: liberty. He intended to hammer this point home as fiercely and relentlessly as possible.

"Don't ask how trade may be increased or how to become a great and powerful people," he bellowed. "Ask how your liberties can be secured." His hands were clenched into fists as though he were ready to wage battle against the idea of tyranny. "For liberty ought to be the direct end of your government. Is the end of trial by jury and the liberty of the press necessary for your liberty? Will abandoning your most sacred rights secure your liberty? Liberty, the greatest of all earthly blessings— give us that precious jewel, and you may take everything else!"

The barren landscape of vanished liberties that Henry sketched was having an effect. An onlooker in the gallery turned to Robert Morris. He wanted to speak but he could not find the words. A scream welled up deep inside him as he felt the cold and hard iron fetters of a devilishly new form of tyranny already pressing upon his flesh.

Henry saw the faces of those in the gallery and knew his warnings were hitting their mark. He sensed a power welling up within him. He would lacerate every argument proposed for this new Constitution— and many that had not even been considered yet.

James Madison sat uneasily in his chair as he listened to Henry dismantle the Federalists' arguments, point by point. He slowly brought his hands together, almost as if in silent prayer. *Yes*, he thought, in silent answer to Henry's latest argument against the need for a national army, *an adequate military and this Constitution are necessary to protect freedom.*

After watching the faces of his fellow delegates as Henry spoke, he was no longer so sure that a majority felt the same way.

Richmond, Virginia
Theatre Square ("The New Academy")
Broad Street, between Twelfth and Fourteenth Streets
June 9, 1788

Tempers ran high. Civility ran on empty. The time for arguing over articles and amendments, taxation and treaties, term limits and war powers, was passing fast.

The time for arguing personalities had arrived with a great roar.

Patrick Henry, refreshed by a good night's rest, took the floor again and skewered the Federalists' boasting of the "checks and balances" in their new system. "What are the checks of exposing accounts?" Henry baited them, pacing about the floor with great energy, "Can you search your President's closet? Is this a real check?"

At just the right moment, Henry tossed another major bombshell into the proceedings. He had somehow secured a copy of a letter his hated opponent Thomas Jefferson had written four months earlier to an old friend. In it, the principal author of the Declaration of Independence and former governor of Virginia had cast doubts on the wisdom of the new Constitution.

Spreading his arms before him, like an eagle about to swoop down on its prey, Henry added to the drama by slowly introducing the letter to the gallery. "We have information that comes from an illustrious citizen of Virginia, who is now in Paris, which *disproves* the suggestions of such dangers as Madison and company have alleged," he announced.

"I might say," Henry continued, oozing with pleasure at the opportunity to summon his archrival Jefferson as a surprise witness, "not from public authority, but good information, that his opinion is that you reject this government!"

The crowd stirred and Henry paused to let the murmuring die down before continuing. "This illustrious citizen advises you to reject this government till it be amended! His sentiments coincide entirely with ours! Let us follow the sage advice of this common friend of our happiness."

An uproar came from the gallery: Huzzahs from one faction; harrumphs and catcalls from the other. Henry simply smiled. There were not many people you'd rather have on your team, personal feelings aside, than Thomas Jefferson.

Henry continued, flitting from one topic to another, attacking each and every thing about the Constitution. When he finally finished, a raging Governor Randolph again took the floor. On Saturday, Henry had slyly puzzled over Randolph's sudden support for adopting the Constitution without amending it first, broadly hinting that Randolph might have been bribed to support the document. He'd even suspected George Washington himself of offering the prize.

For two days, Randolph had fumed over Henry's insinuations, barely able to restrain himself from physically confronting the older man. Now, standing in the hall, Randolph had everyone's attention and he was not about to let the moment pass without taking direct aim at Henry's allegations. "I find myself attacked in the most illiberal manner by the honorable gentleman," he sputtered. "If our friendship must fall, let it fall, like Lucifer, never to rise again!"

The crowd gasped. Those were fighting words in Virginia.

The chair gaveled furiously to silence the murmuring. Henry, visibly shaken, rose to respond and solemnly avowed that he had no intention of offending anyone, particularly the "honorable gentleman"—but that hardly calmed Randolph. If anything, he grew even more inflamed, rising to tell the gallery that, if not for Henry's apology, he'd been prepared to reveal certain unpleasant facts about Henry that would have made some men's hair stand on end.

Henry did not take the threat well. "I beg the honorable gentleman to pardon me," Henry said, his voice rising with every word, "for reminding him that his historical references and quotations are not accurate. If he errs so much with respect to his facts, as he has done in history, we cannot depend on his information or assertions."

The gallery seemed to be in shock. Two of the greatest patriots in the history of the commonwealth stood at the precipice. Another insult, real or perceived, could quite possibly put them, and perhaps the entire convention, over the edge.

Fortunately, reason, and a good night's rest, finally took command. The battle for the Constitution would continue to be waged with words—hot, vitriolic, and passionate words—instead of fists or pistols at twenty paces.

The Swan
North side of Broad Street
Richmond, Virginia
Evening of June 13, 1788

The Federalists had given it their best, but were worried that it wouldn't be enough to counter the brilliance of Patrick Henry. He was not, after all, simply an orator; he was a force of nature.

James Madison thought long and hard about the events of the last
week. His initial euphoria had long since vanished. Tonight, he again
took pen to hand and reported to George Washington. But this time,
his letter was much more dour, reporting that the Federalists' chances
for success were growing less favorable each day. He did not enjoy writing those words.

"Our progress is low," he wrote. "The business is in the most tick-
lish state that can be imagined. The majority will certainly be small, on
whatever side it may finally lie; and I dare not encourage much expecta-
tion that it will be on the favorable side."

James Madison sealed the letter and collapsed into bed. He was exhausted, but sleep came only in fits and starts. When he did drift away,
he dreamt only of defeat.

Theatre Square ("The New Academy")
Broad Street, between Twelfth and Fourteenth Streets
Richmond, Virginia
June 24, 1788

A thousand sweating, jostling spectators crammed the galleries. One
way or another they would soon witness history being made. The time
for talk was drawing to a close; the time for voting was drawing near.

First, however, Patrick Henry was about to drop another bombshell
onto the convention. He rose and surprised everyone by presenting a
series of amendments. He'd gone from opposing the entire Constitution and arguing against nearly every facet of it in great detail, to now
suddenly accepting George Mason's position: ratification, but with
amendments and a Bill of Rights. Some delegates wondered if that had,
in fact, been Henry's position all along. Had he and Mason merely
been playing a clever, protracted game of "Good Constable, Bad Constable"?

James Madison, who had been oddly quiet for the last few days, now
rose in an effort to reframe their duty as one of world-changing signifi-
cance. "Nothing has excited more admiration in the world," he began,
"than the manner in which free governments have been established
in America." But there was more work to be done. State governments

were one thing, but if America could craft a well-functioning federal system then they would turn even more heads.

Turning to the debate at hand—the issue of amending the Constitution before or after ratification—Madison appealed to both common sense and fear. He explained that if the anti-Federalists were to win, the other nine states that had already ratified would have to reopen their conventions to address the new amendments. Anything could happen at those new conventions—from new amendments proposed to votes being changed. The entire process, Madison told them, could be derailed by Virginia's stubbornness.

Then, perhaps playing a game of "Good Constable, Bad Constable" himself, Madison offered an olive branch to Patrick Henry. "His proposed amendments could be subsequently recommended," he told the crowd, "not because they are necessary, but because they can produce no possible danger, and may gratify some Gentlemen's wishes. But I can *never* consent to his previous amendments because they are pregnant with awful dangers."

Henry fumed. *These amendments aren't necessary?* he thought, his face crimson with rage. *Freedom of religion is not necessary? Trial by jury is not necessary? The right to bear arms is not necessary? If a Declaration of Rights is necessary in enlightened Virginia, how much* more *vital is it in the mighty consolidated government these Federalists have cooked up for us?*

"Madison," he bellowed, his voice drawing out the name into three very distinct syllables, "tells you of the important blessings which he imagines will result to us and to mankind from this system. I see the awful immensity of the dangers with which it is pregnant. I see it. I feel it." Henry's voice rose higher and higher. "I see beings of a higher order anxious concerning our decision. We have it in our power to secure the happiness of one half of the human race. Its adoption may involve the misery of the other hemisphere."

And, suddenly, those "higher beings" seemed to personally invade the debate. A distant thunder drew near, and then cracked close by. The skies grew black, then bright white as lightning streaked through overhead. The storm seemed to want to sever the building's roof from its walls. Heavy oak doors slammed shut from the force of the mighty winds. Lead windows rattled and seemed ready to crack and explode into a thousand violent shards.

Patrick Henry stood silent and passive, a calm eye at the center of a great tempest. The chair furiously banged his gavel for adjournment. There was no way anyone could proceed in the midst of this chaos.

Those in the balcony simply stared and marveled at Patrick Henry, the man who could seemingly call down the heavens as his witness.

Theatre Square ("The New Academy")
Broad Street, between Twelfth and Fourteenth Streets
Richmond, Virginia
June 25, 1788

Patrick Henry sensed trouble was brewing.

The roll call commenced on the series of prior amendments Henry had proposed to ensure American rights. This vote was everything. If the delegates decided to shoot down the idea of ratifying with amendments, then Henry knew he would lose the larger battle as well.

He watched intently as the votes began to come in. Delegates from Virginia's first four counties all voted "no"—against the prior amendments, and against Henry. Back and forth it went.

James Madison rose from his chair to gain a better vantage point of what votes remained. A glare from Chairman Pendleton quickly forced him down. With 160 votes counted, the vote stood even. George Mason slumped. He knew that many committed Federalists were still left to vote. If the anti-Federalists were to win, it would have to be on a final flat-footed tie. One by one, the remaining delegates voted, solidly and firmly: "No."

There would be no prior amendments.

Henry and Mason knew that the final vote on ratification of the Constitution itself was now a foregone conclusion. The tight margin, 89–79, belied the anticlimactic nature of the roll call. With Virginia on board, the Constitution and a new nation built around a far stronger federal government would now move forward.

No cheers greeted the final tally. The vote had been too close for that. There had been too many good patriots on either side. And there still remained much work to do. There might be no "previous" amendments, but, in the end, Patrick Henry and George Mason would win their fight for "subsequent" amendments and the badly needed Bill of Rights.

EPILOGUE

James Madison and Edmund Randolph rose from their seats and walked out toward the street. Nobody spoke, but James Madison heard a voice in his head. It was Patrick Henry's, and the words that came to him were the same ones Henry had spoken over the previous two weeks.

"Virtue will slumber," Henry had warned. The Constitution could not hold it up. "The wicked will be continually watching," he cried to the heavens. "Consequently you will be undone."

The words repeated themselves, over and over again, faster and faster, in James Madison's mind. *Virtue will slumber. The wicked will be continually watching. Consequently you will be undone.*

He tried to vanquish the thoughts from his head but instead the warnings grew louder and faster. What if, Madison thought, factions *did* arise, taxation *did* become oppressive, or the government *did* become consolidated? What if the states became impotent in the face of an ever-growing central government? What if foreign treaties endangered our freedoms and crushed our sovereignty? What if this new government eventually moved so far away from the principles they'd all agreed on that it could not even pay the interest on its legal debts? What if privacy was no longer respected? What if the press was not independent and instead an instrument of the state?

Virtue will slumber. The wicked will be continually watching. Consequently you will be undone.

And then Madison heard the words of anti-Federalist James Monroe: *"There are no limits pointed out. They are not restrained or controlled from making any law, however oppressive."* These words melded with Henry's, creating a great, pounding prophetic cacophony of trepidation, as disturbing as any storm of thunder and lightning.

Madison shook his head and took a deep breath. *No,* he thought, *these things could never happen. The Constitution—and, certainly this Bill of Rights they've insisted on—would hold such tyranny at bay. Not even in three hundred years could these iron bulwarks we have erected fail to protect our hard-fought liberty.*

But Patrick Henry, unable to rise from his chair inside the hall, silent and speechless for once in his life, feared otherwise.

4

The Barbary War:
A Steep Price for Peace

Chambers of Abd al-Rahman
London, England
March 28, 1785

The ambassador shifted in his seat. It had been twenty minutes and mysterious odors were beginning to waft into the waiting room from the kitchen. He impatiently glanced at the Arabic script and mosaic tiles covering the walls and heard his stomach growl. He missed his Virginia plantation and the meals his slaves cooked for him.

The ambassador was a man of contradictions. He was a revolutionary, but he'd never fired a gun in anger. He was a profligate spender and chronic debtor, but he hated government expenditures and fought ferociously against a national debt. And he was a well-known slave-holder, who was also his country's most eloquent advocate for liberty and equality.

The only contradiction that currently mattered, however, was Thomas Jefferson's attitude toward the ongoing hostage crisis in the Mediterranean. Hundreds of American sailors, the victims of pirates backed by petty dictators on the Barbary Coast, were languishing in North African prisons. These pirates had also confiscated thousands of dollars' worth of ships and goods. Jefferson hated the Europeans' policy of ransoming their hostages and buying peace by bribing the marauders, but he was equally distrusting of the strong central government that would be required to build a navy strong enough to protect American commerce with force.

At last, a figure approached, silhouetted against the arched hallway. Jefferson stood and turned his tall, thin figure toward Abd al-Rahman, the personal representative of the Pasha of Tripoli, Ali the First. Though nominally part of the Ottoman Empire, Tripoli was a quasi-independent state that, like Tunis, Algiers, and Morocco, had been harassing American ships.

Rahman wore a flowing white robe and dark turban. His scarred and pocked face reflected the brutal land he'd left behind. After some brief pleasantries, Rahman turned to the matter at hand, alternating his language between Italian, Spanish, and French, depending on which word he remembered first as he struggled to translate from his native Arabic. "The United States is our enemy," he said, with a candor Jefferson had not been expecting. "Peace is possible, but peace has a price. One hundred eighty-three thousand guineas, to be exact. Otherwise, we will extract our fee by continuing to pillage your ships."

Jefferson converted guineas to dollars in his head. The total owed to Tripoli and the surrounding Barbary States would approach $1 million. That was one-tenth the entire annual budget of the United States.

"Monsieur Rahman, our countries are being drawn toward a universal and horrible war," Jefferson replied in flawless French, speaking slowly to make sure the Pasha's envoy understood him. "We have no interest in sending soldiers across the Atlantic to fight your men."

Rahman took a deep breath. He understood Jefferson's words just fine but doubted that the young republic this man represented was really prepared to stand behind them. Far larger nations with far stronger militaries had chosen to pay for peace. He had no doubt that this one would as well.

"It is written in the Koran," Rahman said, "that all nations without acknowledged Islamic authority are sinners. As Muslims, it is our right and duty to make war upon whomever we can find and to make slaves of all we can take as prisoners."

Jefferson knew before he'd even arrived that he, as the United States Ambassador to France, was unlikely to succeed where the Ambassador to Britain, his friend John Adams, had already tried and failed. And now, as he listened to Rahman lecture him about the Koran and infidels and slaves, Jefferson knew he'd been right.

Dartmouth College
Five years later: August 1, 1790

There was no doubt that William Eaton liked the girl. He probably even loved her. But the line between love and infatuation was a bit too fine for the twenty-six-year-old recent college graduate. He had courted her, kissed her, and proposed to her. He would gladly promise to love her and honor her. But he wouldn't obey her. Frankly, he wasn't ready to obey anyone. So when this girl, his college sweetheart, said she'd only marry him if he promised to stay in New England and forgo his plans of returning to the army, he had no choice but to give up on her.

"My dear," he said, kissing her cheek, "no man will hereafter love you as I do—but I prefer the field of Mars to the bower of Venus."

A few years later, William Eaton joined the U.S. Army.

Washington, D.C.
Eleven years later: March 4, 1801

The inaugural address was eloquent. How could it not be? Even the new president's fiercest enemies—he had many of them—had to admit that Thomas Jefferson had a way with words.

"We are all Republicans, we are all Federalists," he told the audience gathered in the Senate chamber that day. The high-minded sentiment was quintessential Jefferson.

As Jefferson took office, a familiar problem nagged at him. His meeting with the Pasha's representative sixteen years earlier had only led to another in a long line of expensive bribes. By 1801, the young republic was spending approximately 20 percent of its annual budget paying off the Barbary dictators. It sent ships brimming with gold, precious stones, lumber, spices, cannons, and powder in return for safe passage, but the bribes only invited even more aggression. Ships were still being captured, loot confiscated, and sailors held hostage for ransom.

The Barbary appetite for riches was apparently insatiable.

Jefferson distrusted the Barbary dictators and disliked appeasing them. He believed that war was, in the long run, more economical and more honorable than bribery. He knew there was no end to the demand for money, nor any security in their promises. Blackmail, he believed, would have to be replaced by gunpowder and cannonball.

But Jefferson's actions were not always as resolute as his words. As George Washington's secretary of state, he had personally overseen a policy of ransom and tribute to the Barbary states. As the champion of rural farmers, he had long opposed the creation of a navy and, in fact, was planning to decommission warships built to patrol the Barbary Coast. The budget, after all, had to be balanced.

Tunis
May 15, 1801

The short, muscular consul to Tunis was, after all these years, still looking for another fight. As a boy, the excitable lad had run away from home to fight the British. As a young man, he had chosen the U.S. Army over his would-be fiancée. And now, after service in the Indian war, a court-martial for disobedience, and a dishonorable discharge from the army, William Eaton had a new war in mind. This would be a war to accomplish a task America had never before tried: regime change.

Eaton's mood today was even more bellicose than usual. The blue-eyed, bulldog-faced consul had just heard news of an attack on the American consulate in Tripoli. Without a Tripolitan Congress to pass an official declaration of war, the Pasha's soldiers had followed their traditional process of chopping down the flagpole at the U.S. consulate.

For the first time in its history, America found itself at war in a foreign land.

William Eaton could not have been happier.

Philadelphia, Pennsylvania
Two years later: June 13, 1803

William Ray was having a bad run of luck. Over the past few years, he had lost a string of jobs as a newspaper editor, schoolteacher, and general-store owner. Then, to top it all off, he'd found his girlfriend in the arms of a stranger—a Frenchman who, unbeknownst to Ray, was her husband.

After heavy drinking at a succession of pubs, the morose, frail thirty-four-year-old stumbled down to the banks of the Delaware River. His life a mess, he was ready to drown himself in the river's muddy waters but something made him pause. It was a noise, distant but steady: the beating of a drum.

His curiosity piqued, Ray looked down the river in the direction of the sound. Through the fog he saw the hulking outline of the largest warship he had ever seen. Perhaps because he could think of nothing better to do, or perhaps because he wasn't yet ready to meet his maker, Ray staggered along the riverbank toward the ship.

When he neared his destination—a thirty-eight-gun frigate with U.S.S. PHILADELPHIA stenciled in large letters on its side—he discovered a man in a blue and red uniform standing on the dock looking for recruits. "See the world!" shouted the Marine over the banging of the recruiting drum. "Serve your country and see the world!"

At the time, there were fewer than five hundred United States Marines, and it was not difficult to see why. Their pay was the lowest in the American military; their duties—mainly policing sailors and preventing mutiny—were the least glamorous; and their nickname was curious: *leathernecks*. The term had come from their dress uniforms, which included tall, stiff leather collars that made it difficult for a Marine to turn his head, or, more important, to lose it to the blade of a Barbary pirate's saber.

At that moment, however, none of those things really mattered to William Ray. Guaranteed meals, shelter, and a distraction from his duplicitous girlfriend were all the compensation he needed.

What do I have to lose? he thought as he shook hands with the Marine and boarded the ship for a personal tour.

Washington, D.C.
July 1, 1803

Thomas Jefferson rubbed his temples. The candles didn't shed enough light to prevent his aging eyes from straining, and it was starting to give him a headache. Everyone else in the executive mansion had already gone to bed.

Jefferson had spent the day wrangling with the domestic problems of state, but by evening he had turned his attention to international troubles. Chief in his mind was the situation on the Barbary Coast. It had been more than two years since the Pasha attacked the U.S. consulate in Tripoli and declared war on them, and, so far, the American war effort was going nowhere.

The first squadron Jefferson sent to blockade the enemy port had returned before its timid leader even put up much of a fight. The second squadron's leader, a dilettante named Commodore Richard Morris, had spent more time at parties than at sea. All the while, gold and hostages kept disappearing into the black hole that was Tripoli.

Now what? Jefferson heard the advice of his bitterly divided cabinet members in his head. Robert Smith, his hawkish Secretary of the Navy: "Nothing but a formidable force will effect an honorable peace with Tripoli." Albert Gallatin, his dovish Secretary of the Treasury, had the opposite view: "I sincerely wish you could empower our negotiators to give, if necessary for peace, an annuity to Tripoli."

Jefferson rubbed his temples again. *Damned pirates*, he thought. *We have enough problems to worry about here.* From debates over the size of the national debt and tensions with some American Indian tribes, to congressional ratification of the Louisiana Purchase, Jefferson already had his hands full domestically.

After a few more torturous minutes Jefferson made a decision: He'd send one more squadron. He had heard good things about a frigate christened the USS *Philadelphia*. The name was a good sign: Philadelphia was where the colonies had voted to take a stand against tyranny; perhaps the *Philadelphia* would finally take a stand against piracy. In either case, Jefferson was determined to not go down in history as the first American president to lose a war.

Mediterranean Sea
Off the North African Coast
Aboard the USS *Philadelphia*
October 31, 1803

The wooden decks were bleached white from the hot Mediterranean sun. The sails on the three masts strained against the riggings in the stiff breeze off the Sahara. The yellow sands of North Africa that stretched endlessly south were now just a mile or two away.

These were the shores of Tripoli.

William Ray had heard all the stories about the desolation, the punishing climate, and the inhospitable people—many of whom were Muslim holy warriors who made no secret of their hostility to infidels.

Three months at sea had taken a toll on the crew of the *Philadelphia*. Morale was dragging and brotherly love was in short supply. The salt tack was mealy and the grog perilously low. The holds emanated a pungent stench of old seawater, rotten fish, and body odor, all tinged with excrement. The smell generated by 307 men crammed into three decks on a 157-foot vessel made many sailors retch and heave. They grumbled in hushed tones about making it back home before Christmas and before the winter gales off Greenland made the long voyage even more hellish.

Making matters worse, the men felt useless. Like all the troops fighting in the war against Tripoli, they had done little to assert American power, free American hostages, or protect American ships. The men of the *Philadelphia* were fighting in a war stuck in the mud.

Ray, lost in thought as he stared off at the distant shore, heard a shout from the crow's nest. "Enemy ship ahead, port side!" He looked to the left, and saw, a mile or so in the distance, the *Philadelphia*'s prey: a small ship flying the colors of Tripoli. This, no doubt, was one of the marauders guilty of harassing merchant vessels in the area. There had been little fighting during the *Philadelphia*'s three months at sea. Now, William Ray thought, adrenaline coursing through his veins, perhaps that was about to change.

The eighteen cannons along the leeward side were locked into position as the *Philadelphia* quickly closed the distance to the enemy ship. "Full speed ahead!" ordered the captain.

They were close enough for Ray to now make out the panicked faces aboard the Tripolitan vessel ahead. These pirates knew what was about to happen next: the *Philadelphia* would pull alongside and unleash a fierce volley of cannonballs that would tear into them and likely send their ship to the bottom of the Mediterranean.

A smile formed on William Ray's face as he thought of all the terror these pirates had inflicted on his countrymen. This would be payb— CRACK! His thoughts were interrupted by the piercing sound of splintering wood. The *Philadelphia* lurched to a stop, Ray and the sailors around him spilling forward from the sudden reversal of momentum, some falling over onto the deck and into the ocean below.

Ray looked over the side of the warship and saw a vast reef in the shallow water. They were stuck—dead in the water.

The Tripolitan pirates in their smaller, lighter ship had known the reef was there and had baited the *Philadelphia* right into it.

Ray looked back at the pirates and realized instantly that he'd been wrong: It wasn't panic he had seen on their faces.

It was anticipation.

Tripoli
Two months later: December 25, 1803

After the *Philadelphia* had beached itself on the reef, Tripolitan ships had surrounded it, leaving the captain no option except surrender. Relieved of their uniforms, the sailors and Marines were brought, naked and shivering, into port and jailed. The Pasha of Tripoli renamed the ship *The Gift of Allah*.

William Ray and hundreds of other U.S. sailors and Marines were his prisoners.

Now, almost two months into their captivity, Ray stood with an empty stomach in the bitterly cold ocean, shoveling sand from the seafloor. The Pasha's cruel slave masters seemed to take joy in the prisoners' suffering. Each day, from sunrise through midafternoon, the Americans were kept in the ocean without so much as a morsel of bread. When men fainted from exhaustion, the guards beat them until they somehow found the strength to rise again.

In the afternoon, the sailors and leathernecks were usually given some water and black bread. As they ate, Ray and the others tried everything possible to get warm, from clapping their hands to running in place. They were then returned to the freezing water to work until sunset. Bed was a stone floor covered in tiny rocks. They slept in the same cold, wet clothes they worked in.

William Ray had not always been a praying man, but on this night his plea was solemn and sincere. "Dear God," he whispered, "I pray that I might never experience the horrors of another morning." Ray thought back to that night on the bank of the Delaware River and wished that instead of turning his head toward the sound of the drum, he'd stuck it under the rushing water.

Mediterranean Sea
Off the North African Coast
Aboard the USS *Essex*
February 16, 1804

Stephen Decatur paced from starboard to port and back, unable to hide his anxiety. His commodore had asked him to undertake a suicide mission. Always the loyal officer, Decatur hadn't hesitated to accept. When he asked his crew for volunteers, none of them had hesitated, either.

"We are now about to embark on an expedition which may terminate in our sudden deaths, our perpetual slavery, or our immortal glory," he said to the sixty-seven men gathered on the deck of the USS *Essex*.

At sunset that evening, Decatur and his men—all dressed as Maltese sailors—left their frigate and boarded an aptly named ketch called the *Intrepid*. The *Intrepid* would attract less notice than the *Essex* both because of its smaller size and because, as a ketch that had been previously captured from the enemy, it would not look to the Tripolitans like a threat.

The course was set for the port of Tripoli, only a few miles in the distance. At nine thirty the silhouette of the city's ramparts, dimly lit by lanterns, appeared on the horizon. A few minutes after that, the three masts of the captured USS *Philadelphia*, now *The Gift of Allah*, came into view. They glided silently forward, knowing that if Tripoli's sentries were alerted they didn't stand a chance.

"Man hua?" a voice cried out. Who goes there?

Decatur didn't speak any Arabic, but his helmsman did. He yelled back that they were Maltese traders seeking port for the night.

"Tayyib." Very well.

With the wind dying down in port, the sixty-foot ketch coasted on its own momentum toward the docks. Its destination was not, however, any slip.

It was the *Philadelphia*.

Silent, except for the heavy breathing of the crew and the lapping of water against the hull, the ketch maneuvered alongside the great warship. *It's a shame it has come to this*, Decatur thought.

His men grabbed the cannon nozzles of the *Philadelphia* and affixed ropes to the hull.

"Board now," Decatur whispered. The sailors clambered over the gunnels.

"Amreeki!" Shouts rang out from ship—Americans! Twenty Tripolitan guards on board the *Philadelphia* had seen Decatur's men. They were swiftly silenced with muskets, but the secret was out.

Decatur's men turned the *Philadelphia*'s great cannons toward the city, launching volley after volley and making quick work of the clay and brick buildings in port. Then they lit a fuse to the ship's store of gunpowder and jumped back aboard the ketch.

Whether it was called the *Philadelphia* or *The Gift of Allah*, the once-mighty warship, now burning from bow to stern, would soon be of no further use to anyone.

U.S. Capitol
Washington, D.C.
March 26, 1804

The president appeared to be enjoying himself at this most unusual party. Two years ago, supporters had sent Thomas Jefferson a twelve-hundred-pound block of cheese. Today, starting at noon, Jefferson—with the help of an equally massive loaf of bread and an open invitation to the public—expected to finally finish it off.

Guests at the Capitol ranged from farmers to fishermen, politicians to proletarians, and slaveholders to, according to one senator, their slaves. Some came for the cheese, which had become famous, others came for the alcohol, which was in great supply, but William Eaton was there for something else.

"Mr. President," said the former consul to Tunis, several hours into the festivities, "if I could just have a moment of your time."

Jefferson, Eaton knew from watching closely, had already enjoyed a few drinks. Maybe a few too many. But perhaps, he thought, the president's temporary reduction in inhibitions might work to Eaton's advantage. Perhaps he had caught Jefferson at just the right time.

"Of course," said the self-styled president of the common man. Hearing from his people was, along with the consumption of the large block of cheese, the purpose of today's party. If he was looking down on Eaton, it was only because his excitable guest was six inches shorter.

After a brief introduction, Eaton jumped right into the matter on his mind. "Sir, the capture of the *Philadelphia* is the latest outrage in a war we are losing." If Jefferson was taken aback by Eaton's abruptness, he didn't show it. He had, after all, read equally blunt appraisals of the war effort.

"Our navy doesn't have enough ships to win this war," Eaton continued. "And our commodores don't have enough boldness. The last commodore spent seventeen months in the Mediterranean but only nineteen days before the enemy's port! A fleet of Quaker meeting-houses would have done just as well!"

The president tried to interrupt Eaton, but he was just getting warmed up. Interspersing his passionate plea with lines he had delivered to congressmen a month earlier, Eaton told Jefferson, "There is no limit to the avarice of the Barbary princes. Today Tripoli demands three million dollars. Next year the Pasha will want ten million. Like the insatiable grave, they can never have enough. The solution is not to be found in blockades and bribes but in a change of regime!"

Jefferson, even in his state of mild inebriation, appeared skeptical.

Eaton pushed. "The project is feasible! I have met a man named Hamet Qaramanli, who is the rightful Pasha." Nine years earlier, Hamet's younger brother, Yussef, locked Hamet out of his own palace in Tripoli. In one day, he had lost his throne, his country, the loyalty of his brother, and the company of his wife and children, who had become Yussef's first hostages.

"He is an enemy of piracy," Eaton continued. "He is a friend of America. He belongs on the Tripolitan throne. And with your support, I can put him there."

"Is that so?" asked a still-doubtful president.

"I can march with Hamet Qaramanli from Cairo to Tripoli. His people will rally to his flag. With an Arab army, we can attack by land and put a true friend on the throne. He will release the men of the *Philadelphia* and swear to never kidnap Americans. Nor will he demand a dollar of tribute from the United States. I need only some money and Marines."

Jefferson knew the naval war was producing no results and he understood the public's anger over the capture of the *Philadelphia*. He was angry, too.

It might be the alcohol, he thought to himself, *but this Eaton fellow is making a lot of sense.*

Tripoli
May 1, 1804

William Ray awoke as he had every day for the last seven months: in hell. Damp clothes, a grumbling stomach, and a full day of backbreaking work were ahead. Ray had no way of knowing that this day was different. Help was finally on the way.

Four days after the cheese party at the Capitol, President Jefferson had given William Eaton the title of "Agent of the United States Navy" and the promise of forty thousand dollars. His mission was to put Hamet Qaramanli on the Tripolitan throne.

William Ray had never heard of William Eaton or Hamet Qaramanli. The only "Qaramanli" he knew was his captor and torturer: Yussef, the Pasha of Tripoli. Unaware that a rescue plan was in place, Ray and his fellow prisoners remained careful never to offend their guards.

So far, they'd managed to escape the most extreme forms of torture. Simple beatings, however, were another matter. Today, for their captors' amusement, one American slave had received the traditional Tripolitan beating: bastinados.

Ray watched with resignation as the Marine was thrown onto his back, his feet tied and raised above his head so that he was hanging upside down. Then a slave master slammed a wooden rod into the soles of his feet as hard as he could. Then he did it again, and again and again.

The slave cried out, but his pain only seemed to encourage them.

Another blow came.

And then another.

And then two hundred more.

How long, William Ray thought, *will my country let us languish in this hell?*

Five hundred miles east of Derna
Ten months later: March 12, 1805

Five days earlier, William Eaton, Hamet Qaramanli, and their army of approximately four hundred Arabs, European mercenaries, and United States Marines had left Alexandria, Egypt. Their first mission was to march across the desert to the city of Derna, a coastal jewel in the Pasha's crown located about four hundred miles to the east of the capital, Tripoli City. If they could capture Derna, they knew they would demonstrate their ability to capture the city of Tripoli itself. For that reason, and because Eaton had promised many of the Arabs in his army that they could make money by looting Derna, it was essential to take this city first.

Derna was still five hundred miles away, but Eaton and his army were already in trouble. "Stop!" he yelled, "I will cut off the head of any man who dares to fire a shot!" Waving his scimitar above his head, Eaton found himself squarely in the middle of a closely packed mass of screaming, angry Christians and Muslims.

Earlier that week, Eaton—who had started to call himself "General" Eaton even though no one in his chain of command had approved the promotion—had lost an entire day trying to persuade his camel drivers, who continually asked for more money, to stay with the expedition. Without them there would be no way to bring along the food and supplies necessary to make the rest of the trip.

Money, however, was becoming an issue. The self-proclaimed general had already pledged $100,000 to the ninety Tripolitans, sixty-three European soldiers of fortune, 250 Bedouin accompanying Hamet, eight leathernecks, and a lone navy midshipman on the journey. These promises more than doubled the budget President Jefferson had authorized, but Eaton was sure he could pay his bills once Derna and Tripoli were captured and looted.

Today's crisis began with a rumor that the citizens of Derna had rebelled against the Pasha and were waiting for Hamet to arrive and seize power. Excited by the news, Hamet's Tripolitans fired their guns into the air in celebration. The Bedouin camel drivers, who lagged behind the rest of the group, heard the gunfire and assumed the makeshift army was under attack by other Bedouin. Rather than coming to their defense, the camel drivers rushed ahead, intending to grab a share of the loot. Eaton's European soldiers of fortune, unsure why they were being attacked, formed a defensive line to fend off the charging camel drivers.

In the midst of the confusion and chaos, Eaton ran out between his camel drivers and soldiers, waving his scimitar and demanding they hold their fire. As he explained the situation—a false rumor and a misguided celebration—silence fell over his army. The Bedouin drivers backed away and catastrophe was temporarily averted. This dysfunctional group of Marines and mercenaries had survived to march another day.

Three hundred miles east of Derna
March 18, 1805

William Eaton's army had now been marching for eleven days. Their supply of food was ample, and the water wells in this region were plentiful, but so, unfortunately, was his men's distrust of each other.

This night, it was about to get even worse.

A pilgrim traveling from Morocco to Mecca brought news that the Pasha was sending an eight-hundred-man army to defend Derna. The garrison at Derna was already more than twice the size of Eaton's army. If the Pasha's reinforcements beat them to the city, its fort and barricades would be virtually impregnable. If Eaton's army couldn't get in, it wouldn't be able to loot the city, and his Arab soldiers would likely quit.

Eaton's instinct was to march faster, but his Arab allies refused. They'd been promised that the U.S. Navy would support the attack on Derna with a bombardment. Now they demanded that Eaton send an advance scout ahead to see if the American ships had arrived. When Eaton refused, the Bedouin camel drivers left.

Eaton was livid. *We have marched a distance of two hundred miles*, he lamented in his journal, *through an inhospitable waste of a world*. Over burning sands and rocky mountains, Eaton had held together his band of misfits by begging, borrowing, and bribing. Earlier that day, he had met the Bedouin's latest demand for more money by borrowing $673 from the Marines and European mercenaries, promising to repay them when they rendezvoused with the U.S. Navy. Now, despite having been paid, they were gone.

Once again, Eaton had no choice but to comply with their demands. Reluctantly, he sent a scout ahead to look for American ships. The next day, enough of the camel drivers returned to allow the ragtag army to continue its march toward Derna.

Tripoli
March 29, 1805

William Ray was in his seventeenth month of captivity. His living conditions remained foul. His daily labor remained backbreaking. His captors remained merciless.

As Ray walked by the gates of Tripoli, daydreaming of a rescue that seemed to grow more unlikely by the day, he spotted two African slaves, straw rope wrapped around their necks, still alive, swinging from the city gates.

"What was their crime?" he asked a fellow captive.

"Accused of murder and robbery. But they probably didn't do anything worse than anger the Pasha."

Ray didn't doubt this. The Pasha seemed to be in control over everything except his own erratic and violent whims. "How long have they been hanging there?"

"About two hours," said the sailor. "Two hours in the sun wearing nothing but a shirt. They'll die in another hour or two, but the birds and bugs will get to feast on them first."

130 miles east of Derna
April 10, 1805

The meat was gone, as was the bread. After thirty-four days of marching, all that was left was rice. And distrust.

"I have heard a rumor that you aim only to use me for the purpose of obtaining a peace with my brother," Hamet told Eaton.

"That's absurd," Eaton replied. He wanted to free the prisoners from the *Philadelphia*, but he wouldn't trade Hamet for them. Nor would he trade Hamet for a peace treaty. Any peace that ended with the Pasha still on the throne would be a short-lived and worthless one.

Besides, today was not a day for pessimism. The scout who'd been sent ahead to search for American ships had just returned with great news: they were just a week's march ahead. Reinforcements were close—if only Eaton could keep his army together that long.

65 miles east of Derna
April 16, 1805

Eaton's army, which had grown to more than six hundred men, was too weak to march. The new soldiers, most of them Bedouins who'd been attracted by the promise of payment and the prospect of looting Derna, had put a heavy strain on their supplies.

A few days earlier they'd finished their last ration of rice. The next day they had killed a camel for food.

The hunger exacerbated the distrust. Eaton was worried that the foreign soldiers might soon rebel against him for leading them into this debacle. And he still wasn't sure if Hamet believed that he wouldn't be used as a bargaining chip. The whole expedition seemed to be hanging by a thread.

That evening, a foreign soldier ran into camp, pointing frantically toward the ocean. Eaton ran to the shore and understood immediately. Out where the horizon met the sea, a ship had appeared.

A United States warship.

It would, Eaton knew, have guns, gold coins, and, most important, enough food to feed an army ten times the size of the one he currently had.

For the first time that month, Eaton and his men knew they would not go to sleep on empty stomachs.

At the gates of Derna
April 26, 1805

After five hundred miles, six weeks, and several near mutinies, William Eaton and his army had made it to the gates of the great port city of Derna. His rabble had not only survived intact, they had also beaten the Pasha's reinforcements in the race to the city.

After issuing a "Proclamation to Inhabitants of Tripoli," which described in detail the founding of the United States and informed the city's Tripolitans that Hamet was their rightful ruler, Eaton wrote a short letter to Governor Mustafa, cousin of the Pasha and commander of the Pasha's troops in Derna.

"Sir, I want no territory," Eaton began. "With me is advancing the legitimate Sovereign of your country. Give us passage through your city and the supplies we need and you shall receive fair compensation."

For once, Eaton's promise of compensation was not wholly unrealistic. Navy ships were nearby—one of them being the ship that had come to Eaton's rescue ten days earlier. If the governor opened the city to Eaton, the ships would bring him a healthy reward for his cooperation. If he fought, the ships would shell the city.

"Let no difference of religion induce us to shed the blood of harmless men who think little and know nothing," Eaton told him. "If you are a man of liberal mind you will not have to think long about my propositions. Hamet pledges himself to me that you shall be established in your government. I shall see you tomorrow in a way of your choice."

The governor's terse reply did not take long to arrive, and it did not require much interpretation.

"My head or yours."

Derna
April 27, 1805

The battle with Governor Mustafa's forces was just over an hour old, but it was already turning into a catastrophe. Eaton's army was pinned down at the southeastern edge of Derna by an enemy twice its size. As bullets flew past them from the barricades defending the city, Eaton's men were approaching a state of panic. His European mercenaries were faltering and his Arab allies were ready to retreat.

Eaton, however, remained calm. He had waited his whole life for a battle like this. Decked out in the white, homemade officer's uniform he'd designed himself and worn since leaving Alexandria, Eaton surveyed the scene. He tried to imagine what the great military minds of his favorite history books would do in this situation.

Ahead of him was a well-entrenched, superior enemy. To advance into Mustafa's seemingly impregnable line was to invite death, but to remain pinned down and panicked was unacceptable. And to retreat . . . No. He caught himself. He would never entertain the thought. William Eaton had not crossed a desert and defied hunger, desertions, and near mutiny only to run from the first sight of bullets.

"Fix bayonets!" he yelled over the crash of the cannonballs launched from the naval ships on Eaton's flank.

The word was passed down the line, disordered as it was. It was hard to hear over all the noise, and for a moment, it looked like the orders had been lost. Then, a few of the Marines, the ones closest to Eaton, attached the sharp blades to the ends of their muskets, and the rest of his misfit army followed suit. The next order was the one Eaton believed he was born to give.

"Charge!"

Racing ahead of his men, his eyes flashing with excitement, he sprinted for the barricades. He knew the eight blue-and-red-clad leathernecks would follow him, but he wasn't sure about the others. The hired guns had barely followed him out of Alexandria; would they really charge with him into a hailstorm of musket fire?

The answer, Eaton quickly saw, was yes. Whether it was out of a self-ish desire to loot Derna, a dream of putting Hamet in the Tripolitan throne, a fear of retreating and starving in the barren desert, or some-thing else entirely, did not really matter. What did matter was that they were now following Eaton and the Marines, rushing headlong into a wave of heavy fire.

Their shouts came in at least half a dozen different languages, but they were all the same. "To Derna!" "To Tripoli!" And, in Arabic, "Hamet Qaramanli!" from those with their scimitars held high.

As bullets whizzed by Eaton's head, he leapt over the barricade and into the enemy line, his army at his heels. An enemy soldier lunged at him with a bloody sword, but Eaton ducked, dropped to the ground, and rolled past his attacker. His foe spun around but was too slow. Eaton plunged his bayonet into the Arab's stomach.

The leathernecks fired their muskets into the chests of the enemy at point-blank range. Through the cloud of noise and dirt, one unlikely reality was quickly becoming clear: Mustafa's soldiers were panicking. They hadn't expected the audacious bayonet charge and now they were in a mad rush to retreat.

The bravest enemy soldiers, Eaton saw through the chaos, were fir-ing through the swirling dust, then running for cover, reloading and firing again. It was one of those soldiers who took direct aim at him. Eaton heard a "thwack!" and felt a piercing pain. The bullet had been aimed at his heart.

It had only missed by inches.

Eaton fell to the ground as his triumphant leathernecks, mercenar-ies, and Arabs—their swords and bayonets colored red with blood—rushed past him in pursuit of the retreating enemy. He clenched his teeth and wrapped his wound. His limp arm, which had taken the brunt of the enemy bullet, was not able to hold a musket any longer.

Eaton drew his pistol and charged ahead, firing into any enemy soldier brave or foolish enough to still resist.

Finally, after four hours of fighting, Derna fell silent. Atop Derna's highest flagpole, the Stars and Stripes flapped in the wind.

The city now belonged to the United States.

Eaton took a deep breath. He was pleased, but he wasn't finished. He would not be satisfied until the same flag flew over the Pasha's palace in Tripoli.

Derna
May 31, 1805

In the month after Derna fell, the enemy continued to fight. The Pasha's late-arriving reinforcements surrounded the city and outnumbered Eaton's force. But Eaton had something the Pasha's troops did not: a navy. With warships supplying Eaton with food, weapons, and money, the Pasha's troops soon began to realize that the American army could hold out for as long as it took. Many of the Pasha's men deserted and one enemy commander even approached Eaton about defecting.

On this late spring morning, Eaton was pleased to see a new frigate, the USS *Constellation*, pulling up at the dock. An hour later, a messenger from the warship approached Eaton as he sat down for lunch.

After briefly exchanging greetings the messenger got right to the point. "Sir, I am here to advise you that President Jefferson has revised his orders."

Eaton had expected news about additional weapons or troops. He was confused.

"I'm sorry, I'm afraid I don't quite know what you are talking about."

The messenger continued: "When you took Derna, the Pasha quickly realized that he could lose the throne. So he sued for peace. He told President Jefferson that he would stop all attacks on American ships and release the *Philadelphia* prisoners in exchange for sixty thousand dollars. It is my duty to inform you that the United States government has decided to accept his offer."

Questions raced through Eaton's mind. *Why would the United States*

*allow a tyrant to remain on the throne when his defeat was imminent? Did they
really expect him to live up to his word? What would happen to Eaton's Arab
allies? To Hamet?*

The messenger, sensing Eaton's apprehension, continued. "I am
here under orders from the president to escort Hamet Qaramanli and
all American troops to Sicily. I can also transport your European soldiers and a few of the Arabs. The rest must fend for themselves."

Tripoli
June 4, 1805

William Ray had lived as a slave for nineteen months. He ate when
the Pasha's men said he could eat. He worked when the Pasha's men
ordered him to work, which was from sunrise to sunset, seven days a
week. He slept when the Pasha's men allowed him to sleep.

But today was different. When he'd woken up this morning, no one
was there to drag him out to the sea.

The captain of the *Philadelphia* called together his former crew
and told him what he'd learned: reports of a treaty. Details were still
sketchy, but the Pasha had granted their release.

"We are free," the captain told them. "And tomorrow, we're going
home!"

For the second time, William Ray's life was saved from suicide—
which he had contemplated many times in the last nineteen months—
by the words of a sailor in the United States Navy.

At sea; Washington, D.C.; Sicily
June 20, 1805

William Ray and the men of the *Philadelphia* were emaciated and exhausted, but they were also elated. They were sailing home to the
United States, where a hero's welcome awaited them.

In Washington, Thomas Jefferson was triumphant. He was being
heralded as the commander in chief that freed three hundred American hostages. Now he could use that success to reduce the size of the
American navy and get the budget in order.

On the island of Sicily, Hamet Qaramanli was dejected, but grateful to William Eaton and his troops. As a token of his appreciation, Hamet presented Presley O'Bannon, the officer in charge of the departing Marines, with Hamet's most prized possession: a weapon he had carried from Alexandria to Derna. Its slim blade was slightly curved. Its ornate handle was shaped like the letter *J*, and running the length of the sword—a scimitar, to be precise—were engraved Arabic words.

William Eaton, on the other hand, was not so grateful. In fact, he was bitter. He was willing to concede that the treaty with the Pasha was "more favorable and—separately considered—more honorable than any peace obtained by any Christian nation with a Barbary regency at any period within a hundred years." But he raged at the opportunity that had been lost. "I firmly believe," he later told a friend, "we would have entered Tripoli with as little trouble as we did Derna."

EPILOGUE

Monticello; Washington, D.C.; Tripoli
June 1815

At seventy-two years old, Thomas Jefferson looked back on a life full of historic accomplishments. With the Declaration of Independence he had given his new nation its creed. With the Louisiana Purchase he had doubled its size. His ideas about religious freedom would inform the nation's First Amendment, and his belief in small government would inspire generations of Americans to remain skeptical of centralized power.

The Barbary War was not, however, one of Jefferson's finest moments. By allowing Pasha Qaramanli to remain on the throne, he had chosen compromise over victory. He had shown weakness, and that weakness had provoked more aggression. It was a great irony that, after a daring, five-hundred-mile march to Derna, the Pasha of Tripoli would keep his job, while many officers of the American navy would lose theirs.

In the ten years after the release of the *Philadelphia* prisoners, the Pasha had broken almost every term of the treaty. Tripoli and the other

Barbary states had resumed their attacks on American ships. Now another U.S. president was again forced to deal with the situation.

At just five foot four and barely one hundred pounds, James Madison could appear, upon first impression, weak and frail. But his looks were deceiving. Madison built America's first great navy. He led the United States to victory over Great Britain in the War of 1812. And he was determined to do what his country had failed to do ever since Thomas Jefferson met Abd al-Rahman in London: He would achieve peace through strength, not appeasement. Madison made it the "settled policy of America, that as peace is better than war, war is better than tribute."

While Jefferson rested at Monticello, an armada was parked in the port of Tripoli with enough firepower to turn the city into rubble. One ship brought a personal message for the Pasha from James Madison himself. "The United States," the president had written, "while they wish for war with no nation, will buy peace with none."

The American captain who delivered the president's message was Stephen Decatur, the same man who'd led the daring mission to destroy the USS *Philadelphia*. Decatur, at Madison's behest, had also delivered the same ultimatum to the Barbary states of Algiers and Tunis.

After the capture of thirty-five American ships and seven hundred American hostages, the United States' thirty-year war with the Barbary pirates was finally over. It had not ended with a bribe, or a treaty, but with a demand for peace, backed by a credible threat of overwhelming force.

Today, a scimitar modeled after the one given by Hamet to Presley O'Bannon hangs at the side of every United States Marine officer in dress uniform. The "Marines' Hymn," which is the oldest official song in the military, contains a reference to the war where American leathernecks first proved their incredible resilience:

To the shores of Tripoli.

5

Edison vs. Westinghouse:
An Epic Struggle for Power

New York City
Spring 1885

"Fifty thousand dollars? You *are* mad."

Nikola Tesla straightened his shoulders. His eyes never wavered from Thomas Edison. He responded, "You promised me fifty thousand dollars if I resolved those engineering problems." He lifted his chin slightly. "The designs are complete."

Edison wondered if he had made a mistake hiring this strange young Serb from Continental Edison, his subsidiary in Paris, nine months earlier. Edison had tasked him with designing an improved method of power transmission, but instead of working with direct current distribution—the technology that Edison had championed—he'd concentrated on alternating current. Tesla insisted that alternating the direction of electrical charges was better than a constant flow in a single direction because it allowed electricity to be transmitted from great distances with less power loss. Edison—both for practical and financial reasons—vehemently disagreed.

Edison rose from his chair so he was level with the standing Tesla. "You misunderstood. Now, if you'll excuse me, I have work."

"I won't leave without my money."

Edison knew Tesla was odd, but he never expected to be confronted in this fashion. Tesla counted every step he took, worked only with objects and numbers divisible by three, seldom shook hands, and refused to touch another person's hair. His fastidious attire and precise English annoyed the untidy Edison. *Does Tesla really believe that being neat makes him a better man?* Edison thought to himself. *A better inventor?*

"This is absurd, Nikola. You earn eighteen dollars a week, a generous salary. Didn't we just deny your request for a seven-dollar-per-week raise? How could you possibly believe those designs were worth fifty thousand dollars?"

"Because you promised."

Edison stared disapprovingly at him, a practiced look that was sufficient to dissuade most employees.

Tesla was not so easily put off. "And because I need the money for my work with alternating current."

Edison chewed his unlit cigar. This last statement irritated him to no end. Edison had reservations about direct current technology, but he was deeply committed to it. Most of his inventions, the expertise of his companies, and his factory tooling were all aimed at direct current. Was Tesla trying to wreck everything Edison had built?

"Nikola, you have splendid ideas, but alternating current is utterly impractical. I need your mind on your assigned work."

"Yes, and I've completed my assigned work. Now I've come for the bonus you offered me to improve the electrical distribution system."

"To finance work on alternating current?"

"How I use the money is not your business." The dapper, twenty-eight-year-old engineer looked down for a moment, as so many others had done when coming face-to-face with Edison. But then he quickly lifted his head back up. "Mr. Edison, with deference to your grand accomplishments, the future is alternating current. It's the only way to transmit high-voltage energy over long distances."

"You're wrong Nikola. Now good night."

"You are not going to pay me?"

"I *already* paid you—the eighteen dollars a week we agreed to."

"Then you leave me no alternative but to resign."

Edison removed the cigar from his mouth and, after a heartbeat, waved it dismissively. "Then go."

Edison stood by the window and watched Tesla leave his office. He was sure that Tesla would reconsider the second he stepped out of his headquarters and onto Fifth Avenue. But Edison, his mind always racing, quickly realized the flaw in his thinking: Tesla was far too stubborn and fanatical; he would never be dissuaded from pursuing alternating current. Edison wondered if he should run downstairs and stop Tesla from leaving the brownstone. *Perhaps,* he wondered, *the old adage about keeping enemies close might apply here.*

Edison shoved his cigar back in his mouth, his decision made. He plopped back into his chair and spun it toward his cluttered desk.

No. It was best that Tesla leave and never return.

Great Barrington, Massachusetts
March 1886

George Westinghouse tugged the lapels of his coat until the finely woven fabric snugged properly against his broad shoulders. He licked his fingers and smoothed his expansive handlebar mustache. He was pleased with his reflection in the mirror.

A voice came from behind him. "We should alert the newspapers."

William Stanley had invented an alternating current transformer. His outsized ambition, along with his oversized ego, made him eager to make a name for himself. A story in the newspapers would help.

"No. Alerting newspapers also alerts Edison and his backers," Westinghouse said. "It's better that reporters cover the story as just another electrification." He used the fingers of both hands to fluff his mutton-chops.

"Engineers will be impressed that we are making a leap in technology," Stanley said. "This is a major breakthrough—we both know that. We're changing the direction of electricity, after all. What do we gain by introducing it so quietly?"

Westinghouse turned from the mirror to face Stanley directly. "Edison likes to shout about his accomplishments from the rooftops. I prefer to simply deliver on my commitments. My ambition is to provide employees an opportunity to make their lives better. That is the reason I build large companies. I pay living wages that are higher than other manufacturers, and my companies are pioneers in safety, benefits, and pensions. Personal glory is not among my concerns."

Westinghouse saw by Stanley's expression that he didn't like his answer.

After a silent moment, Stanley gently took him by the elbow and guided him toward the window. There was a large crowd gathering below. "Mr. Westinghouse, this twilight will soon turn to dark, and then we'll turn that darkness back into light. Those people think it's magic, or nearly so."

"Then why should we disillusion them? There is nothing wrong with magic. Besides, we'll only incite our competitors if we crow about this evening."

Westinghouse knew he was not nearly as famous as the flamboyant Wizard of Menlo Park. Edison had a carefully crafted image as a disheveled genius who lived off apple pie. Reporters lionized him as a selfless giant dedicated to changing the world.

Westinghouse, on the other hand, was just another Pittsburgh inventor and manufacturer. He refused interviews. He didn't make good copy. He was dull. Sure, he was successful and rich, but his wealth came from arcane industries that received little public attention. Electricity, however, was different. Unlike trains, telegraphs, or steam engines, electricity came into the home and made everyday life easier, cleaner, and less expensive. Electric light was soft, odor-free, flicker-free, clean, cool, and soundless—all the things gaslights were not. People believed it was magic.

Electricity was becoming so popular that small companies were formed almost every day in almost every city in the nation. Most were doomed to fail, especially those run by electrical neophytes. So, on January 8, 1886, when Westinghouse incorporated his fifth business, the Westinghouse Electric Company, no one took much notice. He believed it was in his interest to keep it that way.

Tonight, they were going to illuminate the town of Great Barrington with electricity generated many miles away. This was an important milestone because the direct current used elsewhere needed to be generated within a half mile of where it was used due to heat and energy loss. This was somewhat workable in cities, but in a rambling town like Great Barrington, it meant that each business and home would need to install a private generator. Whether placed in the basement or down the block, these generators spewed coal dust, smoke, and noise.

Westinghouse's alternating current technology made it possible for power stations to be located close to their fuel source, well outside of neighborhoods. It wasn't hard to see the vision: Westinghouse would build large generating facilities far from population centers and then sell that electricity to the citizens of each city. It would be cleaner, quieter, safer, and far more efficient.

Westinghouse patted Stanley on the shoulder. "Now, let's go give these fine people a magic show."

West Orange, New Jersey
December 1887

"Here are today's copper prices."

The aide handed Edison the ticker tape and scurried out of his office, indicating the tape carried bad news. *Up another penny! Damn the French!* He threw the tape into the ash can.

A French consortium had cornered the copper market and driven the price from ten cents a pound to sixteen cents. Even for short distances, direct current required expensive, thick copper wire. He looked at the budget for his latest proposal. Every penny increase would cost him an additional three thousand dollars for copper wire on this one contract alone. He didn't need another headache right now.

Westinghouse had come out of nowhere to invade his territory. He was making far too much headway with his alternating current schemes and now, because his method used far less copper, the increasing prices were pushing the edge even further in his favor. Edison knew that Westinghouse, through no effort of his own, was gaining an economic advantage.

Edison had fought off competitors like gnats when he'd first electrified Wall Street five years earlier. After he had emerged supreme his name became synonymous with the fastest-growing industry in the world: electrification. His businesses had grown so large so fast that he no longer knew the names of all the people he employed. Was it possible that everything could now be at risk? He had never felt fear like this before. He tried to shake it off, but the foreboding lingered.

Westinghouse's companies were thriving and he was expanding his electrification reach almost every day. Westinghouse had concentrated on delivering power outside the large metropolitan areas, but he recently captured New Orleans, the tenth-largest city in the country. Edison's salesmen were now writing letters to headquarters, pleading for help. Westinghouse had to be stopped.

Edison believed he understood Westinghouse because they had followed similar paths, each of them having invented a vital component for one of the two most important industries in the nation. Edison created the Quadruplex Telegraph, and Westinghouse developed air brakes for railcars. Both were fine inventions, but telegraphs and trains were no longer on the technical or financial frontier. Now Wall Street was rushing to invest in electricity, an industry Edison practically owned until Westinghouse had invaded his arena. He knew he had to do something about it.

Edison picked up a letter that had been sitting on his desk and made a decision.

Last November, Thomas Edison had received a letter from Alfred P. Southwick, a dentist who had been appointed to the Commission on Humane Executions for the state of New York. Southwick wanted Edison's opinion about execution by electricity. Because of his opposition to capital punishment, Edison had declined to offer advice, but Southwick would not be put off. When Edison received a follow-up letter, he began to think about the question more deeply.

Electricity was, by its very nature, dangerous. New York City, for example, was a web of overhead electric lines. Dangerous lines. When they fell, pedestrians were at risk of electric shock.

When Edison entered the New York market, he had insisted on burying his electric wiring in iron pipes. Trenching had been costly and slow, but safety was of utmost importance—and his focus on it ultimately helped him to win popular support. In the end, his competitors went under, retreated to a remote corner of the electricity business, or were forced to move to an entirely different industry.

Now he would use the same strategy—a singular focus on safety—to destroy Westinghouse.

He began to compose a letter back to Southwick, the dentist.

The best appliance for humane execution is one that will perform its work in the shortest space of time, and inflict the least amount of suffering upon its victim. This I believe can be accomplished by the use of electricity and the most suitable apparatus for the purpose is that class of dynamo-electric machine which employs intermittent currents.

The most effective of these are known as "alternating machines," manufactured principally in this country by Mr. Geo. Westinghouse, Pittsburgh.

Pittsburgh, Pennsylvania
June 1888

Westinghouse seethed. He read aloud the line again. "Just as certain as death, Westinghouse will kill a customer within 6 months after he puts in a system of any size."

Nikola Tesla stood very still, his hands folded in front of him. "He wrote that to the president of Edison Electric with full knowledge that the prediction would get whispered around until it became public."

Westinghouse threw the newspaper onto his desk. "Edison's trying to paint me as a killer."

"Precisely," Tesla said.

"Why is he using such underhanded tactics?" Westinghouse asked. "Why not just come out and say it directly? It's not as though he doesn't have access to the newspapers."

Tesla moved his arms and re-clasped his hands behind his back. "He is wrong about alternating current . . . and at some level he knows it. He's afraid his preeminence will fade." He shook his head. "I warned him about this years ago."

"Nikola, do you have advice for me?"

"Do not underestimate Tom Edison. He's clever, and he has a knack for grabbing headlines. He used a thousand-volt Westinghouse generator to kill dogs, horses, and even cows. It is impious, but he claims he is researching the relative dangers of direct and alternating current. He says his only interest is in protecting the public, especially children."

"I meant advice on what action to take," Westinghouse said, with more irritation than he'd intended.

"You must defend alternating current. You must be its champion. Call reporters and tell them our side of the story. The newspapers sensationalize human deaths from alternating current, but they've all occurred from obsolete outdoor arc lighting. There has never been a death associated with Westinghouse Electric."

"Except for dogs!"

"Mr. Westinghouse, I understand your disgust with what he is doing to animals, but he will not stop there. There are rumors he is helping New York State use electricity for capital punishment." Tesla paused for dramatic effect. "He intends to use alternating current."

Westinghouse paced his office. Edison had started this damn war between direct and alternating current and there was no need for it. There was enough business for both of them. The whole world needed electricity.

He understood Edison's desire to protect his investment; Westinghouse had a similar motivation. He had recently paid Tesla $60,000, plus royalties of $2.50 per horsepower of electrical capacity sold, to use his patents. Westinghouse had further invested in factories, salesmen, and research dedicated to alternating current. He and Edison both had a lot to protect—and Westinghouse had come a long way.

After only two years, Westinghouse had over half as many generating stations as Edison, but mostly in smaller markets. Edison had New York City; he had Buffalo. Westinghouse had commercialized alternating current so electricity would become more than an urban luxury, but now he needed to expand into those larger urban areas as well— which was one reason he had bid below cost to win New Orleans.

"Thank you, Nikola."

That was a dismissal, but Tesla did not move. "What are you going to do?" he asked.

"I'm not going to fight this war in the press. Not yet anyway. Please give me some privacy so I can compose a letter."

"You will not dissuade Edison with a letter."

"Nikola, need I be rude?"

Tesla nodded gently and departed.

Westinghouse struggled with the proper tone for the letter to his nemesis. He decided the best approach was to pretend that Edison was not personally behind this seedy campaign. It would offer him a way out. They could both be disgusted that someone was trying to impugn the safety of something they'd each invested so much in.

I believe there has been a systemic attempt on the part of some people to do a great deal of mischief and create as great a difference as possible between the Edison Company and The Westinghouse Electric Co., when there ought to be an entirely different condition of affairs.

As he sealed the letter and flipped the envelope into his mailbox, Westinghouse realized that Tesla had once again been right. In all likelihood, Edison's response would not come via letter, but instead via another headline in the newspaper. This vicious competition, Westinghouse understood, would not end with a letter or with a partnership; it would only end when one of them emerged as the clear victor.

This was to be a war.

West Orange, New Jersey
July 1888

"You wrote a fine letter," Thomas Edison said, holding up the weeks-old newspaper so that Harold Brown could see it.

On June 5, Brown had sent a letter to the *New York Post* describing an accident where a boy had died after touching an exposed wire operating on alternating current. At the time, Brown had been a salesman for Brush Electric Company—basically a nobody in the electrical industry—but he had made such an effective argument against alternating current that Edison kept the newspaper on his desk to read aloud to any and all visitors.

"The only excuse for the use of the fatal alternating current," Brown wrote, "is that it saves the company operating it from spending a larger sum of money for the heavier copper wires which are required by the safe incandescent systems. That is, the public must submit to constant danger from sudden death, in order that a corporation may pay a little larger dividend."

The letter went on to recommend a new law to limit alternating current transmissions to 300 volts. This restriction would remove alternating current's advantage of transmitting high voltage to customers who lived a good distance away from a power plant.

Shortly after the letter was published, Edison had secretly hired Brown and given him use of his lab so he could continue experimenting with electricity on animals.

"Thank you, sir," said Brown, attempting to stifle a grin.

"I also want to compliment you on the demonstration at Columbia."

Brown had proven himself to be a zealous executioner. Along with his assistant, Dr. Fred Peterson, Brown had demonstrated the lethal characteristics of alternating current at Columbia University by administering a series of 1,000-volt direct current shocks to a large Newfoundland dog. The dog writhed in agony but quickly recovered after the electric current was shut off. Brown finished the demonstration by killing the dog with an alternating current of only 330 volts. The raucous display in an academic setting had garnered national publicity.

"I apologize it didn't go better. Some of the audience left in disgust."

"Nonsense. That only made it bigger news. You and Dr. Peterson showed that direct current only induced pain but that alternating current killed, and at much lower voltage levels. The pain may be pitiful to inflict, but there is no permanent damage. I heard there was some heckling, but don't let it worry you—it all added to the theater." Edison chuckled. "I also heard that the Society for the Prevention of Cruelty to Animals won a reprieve for a second dog. Splendid."

"Yes, I've heard that as well," Brown said. He seemed to relax after hearing that Edison had not brought him here for a reprimand, but he kept respectfully silent.

Edison continued: "Harold, as you know, the legislature passed an electric execution law. In the same session, they set up a committee to decide between using direct current or alternating current. My friends have gotten Dr. Peterson appointed as chair of the committee. I presume you've heard."

"Yes. It shouldn't take too much of Dr. Peterson's time. We can continue our research."

"Good. We need more newspaper articles to get our legislators off their duffs. First, we mold public opinion, then we use government power to squash Westinghouse and Tesla."

"It will be my pleasure," Brown responded.

"Yes, I believe it will." Edison made a backward wave with his hand. "You may go. I'm sure you have important duties awaiting your attention."

After Brown left, Edison fingered another paper he kept on the top of his desk. It was a letter from Westinghouse. Edison had taken the letter as a sign of weakness and had, of course, immediately rejected his rival's feeble peace proposal. *Westinghouse is crumbling*, Edison thought. Now it was time to send him back to the simple world of railcars.

Pittsburgh, Pennsylvania
New Year's Day, 1889

"The New York electrocution law goes into effect today," Tesla said.

George Westinghouse frowned. "Not the best start of a new year, but we're winning in the marketplace."

"That is not enough," Tesla countered.

"It is. Edison's costs are high. City property is expensive. I build my generators on cheap land. Copper alone may bring him down." Westinghouse paced his spacious office, speaking hurriedly as he walked. "That's why he's attacking me on safety. He needs a nonfinancial reason for cities to reject alternating current."

Tesla remained still, watching Westinghouse wear a pattern in his Persian rug. "Copper prices will drop," he said. "Probably soon."

Westinghouse quit pacing. "Why do you say that?"

"The French cornered production channels, but they forgot about scrap. Every boy over six is scavenging copper. The consortium will fail and copper prices will collapse. Don't count on that advantage lasting. You must defend alternating current against these safety attacks."

"I wrote an article that was published in the New York papers doing exactly that," Westinghouse replied.

"You defended Westinghouse Electric, you did not attack Edison."

"I'll attack in my next bid."

"Sir, you must refute Edison's claims or you'll be branded a killer. Harold Brown and Dr. Peterson have the commission to design an electric chair under their thumb. You know what they will do."

Westinghouse resumed pacing. He knew that Brown and Edison were up to no good when he had received a request from New York State to buy three Westinghouse alternating-current dynamos. He refused, but Brown—determined to execute someone with a Westinghouse dynamo—deceptively bought the generators through a third company that was in merger talks with Edison Electric.

Westinghouse knew he could handle the public indignity, but Edison's minions were now working state legislatures all over the country. If they succeeded in restricting or limiting alternating current, Westinghouse Electric was doomed. He hated politicians, especially crooked or stupid ones, and he believed there were very few who didn't fall into one of those two categories.

"I have my own plan, Nikola."

"May I ask what it is?"

"I'm going to illuminate the World's Fair."

"Mr. Westinghouse—" Tesla was at a temporary loss for words. Finally, he sputtered, "Sir, that is four years away! It will be much too late."

Westinghouse's pace quickened. "Only three years until the contract is awarded. And it won't be too late if I follow your advice. We'll challenge Edison on safety. There'll be many skirmishes during the next three years, but the deciding battle will be the World's Fair. That is where we will establish alternating current as the way of the future."

Westinghouse stopped directly in front of Tesla. "In the meantime, I've hired a lawyer with enough clout to bury the legislation in committees."

New York City
July 1889

Thomas Edison scooted his chair closer to W. Bourke Cockran. He was infuriated, but he had to put on a good face.

"Would you please repeat the question?" Edison spoke loudly as he played with an unlit half-smoked cigar. "My hearing is not what it used to be."

Cockran nearly yelled the question. "In your judgment, can alternating electric current be generated and applied in such a way to produce death in a human being in every case?"

"Yes!" he shouted back.

"Instantly?"

"Yes."

Edison was pleased to see frustration on Cockran's face even as he worked to keep his own expression blank. Cockran was a formidable foe. A former New York congressman and kingpin in the Tammany organization, he was now a powerful attorney with one of the most prestigious lists of clients in the city. Westinghouse had secretly hired Cockran to appeal William Kemmler's death sentence by electricity. Unless someone intervened, Kemmler was going to be the first condemned man to die this way.

More than a dozen journalists were crammed into Cockran's grand office in the Equitable Building, all there to report on an appeal that would determine if electrocution violated the constitutional restriction on "cruel and unusual punishment." The hearing had been going on for nearly a week and Edison was losing. Cockran had called a string of witnesses who had survived accidental electric shocks or lightning strikes. Academics and government researchers had testified that Kemmler might be set on fire instead of killed instantly. And he'd even called Dash, a dog who had survived contact with a dangling Western Union line, as a witness.

Harold Brown convinced Edison that he needed to testify to turn the momentum around. But Cockran, Edison knew, would not go down easy; Westinghouse had done well to make him the public face defending alternating current.

"What is your relationship with Mr. Harold Brown?" Cockran asked Edison.

"He's an independent engineer. I allow him to use my laboratories. I let many researchers use my labs. They're the best in the world."

"He is not in your employ?"

"No."

Cockran looked amused. He leaned forward and struck a match to light Edison's cigar. Edison took two healthy puffs and eyed Cockran quizzically.

"You're excused," Cockran said.

Edison stood to the screech of chairs all over the room, the reporters eager to follow him out. Since he hadn't made a public appearance in the last eighteen months, he knew that he was the news, not this hearing.

Edison was pleased with himself. Cockran had tried numerous tactics to rattle him, but Edison either pretended not to hear or gave single-word answers. He didn't dissimulate, volunteer extraneous information, or show any doubt in his answers.

Cockran controlled the questions, but Edison knew that was far less powerful than controlling the answers. *If that's all you've got, George*, Edison thought to himself, *then this is going to all be over faster than I thought.*

Pittsburgh, Pennsylvania
February 1890

A loud noise at the door drew Westinghouse's attention away from his work. Ernest Heinrichs stood at his door.

"Have you read this?" Heinrichs asked, still trying to catch his breath. Westinghouse had recently hired Heinrichs, a journalist, to write articles that presented the viewpoint of the Westinghouse Electric Company. He motioned for him to take a seat.

"We need to say something to discredit these slanderers," Heinrichs said, holding up a copy of a New York newspaper. "They want to popularize the term *Westinghoused*, like Dr. Guillotin's name was attached to decapitation."

Westinghouse held up his own copy of the paper, indicating he'd already read the article. "Don't play the other fellow's game. Edison hopes his power and influence will arrest the march of progress. It won't. I hired you to get our position into the newspapers. Write positive stories about alternating current. Don't return their slander." Westinghouse reached behind him and picked up a sheaf of papers. "This is what you will write. These are notes on the Virginia Senate committee proceedings to limit the voltage of alternating current."

Heinrichs sat up straighter. "We won Virginia?"

Westinghouse handed the papers to Heinrichs. "No, *they* lost Virginia. Edison himself testified—I think he was emboldened after the Kemmler hearing—and they still lost. Edison's attorneys were so bent on attacking us that they never saw the coming assault by the arc lighting companies. Arc lighting may predate Edison's lightbulb, but arc lights are still popular outdoors. They use alternating current, so they're our natural allies. The people who testified against Edison were local businessmen, and good ol' southern boys beat Yankee interlopers every time in Virginia. This was the first state legislative test. I want you to write it up so that it gets national attention."

He picked a pamphlet off his desk and handed it to Heinrichs. "This is my reply to Mr. Edison, published last December. Use it for your articles. In 1888, sixty-four people were killed in streetcar accidents, fifty-five by wagons, twenty-three by gaslights, and five by alternating current. Memorize those numbers. Five is not exactly an orgy of killing. The article points out that at the August meeting of the Edison illuminating companies, a resolution was passed asking the parent company to satisfy criteria that can only be met by alternating current. His own engineers are rebuffing direct current. We now have five times the number of central stations as Edison." He pointed at the pamphlet. "It's all in there. These are the key points I want you to emphasize in the press at every opportunity."

Heinrichs smiled. "You're winning on every front."

"No, not every front. We've lost our appeal for Kemmler so Edison still has his electric chair to use as a club. But I don't want you to write about the new Kemmler appeal. I have others assigned to that battle.

"Mr. Heinrichs, you're young and talented. You have a grand future. Always do your work with self-respect. Forget slanderous attacks. Write about how we are winning in the marketplace, in the state legislatures, and with electrical engineers."

Westinghouse stood, put a hand on Heinrichs's shoulder, and led him to the door.

"Do you understand your assignment?"

"Yes, sir."

"Good. Next time, knock before bursting into my office."

New York City
Six months later: August 1890

"I tell you, this is a grand thing, and is destined to become the instrument of legal death throughout the world."

Thomas Edison couldn't tell if Dr. Southwick believed what he had just said or was simply a fool.

"Doctor, do you wish to know what I think of this first electrocution?"

"I do!" he said eagerly.

The man was smiling. He was an idiot. Edison swiveled his chair to look at Harold Brown, who at least had the wit to look chagrined.

"I invested years in associating alternating current with death," Edison said. "We've successfully killed hundreds of animals with it, yet you can't kill even one deranged axe murderer. Harold, I—"

"Mr. Edison, he's dead," Southwick interrupted.

"Dead?" Edison yelled. "Are you sure? You hit him with seventeen seconds of current and he came back to life." Edison picked up the newspaper account and followed the text with his finger as he read aloud. "One of the physicians yelled in horror. 'Great God! He is alive.' Another screamed, 'See, he breathes.' A witness shouted, 'For God's sake, kill him.' "

Edison threw the paper at Brown, who blocked it with a forearm. Edison continued: "The article goes on to say the warden had to reattach the scalp electrode to do the job again. Kemmler caught on fire and smoked. Most of the newspapers say he was roasted. The stench from burnt flesh and feces was unbearable. Several people threw up, adding to the stink. A reporter fainted, the county sheriff started bawling, and everybody fought to get out of that damned chamber."

Edison reached behind him and threw a stack of newspapers at Brown. "They all say the same thing!" Edison swiveled toward the doctor. "And you call this a *grand thing*? You two have ruined me!"

Both men stood up sheepishly.

"Harold, I never want to see your name in print. If I ever see or hear of you again, I'll have you arrested, even if I have to trump up charges. Do you understand me?"

"Yes, sir."

"Good. Now get out."

Edison ran his fingers through his hair and sighed. He told himself his reputation could be salvaged, that he never gave up and had never been defeated. Westinghouse would still rue the day he challenged the Wizard of Menlo Park.

He stood. There were reporters downstairs. He had to face them. He composed himself as he descended the stairs and mustered every ounce of optimism he could.

The first reporter's question was obvious. "What do you think about the electrocution?"

"I have merely glanced over an account of Kemmler's death and it was not pleasant reading."

"Why didn't it go as you predicted?"

"I understand the doctors bungled it. Very unfortunate."

"George Westinghouse said they could have done it better with an axe. Any comment?"

"No." Edison turned and climbed back up the stairs to his office.

Pittsburgh, Pennsylvania
June 1891

"Edison is in Chicago. He wants to electrify the World's Fair." Tesla sounded peeved.

Westinghouse was calm. "It's a good sign. His backers are concerned."

J. P. Morgan, William H. Vanderbilt, and William Waldorf Astor had pledged $15 million to finance the fair if Congress awarded it to New York, but Chicago had won out anyway. New Yorkers had been

stunned when they'd learned about the loss. They'd assumed everything west of the Hudson River was wasteland. Westinghouse, however, knew there were more than two hundred hungry millionaires in
Chicago, all of them craving recognition, status, and respect. They had
met the Wall Street bid and raised it. Edison and his financiers assumed
that an electric contract would automatically come with the fair. Now
that the contract was no longer assured, they had dispatched the Wizard to personally sell his elixir to the fair's governing committee.

Tesla seldom paced, but he couldn't help himself. "Edison can be
persuasive."

Westinghouse smiled. "Sit down or stand still, Nikola. Pacing
doesn't suit you."

Tesla stood still with his hands clasped behind his back. "You should
be worried."

Westinghouse laughed. "You don't see me fret, so you take on the
mantle of worrier? Relax. Edison's in trouble. The Kemmler execution
put a big dent in his armor. He's no longer infallible."

Westinghouse was gaining confidence by the day. The month after
Kemmler's botched electrocution, Westinghouse sales had jumped
to their highest levels in company history. In less than five years, rev-
enue had grown from $150,000 to nearly $5 million. In the meantime,
Edison had allowed his companies to be reorganized as Edison General
Electric. Westinghouse heard that the president of the new company
had once boasted that the new capital meant good-bye to Westinghouse.

Tesla took a deep breath. "You have a plan, don't you, George?"

Westinghouse shrugged. "Not so much a plan as a partner. We'll
feign disinterest in the bidding, but in the end, we'll be in the game."

Thomas Edison had received a large amount of cash as part of the
reorganization, but he ended up retaining only a 10 percent interest in
the new company. That, Westinghouse believed, was a big mistake. One
that he himself would never make. He wouldn't sell his patents and he
would never sell his companies. Ownership was control, and control
was everything.

He suspected that Edison was about to learn a hard lesson about the
ruthlessness of Wall Street moneymen.

West Orange, New Jersey
Late winter 1892

Thomas Edison was surprised to hear that Alfred Tate was downstairs. Tate, who had been serving as Edison's personal secretary for nearly ten years, was supposed to be in New York City at Edison headquarters, not here at Edison's West Orange estate.

"Send him up," Edison said.

When Tate hurried into his private office, Edison cut right to the chase. "Why are you here, Alfred?"

"There's been a merger."

"Who?" Edison was suddenly gripped by a fear that Westinghouse had found a powerful ally.

"Edison General Electric and Thomson-Houston. It's the second-largest industrial merger in history."

Edison leapt to his feet. "My company? How could that happen without me knowing?"

"J. P. Morgan. He struck the deal." Tate paused and looked toward the ground. "Sir, I don't know how to tell you this, but Edison General Electric is the *junior* partner. Charles Coffin, the Thomson-Houston president, will be the president of the combined company."

"No! This cannot be." Edison felt faint. He sat back down and pounded his fist into a pile of papers on top of his cluttered desk. *Damn Morgan.* Edison's first electrification was Morgan's home and now the banker had repaid him by shoving him aside without even the courtesy of a telegram.

How could this happen? Edison thought—but the truth was that he knew how it happened. Even worse, he knew why: He had been maneuvered to relinquish control because of the threat posed by alternating current. The Kemmler electrocution had merely been a public exhibition of his failure to kill this competing technology. Edison salesmen were now clamoring for alternating current and that is what Thomson-Houston brought to the table. *Dammit!* His entire strategy to discredit alternating current had backfired. Instead of proving how unsafe it was, it proved the opposite: It was hard to kill a man with alternating current even when it was hooked directly up to his skull.

After a few moments of silence Edison had regained his composure. "What is the name of our new enterprise?" he asked Tate.

Tate hesitated. "General Electric."

"At least they took my name."

"No, sir."

"I don't understand—you said that the new company was called 'Edison General Electric.' "

"No, sir. There is no 'Edison' anymore."

Chicago
May 1893

Westinghouse was nervous. This was an unnatural emotion for him, but in a couple of minutes he would either rule the electrification world or be the biggest dunce in America. It all depended on the flip of a switch.

It had been a circuitous route to this moment. Westinghouse had publicly stated that his company would not bid on the electrification of the World's Fair. With every other substantial electric company consolidated into General Electric, there was hardly any competition left.

When the bid box was opened, GE's bid surprised no one: $1,720,000. But a second bid was found: $625,600 from a small Chicago firm. It was far less than GE's, but the small company was taken seriously when Westinghouse Electric said it would back the proposal.

Westinghouse had, of course, not relied solely on the bid of a silent partner. In advance of the bidding he had dispatched Heinrichs to Chicago to whip up newspaper animosity toward the haughty New Yorkers. Heinrichs never had an easier assignment. The Chicago reporters hated the New York "electrical trust" and embraced Westinghouse as their champion from Pittsburgh, another industrial town familiar with being disparaged by the high-and-mighty Manhattanites.

Westinghouse, knowing the importance of the World's Fair as a showcase for technology, had surreptitiously worked three years to win the bid. Now the war between him and Edison—between alternating and direct current—all came down to the flip of a switch.

• • •

It had been a long haul. There were business, legal, and engineering challenges. A big-city alternating-current plant might light up as many as ten thousand lights, but the World's Fair was *160,000 lights*, plus a good number of motors. All of this would be powered by twelve oil-fueled engines that had been installed only weeks earlier in Machinery Hall. No dirty coal smoke would rain down to stain the White City—the nickname given the main thoroughfare through the World's Fair due to the white classical buildings that lined both sides of an immense reflecting pool.

As George Westinghouse stood on the bunted platform with other officiating guests, he fretted that it was all now out of his hands. President Grover Cleveland would press the gold and ivory telegraph key to light the World's Columbian Exhibition, which celebrated the four-hundred-year anniversary of Columbus's great voyage of discovery. Westinghouse would just stand there and smile.

Westinghouse didn't realize he had been holding his breath until the lights came on with a roar from tens of thousands of spectators. It was magnificent. Fountains threw plumes of water a hundred feet into the air, flags unfurled, cannon and boat whistles assaulted the ears, and everybody yelled. The elegant White City instantaneously became the Bright City as it burst out of darkness. The gold dome of the Administration Building glowed; crowds on walkways and steps and lawns abruptly came into view; and the peristyle at the far end of the Great Basin seemed to glow from within. This entire spectacle came from Westinghouse lamps and motors powered by Westinghouse engines. All of it was made possible by the genius of Nikola Tesla and his alternating current.

Westinghouse felt himself smiling. It had all worked. The lamps, the motors, the engines, and the transmission lines. It was an entire electrical system fit for a city. Everywhere he looked there was glittering brightness and happy faces.

It was a new dawn, and a man-made one at that.

Coney Island, New York
Ten years later: January 4, 1903

In the decade since the founding of General Electric, Thomas Edison concentrated his talents on industries like mining and motion pictures. His own mines had not been profitable, but his patented techniques for things such as magnetic separation, blasting, conveying, and crushing had proven to be lucrative. His greatest enthusiasm, however, was for movies. He had watched their effect on audiences. One good film could alter the thinking of thousands of people.

The Edison Motion Picture Studio was making history by filming the first ever movie with a story. He was sure that film, *The Great Train Robbery*, would make money, but the movie he was about to make on Coney Island was far more important to him: It would be the first death ever captured on film.

Edison's plan was to film an elephant being electrocuted with alternating current produced by a Westinghouse dynamo. The execution itself would be watched live by thousands of people at Luna Park, but the movie would have a much wider reach.

Edison knew that the war on currents was essentially finished. Even General Electric, the company he'd founded, had embraced alternating current. But he also knew that revenge was best when it was unexpected.

The elephant to be killed was a three-ton female named "Topsy," who was reputed to have killed three people over the last few years. The latest was a cruel trainer who'd tried to feed her a lit cigarette. Her owners, believing she was too dangerous to keep, first attempted to poison her with cyanide. A thousand people gathered to watch the event, but Topsy didn't budge.

With New York having abandoned hanging in favor of the electric chair, Topsy's owners saw the potential for another live event.

So did Thomas Edison.

Sensing an opportunity to strike back against Westinghouse in dramatic fashion, Edison stepped forward to volunteer his electrical expertise on one condition. They'd have to let him film the entire event.

• • •

Edison checked in with his electrical technicians. They assured him that everything was ready. Then he checked in with his camera crew. They were set as well.

Edison waved and a circus trainer led the ill-fated elephant to the electrocution apparatus that he had designed. Edison glanced back and forth between Topsy and the cameraman. The death march was all being captured on film.

Edison directed the filming to stop once Topsy was in position. He did not want to film the long process of fitting Topsy with electrodes and the specially designed copper-lined sandals that would transmit the current.

The trained elephant dutifully raised each foot so the sandals could be slipped underneath. While the animal was being prepared, Edison checked the electrical equipment again and reminded the guards to hold the onlookers away from the camera. There would be only one take.

Finally, all was in place. Edison signaled and the cameraman started filming again.

He waited until he was certain the camera was fully operational, and then he signaled again. Then 6,600 volts pulsed through the sandals and into Topsy.

Smoke billowed from Topsy's feet and she shuttered violently. She tried to shake one of the sandals loose, but quickly convulsed, then tumbled forward onto her head and rolled over to her side. Smoke continued to billow from her until the alternating current was turned off after a full ten seconds.

Topsy never moved again.

EPILOGUE

In 1893, the same year as the World's Fair that had showcased alternating current, George Westinghouse won the Niagara Falls hydropower contract that cemented his company's dominance. After a long and brutal financial battle, New York and Boston bankers gained control of Westinghouse Electric in 1909 and ousted Westinghouse as its chairman. He continued to successfully run his other businesses until his death five years later.

Thomas Edison built a ten-company motion picture trust that tried to monopolize the movie industry. Edison used the trust to limit the length of films to ten to twenty minutes because he believed that was the attention span of audiences. The trust also refused to identify actors by name to prevent them from demanding higher salaries. To escape the Edison Trust, independent producers fled New York for a town in California that was protected by the Ninth Circuit Court of Appeals' distaste for patent infringement claims. The town was called Hollywood.

Alternating current won the war, but direct current has not disappeared completely. Batteries, solar power systems, and electronics with circuit boards still rely on it. However, one of the devices at the center of the Edison-Westinghouse War of Currents does not: the electric chair.

On January 16, 2013, Virginia death row inmate Robert Gleason chose to die from electrocution rather than lethal injection. He was executed with the same system of electricity now used safely in millions of homes around the world: alternating current.

6

The Battle of Wounded Knee:
Medals of Dishonor

Grand River, South Dakota
December 12, 1890

"Rescue me from these traitors!" Sitting Bull shouted.

Lieutenant Bull Head was getting more concerned by the minute. What had started as a relatively simple mission to arrest this Indian chief for his involvement in a Sioux uprising was quickly getting out of hand.

The lieutenant, in response to orders from General Nelson A. Miles, had entered the camp at first light with forty-two other Indian police. They'd hoped to arrest the old chief quickly and quietly, before his hundreds of followers could react.

But that's not at all what happened.

The lieutenant had entered Sitting Bull's cabin and found the chief and his sons asleep. Sitting Bull had been nude and it took a few minutes for him to dress. He had been willing to come quietly at first, but Crow Foot, one of his sons, started to berate his father for not resisting. When the small party stepped outside, the lieutenant saw that armed Sioux had gathered in front of the cabin. Sitting Bull, incited by his son, began to order his people to kill Lieutenant Bull Head. "This man is the leader!" he shouted. "Kill him and the others will flee!"

The lieutenant saw that his fellow policemen were holding back the angry Sioux in a wide arc, but they were surrounded and had no way to get to their horses. *Damn the Ghost Dancers*, he thought. The Sioux danced for days on end in a ritual meant to reunite the living and the dead and eliminate evil, including the white man, from the world. Hundreds of these crazed believers had made camp around Sitting Bull's cabin, and it now seemed that they were all coming to their leader's defense.

Bull Head hated these ignorant Ghost Dancers and what they were doing to the public's perception of Indians. What they practiced, he believed, wasn't a religion; it was wishful thinking. The buffalo weren't coming back, and the white men weren't going anywhere. The Sioux way of life had to change to fit the new reality.

Bull Head knew the Ghost Dancers hated him, as well. They thought he was a traitor to his people for joining the Indian Police. Nonsense. Yes, the Indian Police reported to the U.S. Indian agent in charge of the reservation, but they also kept the white men away from his people. After all, if his unit had not come to arrest Sitting Bull, it would have been a company of cavalrymen.

At this moment, however, that logic was irrelevant. He was holding the Sioux chief, who was still yelling to his Ghost Dancers to attack, by the elbow with one hand, and his army Colt in the other. He wished he could just knock him unconscious; Sitting Bull's yelling was going to get them all killed.

The lieutenant saw motion out of the corner of his eye. He snapped his head around just in time to see a young warrior named Catch the Bear charging at him with a raised pistol. Everything seemed to move in slow motion. He saw smoke come from the pistol's barrel but didn't hear the gunfire. Then he felt a searing pain in his side. He heard his own scream of pain as the shot twisted him back in the direction of Sitting Bull.

As he fell to the ground, only one thought entered his head: kill Sitting Bull. He fired his Colt into the chief just before he saw another bullet shatter his head. Then everything went to black.

Pine Ridge Reservation, South Dakota
December 18, 1890

General Nelson A. Miles read the report on the Sitting Bull incident for a second time. The first time he'd read it to get a general overview of what happened. His second reading was a search for bias or obfuscation. He found neither. Major James McLaughlin, the Indian agent at the Standing Rock Reservation in northern South Dakota, appeared to have written a straightforward recitation of the facts as he saw them. Miles was pleased, but also somewhat surprised. He'd had difficulties with McLaughlin before.

Less than three weeks earlier, the general had asked William "Buffalo Bill" Cody to arrest Sitting Bull. The two men had worked together in Cody's Wild West Show and Miles believed that their existing relationship would ensure a peaceful arrest. Cody traveled to South Dakota with two wagonloads of gifts for Sitting Bull, but McLaughlin went over Miles's head and sent a telegram to Washington, pleading that the order be rescinded. The Bureau of Indian Affairs agreed and Buffalo Bill was sent back to Washington empty-handed.

General Miles thought about how much easier his life would be if he could order the Indian agents around in the same way he did his own soldiers. Unfortunately, his request that reservation duties be run by the military had been rebuffed. The Indian reservation agents remained civilian political appointees of the Office of Indian Affairs. Politicians viewed these positions as spoils and often appointed donors or their relatives to the jobs. Many were corrupt and made Miles's job more difficult by cheating the Indians of food and materials for personal gain.

Agent Daniel F. Royer, the agent at the Pine Ridge Reservation on the Nebraska border, may or may not have been corrupt, but he was certainly, Miles thought, incompetent. Royer, who Miles knew was referred to by the Sioux as the "Young-man-afraid-of-Indians," had sent numerous telegrams to Washington pleading for help with Ghost Dancers. One of them claimed that "Indians are dancing in the snow and are wild and crazy. We need protection and we need it now." Royer's hysteria had prompted the War Department to treat spiritual fervor as a major Sioux uprising.

In truth, Sitting Bull's death was not *all* Royer's fault. Settlers in the area had also persistently complained to Washington about the Ghost Dancers and newspapers around the country had panicked readers with strange stories about crazed Sioux dancing to bring about a messiah who would rid them of the white man.

The government's response was swift and convincing. They mobilized the largest number of troops since the Civil War to head to Grand River, South Dakota. There, under the authority of General Miles, the Sioux were ordered back to their reservations. Those who complied were labeled "friendlies" and those who did not were called "hostiles."

Once in Grand River, Miles had assumed that the legendary Chief Sitting Bull was one of those leading the Ghost Dancers. After the general's attempt to have Buffalo Bill arrest the chief failed, McLaughlin sent a large squad of Indian police to take him into custody. That arrest had been terribly mishandled and ended with the police killing Sitting Bull and his two sons—one of whom was just twelve years old. In addition, six policemen, including their commander, Lieutenant Bull Head, were killed. The entire affair had raised the rage and indignation of both the army and the Sioux. South Dakota was now a tinderbox—and Miles was sitting right in the middle of it.

He tossed the report onto his desk just as he heard a knock at the door. "Come in."

Major Samuel Whitside entered and Miles waved him into a chair. "Major, as you know, many of the hostile Sioux are hiding in the Badlands. For now, they appear content to stay concealed, but these hostiles may go on the warpath any day. It appears Chief Big Foot and his band are trying to join up with them."

"That would make a large force, general," Whitside said. "I don't think that's advisable."

"Good, I'm glad you agree with me. Your orders are to take the Seventh Cavalry, find Big Foot, and escort him and his band back here to Pine Ridge. He's broken his promises to come in before, so don't allow him to make his own way here. You are to stay with him the whole way. Understood?"

"Yes, sir."

"Dismissed."

Wounded Knee Creek, South Dakota
December 28, 1890

Major Samuel Whitside stood in his stirrups to get a better view.

Big Foot's band was moving south, along Wounded Knee Creek toward Pine Ridge. Scouts had reported that the hostile Sioux were hiding to the north in the Badlands, meaning that the rumor about the groups joining forces was likely false. *The first good news of the week*, Whitside thought.

As he and his troops slowly closed in on Big Foot, three Sioux warriors came forward on their horses, a white flag held high by the one on the right. Whitside and two troopers spurred their own horses and galloped out to meet the three in open land between the soldiers and the rest of the Sioux.

When the horses came nose to nose, Whitside asked, "Where is Chief Big Foot?"

"Ill," answered the warrior in the center.

"Bring him. I won't negotiate with anyone else." Whitside didn't trust Big Foot. He had a history of duplicity, and Whitside knew that negotiating with anyone other than the chief was pointless.

After a silent standoff, the warrior spoke in Lakota to the man on his left, who then rode off to join the main party. The three cavalrymen faced the two Sioux in silence until a wagon pulled up carrying Big Foot.

Whitside peeked inside. The chief was indeed ill, very ill. He looked exhausted and pale and was coughing up blood, which made it difficult for him to speak. Whitside sent one of his soldiers for the surgeon, but it looked to him like Big Foot had pneumonia.

Big Foot's informal party consisted of about 120 men and 250 women and children. Whitside realized immediately that this was not a war party. These Sioux were a pathetic collection of refugees.

While they waited for the surgeon, Big Foot had readily agreed to be escorted to the Pine Ridge Reservation. Once the surgeon arrived, they moved slowly toward their destination, carrying Big Foot along in an army ambulance with a cot and medical supplies.

In the late afternoon, a scout reported an open swale at the intersection of several trails ahead. On inspection, Whitside found the location to be suitable to make camp for the night. He ordered army tents erected in five rows facing the Sioux tepees, which were lined up in an arc that followed the contours of a dry ravine. A small open field separated the two groups. Whitside then ordered troops placed on the backside of the ravine, on a couple knolls overlooking the camp, and along the side of the Sioux encampment.

"Sir, should we disarm them?" asked one of his officers.

Whitside thought about it for a moment. The surgeon had earlier confirmed that Big Foot indeed had pneumonia. "No. The Sioux are jumpy and suspicious after the Sitting Bull incident and their chief is ill. Let them see we mean them no harm and get comfortable with our presence. We'll disarm them in the morning after breakfast and then continue on to Pine Ridge."

Whitside ordered three hundred army rations distributed to the Sioux and a stove delivered to Big Foot's tepee. Then he walked the perimeter of the two camps and was pleased, considering the circumstances, that the situation seemed to be under control.

A scout rode up and swung out of his saddle. After a crisp salute, he said, "Colonel Forsyth is just behind me with the Second Battalion. He should arrive about eight this evening to assume command."

Major Whitside breathed a sigh of relief. This was no longer his problem.

Wounded Knee, South Dakota
December 29, 1890

Colonel James W. Forsyth had arrived the prior evening to take command of the combined force of five hundred cavalrymen, plus a company of scouts. Once he was settled, he called Major Whitside over. "Major, please explain to me why these Indians are not being properly guarded."

"Colonel, given Big Foot's illness, the distrust the Sioux have for us, and the fact that the band has peacefully and willingly followed us to this point, I thought it best to place troops only along the backside for now." He swallowed hard.

"That is very logical of you, Major," Forsyth replied. "And very naïve as well. I see you have conveniently decided to postpone disarming them. What do you plan to do when these armed Indians run off or charge us en masse in the middle of the night?"

Whitside knew well enough to remain quiet. These questions were not meant to be answered.

"Major, I want this encampment completely surrounded with troops and Hotchkiss guns. And I want it done now. We disarm them at first light."

"Yes, sir." Whitside snapped off a salute and got to work, though he felt uneasy about it. The troop placements that Forsyth had ordered would form a large square around the Sioux. That might help prevent escapes, but if there was an uprising, it could mean his men would be caught in their own crossfire.

Other than the soldiers getting drunk on a keg of whiskey brought in by a local trader, the night had been uneventful. But as the sun rose over the encampment, things had taken a turn for the worse. Colonel Forsyth was acting so aggressively that Whitside worried he was severely hungover, or possibly even still drunk.

The Sioux had been assembled in front of their tepees at first light, fed a hardtack breakfast, and then ordered to surrender their weapons. Twenty-five old and worn rifles had been collected and stacked in a pile in front of the army officers. Through an interpreter, Colonel Forsyth accused the ailing Big Foot of withholding their best guns. Big Foot conferred with his men, who responded that these were all the guns they had.

"You are lying to me," Forsyth told the Indian chief. Then he turned to a nearby lieutenant. "Assemble a detail and search every man, woman, and child, as well as every tepee, wagon, bush, and bag. Leave nothing untouched."

The lieutenant rode off and returned an hour later with thirty-eight more guns as well as knives, axes, tent pegs, scissors, and other sharp objects that could easily be used as weapons. Whitside and Forsyth stood facing Big Foot and a couple dozen of his warriors as the additional cache of weapons was added to the stack. Troopers lined up on either side of the officers. No one spoke; the tension was palpable.

Except for the warriors standing directly in front of them, the Sioux were now completely disarmed. "Lift your clothing and show us that you are unarmed," Forsyth ordered the men in front of him. The old men complied instantly, lifting up the blankets draped over their shoulders to show they had no weapons, but the young warriors refused.

"I will not ask you again," Forsyth said. "Remove your coverings now or we will search you ourselves."

The young warriors did not budge.

"Very well." Forsyth turned to the same lieutenant he'd sent out earlier to scour the camp. "Search these men, head to toe."

Two guns were quickly revealed before a young deaf warrior named Black Coyote drew a gun from under his blanket and leaped backward. He shook it high over his head and yelled in Lakota. Whitside was pretty sure he wanted to be paid for the expensive weapon.

Two soldiers snuck up behind Black Coyote and grabbed hold of his arm, struggling to seize the weapon.

Bang! The gun discharged into the eastern sky.

Everyone froze.

The shot echoed.

Then, silence.

Colonel Forsyth yelled, "Fire! Fire on them!"

In an instant, the serene South Dakota hills erupted in noise and motion. Soldiers swung their rifles around to aim at the Sioux; young warriors charged at the pile of confiscated weapons, and unarmed Sioux screamed and ran in every direction.

Whitside unbuttoned his pistol case and drew his army Colt. Swiveling his head from side to side he saw Sioux falling everywhere. A few fell while fighting, but most were shot in the back as they ran away. Some Indian boys who had been playing leapfrog moments ago collapsed in a hail of bullets. Gun smoke soon filled the field of fire, but soldiers continued to shoot volleys in the general direction of the Sioux, who were quickly finding that they had no way to retreat—they were surrounded by soldiers on all sides.

Whitside heard a horrific sound. The Hotchkiss guns. He went to one knee to prepare himself for the hail of oversized shells that would be coming in at sixty-eight rounds per minute. As the Hotchkiss guns roared, soldiers started to fall, or were thrown to the ground like rag dolls. Whitside spotted a few wagons and Sioux horsemen attempting escape, but the Hotchkiss guns obliterated them.

Whitside wanted the slaughter to stop, but his head was spinning. He retched. Wiping his mouth with his sleeve, he yelled: "Cease fire! Cease fire!" But it was hopeless. A frenzy had taken hold of his men. On the outskirts of the encampment, he saw women, some carrying babies, being chased down by soldiers on horseback. They were shot without even so much as a warning to stop or surrender. Soldiers streamed through the camp killing the elderly, women, and children—even infants in cradleboards were not spared.

For the first time in years, Whitside prayed.

When the gunfire finally subsided, heavy smoke and screams of pain filled the air. The smell of sulfur, blood, and human excrement assaulted him from every direction. To his left he heard yelling, down by the dry ravine. Whitside ran toward the sound and arrived just in time to see Gatling guns cutting down several groups of Sioux attempting to take refuge in a shallow gully. Soldiers around the perimeter winced as they were hit by shrapnel and splintered rock.

It grew still again and he looked around. It was really over this time. There were no more targets. The only Sioux who moved were those squirming on the ground in agony. It was the most heartrending scene he'd ever witnessed.

Whitside collapsed to his knees.

Major Samuel Whitside stood, his legs still shaking, and glanced at his pistol. It had never been fired. At first he found that comforting, but he knew that if one of the Sioux warriors had charged at him, he would have killed him without a thought. And what then? Would he have joined in the massacre? Would he have shot women and babies? He knew that his own participation didn't matter. He was second in command and he had failed to stop the carnage that now lay out before him.

Dammit. He knew this had been a ragtag band of Indians lead by an old and ailing chief. They were, for the most part, women, children, and infants. When the shooting started, few of the young warriors had even been armed. If not innocent, they had at least been mostly harmless.

Now they were mostly dead.

Whitside began to walk through the bodies and shout orders for the wounded to be tended to. He didn't argue when his troopers received the treatment first. They were his charges, after all.

He returned to check on Colonel Forsyth and found him unharmed. Relieved, Whitside looked toward the ground at the warriors who had been near him when the shooting began. He recognized one of them as the Indian in the center of the three who'd initially come out to meet him on horseback. He recognized the next man on the ground as well. He looked different than the others: older, but also paler, as though he'd been ill.

Whitside gasped.

Big Foot was dead.

Pine Ridge Reservation, South Dakota
December 31, 1890

"Major, what the hell happened?"

General Nelson Miles was angry. After the Sitting Bull debacle, this mass killing at Wounded Knee added another disgrace to his command.

Major Whitside looked around the empty room. He was uncomfortable meeting privately with the general. "Sir, shouldn't Colonel Forsyth be present for this conference?"

"I've already spoken to Colonel Forsyth. If I wanted him present, he would be sitting beside you. Now answer my question."

"Yes, sir." Whitside folded his gloves and hands into his lap and looked directly forward, avoiding eye contact with General Miles. He recited what the general recognized as a well-rehearsed account of the incident.

When Whitside had finished, the general leaned back in his chair and lifted his chin. He spoke in a tone he'd spent years cultivating for the sole purpose of intimidation. "Major, there were sixty-four army casualties—twenty-five dead and thirty-nine wounded. It appears most of our troopers were hit by rifle fire from fellow soldiers or by our own Hotchkiss guns." He waited for Whitside to feel the weight of the coming question. "Why did you order such an inept emplacement?"

Whitside looked conflicted. He wanted to defend himself, but did not want to put the blame squarely onto Forsyth, his commanding officer. The general did not speak, allowing the awkward silence to linger.

Finally, Whitside answered. "Sir, I was following orders from my commanding officer."

"Colonel Forsyth told you to place your heavily armed men in a rough square facing each other?"

"I was instructed to encircle the Sioux so that no one could escape. It was a several-hundred-yard enclosure."

Miles shook his head. He was sure that most of the troopers had been killed or injured by friendly fire. It was ironic, he thought, that the best way for the Sioux to kill his soldiers would have been for them to duck while the soldiers shot each other.

"What happened the night before the incident?" Miles asked.

Whitside shifted his eyes and locked them on to the general. "The night before, sir?"

"You heard me."

"Sir, I presume you mean the celebration of the capture of Big Foot. A few men drank, but not to excess."

Miles nodded. "Okay, then tell me about the morning. Prior to the first shot."

"After voluntary disarmament failed, we initiated a search for weapons. The colonel was highly annoyed with Big Foot's lying about guns and weapons being hidden in camp."

"How did the Sioux react to the search?"

"I saw anger on their faces, but they complied." Whitside hesitated before adding, "The interpreter told us that Big Foot ordered his men to remain calm and allow the search."

"What was found?"

"Colonel Forsyth's anger turned out to be justified. Search teams found more rifles, pistols, knives, tomahawks, scissors, and lances. Everything was heaped onto a huge stack. The colonel lectured Big Foot on duplicity, but I don't think the Indians grasped his meaning. They're naturally deceitful."

Whitside looked like he was waiting for a reaction, but the general

remained stoic. "I understand that Black Coyote ignited the alterca-
tion? He brandished a pistol?"

"Correct, sir. When two cavalrymen tried to take it from him he fired
it into the air. Possibly as a signal."

"Then what?"

"Then all hell broke loose."

"And yesterday?"

"What about yesterday, sir?"

"Why did Colonel Forsyth need to be rescued?"

"We engaged over four thousand Sioux. We had no visibility due to
the blizzard and we were badly outnumbered."

"Colonel Forsyth was ordered to gather up the hostile Sioux at
White Clay Creek and escort them back to the reservation. He ended
up outflanked and pinned down in a valley. If the Ninth Calvary hadn't
rescued him you wouldn't be sitting in front of me today." He paused
to let his words sink in. "Did it occur to you that the hostiles, after seeing what happened to Big Foot, might try to fight?"

Whitside flinched before making eye contact again. "Sir, you should
ask Colonel Forsyth about his command decisions during combat."

General Miles contemplated further questions but decided they
would lead nowhere. The officers and troops were already circling the
wagons, painting a self-serving picture of a stand-up battle where every
soldier had shown forbearance and then, only when absolutely necessary, tenacity and courage under fire.

"Dismissed."

Whitside stood and walked to the door. Then he turned back and
asked, "Does the general anticipate a board of inquiry?"

"I said you were dismissed, Major."

Wounded Knee Creek, South Dakota
January 1, 1891

White Lance examined the ice-covered corpses of his fellow Lakota
Sioux. The blizzard that had rolled in after the slaughter had frozen the
bodies exactly as they'd fallen. He saw depressions in the frozen ground

where some of the bodies had been removed by friends or family to be buried.

At first, White Lance thought himself lucky to have survived the massacre. But now, as he surveyed the pained faces of the men, women, children, and babies strewn about the ground, he was no longer so sure.

The white soldiers, including their chief, a man they called General Miles, kept yelling at him to leave the dead and go to the hills to look for the living, but White Lance pretended not to understand. He had been instructed by his chief to memorialize each of the dead and how they had fallen. Tribal history was an important Sioux tradition and White Lance had been entrusted with the duty to ensure that the real story of what had happened here lived on.

The bodies were cold and stiff, and White Lance often had to turn them in order to see their faces. It was slow, gruesome work. A wagon soon came over a rise with six or seven Sioux huddled in back. General Miles seemed happy to see these survivors and yelled at the doctor to attend to them at once. How could a few live Sioux please a white man after he had killed so many? The world was incomprehensible.

Later that afternoon, the general called the eighty-four Sioux who'd been searching the bodies along with White Lance to gather around a wagon that served as a makeshift speaker's platform. A Lakota interpreter stood by Miles's side and translated.

"Thank you for coming here. It is a sad day and it must be overwhelming for you. We have discovered seven Sioux who would have died in this weather if you had not come to this place, so you have done well."

White Lance wondered how the general would feel if these were his people—slaughtered without mercy. He willed his mind to shed anger because rage would interfere with his attempt to remember every detail of what he saw.

"We will demand an investigation of what has happened here, but there are no more survivors and it is now time for you to return to the reservation."

Two old warriors stood shaking their heads. The eldest said, "You have no right to order us. We are a free people. We stay to bury our dead."

The general spoke for a long time before the interpreter nodded his understanding.

"The great general says that if you return now . . . peaceably, none of you will be punished."

"Punished?" The two old warriors looked incredulously at each other. "We do not understand. Punished for what?"

"You left the reservation. You participated in Ghost Dancing. You prepared for war. These things are against our treaty."

Half of the Sioux stood and yelled. The interpreter did his best to explain their collective complaint to Miles. "They say that the white man has *repeatedly* broken the treaty." The general held up his hand and nodded as if he understood. He spoke several sentences back to the interpreter.

"General Miles says there are food, blankets, and tools in those wagons. If you return peaceably to the reservation, they are yours. He will find out what happened here and those at fault will be disciplined. He also has people coming to bury the dead. It is best now that you leave this sad place. The spirits are not good."

There would be more discussion, but White Lance knew that, in the end, they would leave Wounded Knee without further conflict. He also knew what would happen after they did. Earlier, along one side of the field, he'd seen soldiers drawing a long rectangular outline in the dirt. They were going to toss the bodies of his people into a common grave and throw dirt on them until they disappeared forever.

The white man wanted no reminders of what had happened here.

White Lance would remember everything.

Pine Ridge, South Dakota
January 6, 1891

General Miles flung the magazine onto the table in front of Whitside.

"Did you have anything to do with this story?"

Whitside looked down at an issue of *Leslie's*.

"No, sir."

He threw down a copy of *Harper's*. Then the *Evening Star*, a Washington, D.C., newspaper. Then a heap of other newspapers from all across the country.

"How about these?"

"No, sir."

Miles was furious. "How can I conduct a fair board of inquiry if people believe the lies in these publications?" He picked up the *Evening Star*. "In this story they claim that Sitting Bull ambushed Custer at the Battle of the Little Bighorn and they call him 'the assassin of the brave Custer.' Nothing could be further from the truth! *Custer* was the one to attack and he was outmaneuvered."

He traded the *Evening Star* for *Harper's*. "In this issue, the artist Frederic Remington turns the Wounded Knee massacre into a glorious triumph and writes that Big Foot's band was the worst of their race. His illustrations are pure fiction."

Then he picked up *Leslie's* and read from it. "In the annals of American history, there cannot be found a battle so fierce, bloody, and decisive as the fight at Wounded Knee Creek between the Seventh Calvary and Big Foot's band of Sioux. This affair at Wounded Knee was a stand-up fight of the most desperate kind, in which the entire band was annihilated."

Miles violently swept the newspaper and magazines off the table and onto the floor. Where had this information come from? He did not believe reporters invented stories, so someone had to be feeding these accounts to the newspapers. Ever since he had relieved Colonel Forsyth of his command pending an investigation, army officialdom seemed intent on hiding the real story. He suspected that Whitside was part of the effort to recast the massacre as an honorable battle.

Miles supported his weight with two fists anchored against the table. He breathed hard for almost a full minute before lifting his head and looking Whitside directly in the eyes.

"Major, I called you here for a simple question. I want a yes-or-no answer. Will you testify truthfully at the hearing?"

Whitside answered without hesitation, "Yes, sir."

Pine Ridge, South Dakota
January 14, 1891

"These are your findings?" General Miles asked.

The investigating officers, Major J. Ford Kent and Captain Frank D. Baldwin, had concluded their investigation the day before. They'd found little fault in Forsyth's conduct.

Kent answered. "Yes. Testimony supplied no evidence or indication of fault by Colonel Forsyth."

"I saw the field of battle three days after the incident, but still frozen in time," Miles said. "Anyone with two eyes could see fault. Did you examine Major Whitside's map of the troop and gun placements?"

"We did," Kent said. "It was deemed flawed, but not negligent."

After his personal examination of Wounded Knee, Miles had ordered Whitside to go back and draw a detailed map of the Sioux and cavalry positions. He wanted an accurate drawing for the record because he believed the troop placement had been reckless.

"And all the dead women and children. No fault?"

"Testimony showed great forbearance by our troopers. Major Whitside testified that the Sioux fired fifty shots before his men returned fire. Every witness testified that some noncombatants were unfortunately shot by our men due to the warriors running amongst them, but that Sioux warriors killed the large majority of them by firing into or across their own women and children."

"Do you believe that?" Miles asked.

"We have no evidence to the contrary." Kent glanced at Baldwin for reassurance and got a nod. "The testimony was very consistent."

"I want you to reopen the inquiry. Find testimony that is consistent with the facts on the ground, not a story concocted after the fact."

"But General—"

"That's an order, Major. Dismissed."

Pine Ridge, South Dakota
January 20, 1891

Major Kent and Captain Baldwin sat nervously in front of the general's desk.

General Miles read the conclusion of the revised report aloud: "Colonel Forsyth's command was not held at a safe distance, and the attack of the Indians resulted in a surprise to the troops."

He threw the report on the table, and looked at Major Kent. "That's it? He positioned his troops too close and thus allowed himself to be surprised? That's the most mild censure I've ever read."

"General, we have no evidence of malfeasance . . . and we have a surfeit of testimony to the opposite. We can rule no other way."

"Perhaps, but I can make my own recommendation."

"General, may I speak freely?" Kent asked.

"You may."

"There is word going around that you are intent on railroading Colonel Forsyth because the Sitting Bull and Wounded Knee incidents will hurt your career."

"Does that make sense to you?" Miles asked.

"Sir, I have never known you to be vindictive."

"I was speaking logically, Major. If the army wants to portray Wounded Knee as a stand-up victory over heavily armed savages, wouldn't I be best served by going along with that story? Wouldn't a military victory *enhance* my career?"

Kent looked confused. "Then why so many inquiries, sir?"

"Because I promised the Sioux survivors that I would investigate and punish any wrongdoers."

"Sir? You're doing this because of a promise you made to Indians?"

"No, I'm doing this because it is right."

Washington, D.C.
February 7, 1891

General John Schofield, commanding general of the United States Army, read the recommendation that accompanied the Board of Inquiry findings. General Miles had been harsh on Colonel Forsyth, and, by doing so, had by default been harsh on the United States Army.

"Troops were not disposed," Miles's report read, "to deliver its fire upon the warriors without endangering the lives of some of their own comrades." Later, Miles commented on the fact that many of the Indians had already been disarmed, writing: "A large number of the 106 Sioux warriors were without firearms when the outbreak occurred."

Throughout the document, General Miles had used words like "inexcusable," "apathy," "neglect," "contempt," and "incompetence." He went on to make the worst accusation that can be leveled against a field-grade officer. "Colonel Forsyth was inexperienced in the responsibility of exercising command."

Schofield knew that this report would not only ruin Colonel Forsyth's career, it would reflect badly on the army. And for what purpose? Miles's recriminations were at odds with most newspaper accounts of the battle, not to mention the testimony of soldiers present that day. Even retired general William T. Sherman, who had been Schofield's predecessor as commanding general of the army, had taken Forsyth's side. "If Forsyth was relieved because some squaws were killed," Sherman had written, "then somebody had made a mistake, for squaws have been killed in every Indian war."

Schofield picked up a pen and paused briefly before writing to his boss, the secretary of war.

The interests of military service do not, in my judgment, demand further proceedings in this case, nor any longer continuance of Col. Forsyth's suspension from the command of his regiment. The evidence in these papers shows that great care was taken to avoid unnecessary killing of Indian women and children.

In my judgment, the conduct of the regiment was well worthy of the commendation bestowed upon it by me in my first telegram after the engagement.

He concluded that the soldiers had displayed great forbearance and that units under Forsyth's command had shown excellent discipline.

General Schofield reread his report. He was pleased. This would finally set the record straight.

Pine Ridge, South Dakota
February 17, 1891

Col. Forsyth Exonerated, His Action at Wounded Knee Justified,
Decision of Secretary Proctor on the Investigation—The Colonel Restored
to the Command of His Gallant Regiment

The headline couldn't have been clearer, and General Nelson Miles couldn't have been more depressed.

The crushing futility sapped every bit of his energy. He was not angry, he was not bitter, and he certainly was not surprised—but he was weary. It had been an agonizing political battle, but now it was over and he had lost.

After receiving Commanding General Schofield's report, Secretary of War Redfield Proctor had penned what would become the official government position on the Battle of Wounded Knee.

The disarmament was commenced and it was evident that the Indians were sullenly trying to evade the order. They were carried away by the harangue of the ghost dancer, and wheeling about, opened fire. Nothing illustrates the madness of their outbreak more forcibly than the fact that their first fire was so directed that every shot that did not hit a soldier must have gone through their own village. There is little doubt that the first killing, of women and children was by the first fire of the Indians themselves.

The firing by the troops was entirely directed on the men until the Indians, after their break, mingled with their women and children, thus exposing them to the fire of the troops and as a consequence some were killed. Major Whitside emphatically declares that at least fifty shots were fired by the Indians before the troops returned the fire. Major Kent and Capt. Baldwin concur in finding that the evidence fails to establish that a single man of Col. Forsyth's command was killed or wounded by his fellows.

This fact and, indeed, the conduct of both officers and men through the whole affair, demonstrates an exceedingly satisfactory state of discipline in the Seventh Cavalry. Their behavior was characterized by skill, coolness, discretion, and forbearance, and reflects the highest possible credit upon the regiment.

The concluding sentence crushed General Miles' spirit:

The interests of the military service do not demand any further proceedings in this case. By direction of the President, Col. Forsyth will resume the command of his regiment.

St. Louis, Missouri
June 1891

"General, here are the citations for Wounded Knee."

The staff officer was newly assigned and unaware of General Miles's disapproval of the army's actions at Wounded Knee. At least the general preferred to *assume* that the staff officer was unaware; otherwise he would be annoyed at his cheerful delivery of more than a dozen Medal of Honor citations for bravery at Wounded Knee.

Miles had thought his anger over Wounded Knee had ebbed, but when he'd heard about these citations working their way up to him, he'd lost his temper again. This was the greatest number of Congressional Medals of Honor ever awarded in any single engagement. He should have seen it coming: The army does not merely bury its blunders; it decorates them with so many ribbons that no one can question the veracity of the official report.

There had already been a couple of Medals of Honor awarded, and this new round would bring the total to seventeen. He sighed. *There will be more to come,* he thought.

"Is this an inconvenient time, sir? I can return with them later."

Miles held his hand out. "No. This won't take but a moment."

He rifled through the citations quickly, making scant comments on just a few. He handed them back to the staff officer. "You may forward these to the War Department."

"Sir, if you'll excuse me . . . you hardly added any comments. Would you like to keep them overnight? At this late juncture, there is no hurry." The confused staff officer held up the citations. "These men fought bravely under your command."

"Whatever gave you that idea?" Miles asked testily.

"I read the reports before reviewing the citations."

"You shouldn't believe everything you read. These men didn't fight; they killed. They had disarmed the majority of the Sioux before the first shot was ever fired."

"Sir?" The officer looked thoroughly confused. "Congress wouldn't approve Medals of Honor without endorsement. The president has commended the action. Why would everyone in the chain of command participate in a deception?"

"Because governments do not make mistakes."

EPILOGUE

Pine Ridge Reservation
February 2013

Calvin Spotted Elk had made rescinding the twenty Congressional Medals of Honor awarded for Wounded Knee part of his life's work. So far, that work wasn't going very well. He'd been rebuffed every step of the way.

Elk's ancestor, Chief Spotted Elk, had been killed in the massacre, and Calvin did not believe his spirit would rest as long as the slaughter at Wounded Knee continued to be referred to as a "battle."

In 1917, retired general Nelson A. Miles had written that "[a] massacre occurred, not only the warriors but the sick Chief Big Foot, and a large number of women and children who tried to escape by running and scattering over the prairie, were hunted down and killed."

Calvin Spotted Elk believed that Miles's report was the truth, and he had futilely tried many times over the years to get attention for his cause. Now, with a newly reelected president in office, Elk had hope that something would finally be done to right this historical tragedy. He chose his words to President Obama carefully.

Mr. President, what happened at Wounded Knee was not worthy of this nation's highest award for exceptional valor. The actions of the soldiers have been justly criticized because this was a massacre, not a battle. This tragedy, for many, remains a blemish in American history.

My relatives and I pray for this never to happen again and we pray you will hear our plea to put this to rest. The healing process takes time, but through prayer, acceptance, awareness and forgiveness, it is possible. For many of us, acknowledgment of what happened is at the root of our healing.

Calvin Spotted Elk did not expect a reply, but he added one additional line in the hope of proving to whoever would read the letter that he had good standing in this matter.

For many years, my grandfather, Chief Spotted Elk, has erroneously been known as Chief "Big Foot."

Elk, along with many others who have petitioned the government over the years to reconsider these medals and revise the official report on the Battle of Wounded Knee, is still waiting for a response.

7

Easy Eddie & the Hard Road to Redemption

Executive Management Level
Sportsman's Park
Cicero, Illinois
November 8, 1939

Easy Eddie O'Hare sat down at his fine mahogany desk and placed his glass of eighteen-year-old scotch on the blotter. Then he opened the bottom-left drawer and took out his pistol.

Oiling and cleaning this little .32 had become a thoughtful evening ritual over the last several years, though he'd never felt the need to carry it. But tonight would be different. Tonight, for the drive home from Cicero, he would load his gun and have it holstered beneath his overcoat. At least he'd be armed when they came for him, for all the good that would do.

Even the Chicago mob has laws. Not many, of course, but the few there are have only one penalty. And the mob has got more style in enforcement than the police and the courtrooms. They'll still hold trial and pass sentence, all right, but once a person's condemned they aren't killed right away, not unless it's absolutely necessary. They let the poor sucker walk around free and think about how his days are numbered.

They'd let Easy Eddie think about it for six long years.

He still had a few friends in the outfit; that's how he knew for sure that his number was up. *You shouldn't buy any green bananas, old pal.* The straight-faced warning in that bit of gallows humor was the only help he could expect. No one was going to be caught dead coming to his aid, not with Capone due back in town any time from his extended holiday on Alcatraz Island.

As he finished tending to his pistol, Eddie sat back and looked around the luxurious office that he'd furnished with ill-gotten gains. Not everything here was of great value, though, at least not in the monetary sense. Some items were only mementos, worth little to anyone but him.

There were the old photos of his kids that were just beginning to yellow in their frames. He hadn't seen the girls in years, and his boy had long since become a navy man—a pilot, to be exact.

One of the paperweights on his desk was a dented gas cap from Charles Lindbergh's mail plane, a souvenir pocketed at Lambert Field after a ride-along with that soon-to-be-great man. A pair of blood-flecked boxing gloves that hung on the coatrack recalled a very short match he'd once fought in his misspent youth, an open-call tryout for a pro sparring partner. One quick right cross from his opponent had put Eddie facedown on the canvas and convinced him he was no Jack Johnson. *There must be an easier way to make a million*, he'd thought.

And so there was.

He checked his pocket watch, studied the door for a while, and decided that he wasn't quite ready to walk through it for the last time. Maybe just one more drink, and for old times' sake, just another short stroll down memory lane.

His tired eyes soon found another keepsake, this one displayed on its own side table. It was an artificial rabbit on a rusty metal stand, the odd invention of his first big legal client—and arguably the object that put Easy Eddie on the road to riches and, eventually, to ruin.

But that wasn't really where the story started. For that, he'd have to go back a bit further.

Soulard district, St. Louis, Missouri
Twenty years earlier: December 31, 1919

The baby was crying and, before long, Eddie's young son had joined in the wailing.

He couldn't really blame hungry kids for making a racket, but that night it was just a little too much to swallow. With him and his wife not on speaking terms, Christmas had once again been a dismal, joyless affair. And now New Year's Eve was threatening to turn out the same way.

At one minute to midnight, with no steady job, no prospects, and not a plug nickel to his name, Eddie had made himself a promise, an oath that couldn't have been more solemn if he'd signed it in blood. He would make himself a wealthy man.

The bleak decade he'd just suffered through had finally and mercifully ended. There would be no more hopeless days, no more dead-end laboring just to scrape together another humble meal for the family table. No more drifting, no more despair, no more drafty walk-up apartments that reeked of cold cuts and day-old produce from the grocery store below. Right then and there, with the 1920s set to come roaring in, Eddie swore to change his life and his fortunes.

The next few years were a blur. Between working any job he could scrounge, day and night classes to complete his education at St. Louis University, and later studying law until the wee hours, there'd been far too little time left for his wife and children. But all of this was for them; at least that's the way it had begun.

During his lowest times, Eddie's father-in-law would encourage him with the same words over and over: *Stay with it, son. The day you pass that bar exam, a lot of doors will open.* He was right about that, of course, but if he'd really wanted to help, his wife's old man would have added one more nugget of valuable counsel:

Be awfully careful what you wish for.

Sportsman's Park
Cicero, Illinois
October 3, 1924

The fresh paint had barely finished drying in his first law office when Eddie met Owen Smith, the inventor of a more reliable, new-and-improved lure to entice racing dogs to speed around the greyhound tracks. The two of them were a good match: Mr. Smith needed help to patent his furry little robot, and Eddie needed the fee.

Now, a year into the relationship, Eddie had become Owen Smith's chief business advocate—and business was getting better every day. The two men traveled extensively, selling operator's rights to use the rabbit at dog tracks from St. Louis all the way to Hialeah in southern Florida.

This was their first trip to the Chicago area and, so far, it seemed to be a fruitful visit.

Eddie and Owen Smith had been seated in the track manager's garish corner office, waiting as the man looked over the contract and considered their deal, when the door opened behind them.

Three imposing men entered the room and took stations near the entrance. A gorilla in a pin-striped suit is still a gorilla, but this trio of simians obviously belonged to somebody with a lot of swing. Soon another man appeared—balding, shorter, and stockier than the others.

When his eyes caught this last man, the track manager dropped what he was doing and stood like he'd been called before a hanging judge.

No one spoke up immediately, so Eddie broke the silence.

"We're in the middle of a meeting here, fellas. Can I help you with something?"

The shorter man smiled humorlessly.

"Yeah," he said, "I've heard that you can."

"You've heard I can what?"

"Aw, let's not play coy, counselor. I've heard that you can help me with something."

Eddie blinked, and got to his feet. "I'm sorry, do I know you?"

"You don't, but you should."

The man gave only the slightest gesture and the track manager hurried from the room, followed closely by Owen Smith, who was well-known for his ability to take a hint.

The three big guys also left and closed the door, leaving Eddie and the sharply dressed stranger alone. Only then did Eddie notice the scars that trailed down the other man's face. It looked as though at some point in his youth he'd lost a fight with a broken bottle.

Eddie put out his hand. "I'm—"

"I told you, I know who you are."

They shook, and it felt to Eddie like he'd gripped a cold shank of Easter ham. "So, what can I do for you?" he asked.

"I'm looking to buy myself a little piece of this track," the man replied, "and some people downstate are making things very difficult for me."

"And?"

"And I hear you're a guy who can make things easy."

"I'm embarrassed to say that you've still got me a bit confused," Eddie said. "Who are you?"

The man laughed and pulled the track manager's rolling chair around the desk. He motioned for Eddie to sit, and then he did, too. "You talk real classy. That's good. I like that." His smile began to fade as he continued. "Yeah, I can tell you're a college man, but here's something I guess they didn't teach you in school. See, when you do business in Chicago, the first thing you've gotta do is choose a gang. Fortunately you got real lucky this time, because the gang chose you."

Eddie found that his mouth had grown uncomfortably dry. "And what gang is that?"

The man's next words were spoken low, as if he thought there might be a lawman listening from behind the drawn curtains across the room.

"Pleasure to meet you, Easy Eddie," he said. "I'm Al Capone."

Uptown Chicago
August 9, 1927

Eddie worked his way through the noisy crowd at Capone's favorite club, the Green Mill Lounge, glad-handing the VIPs and passing out tips like peppermint candy. He gave a wave to part owner Jack "Machine Gun" McGurn and got a respectful nod in return. Eddie had his new girlfriend on his arm, an illegal cocktail in his hand, and the band was playing "The Best Things in Life Are Free." He thought that it had been a hell of a day so far.

When they reached Eddie's table, the one always reserved near the stage, they sat and waved for the waiter.

"A gal down at work called this place 'the blind pig,' " his girl-friend said, shouting over the music. "Why do you think she called it that?"

"It's an old-time name for a speakeasy," Eddie replied, "from the last century. Back in your grandfather's day, they'd get around the law by putting a carny attraction of some kind in a room in the back—you know, a two-headed chicken or a three-legged cat—"

"Or a blind pig?"

"Right. And so they'd make you buy a ticket to see the pig, and then they'd give you the whiskey for free. No sale, no crime, see?"

She nodded, and smiled, clearly impressed.

"Thinking up stuff like that; it's kind of what I do for a living," Eddie said.

"That's very clever."

"And you're very pretty."

"Aren't you sweet," she said. She gave him a kiss and a wink and then turned in her chair toward the stage to listen to the band.

Eddie watched her for a moment or two. His divorce had been final-ized not long before, and though the parting had been fairly friendly, it certainly hadn't been a picnic. He thought of his boy, now a teenager, and his girls. The thought of them made him think hard about how his life had changed. A lot of dirty water had flowed over the dam in the last three years.

But a good man doesn't go bad all at once.

His alliance with Capone had started small. Eddie had smoothed the way for deals to establish front-businesses for Big Al, his lieutenants, and, from behind the scenes, the big boss, Johnny Torrio. He'd told himself for a while that he wasn't doing anything that any other ca-pable attorney wouldn't do for his clients. But, eventually, he faced the facts: a man couldn't so much as walk across the street with Capone and stay clean. He was the King Midas of crimes and scams; everything he touched turned to possible jail time.

Even at the track—a seedy enough hangout to begin with—Capone wasn't satisfied with simply gambling; he had to cheat. His favorite sure thing was to feed seven of the dogs a Porterhouse steak before a race and then bet heavy on the last, hungry dog. That was always good for a laugh and a hundred-dollar ticket at twenty-to-one odds.

All the while, little by little, Eddie had traded in his principles for riches, and each step downhill had certainly seemed like a worthy bargain at the time.

But then his affair with the mob took a giant step forward.

Early in 1925, Bugs Moran and the North Siders tried to assassinate mob boss Johnny Torrio. They'd shot him to hell right outside his home; but he'd lived. When he'd recovered, after a brief stint in prison for operating a bootleg brewery, the man they called "the Fox" had finally seen enough trouble. He left for Italy with his family and turned the reins over to his longtime protégé, Alphonse Capone.

On that same day Eddie had also received a promotion he'd never signed up for. One minute he was just a lawyer with a few loose connections to organized crime. The next he was the reluctant chief counsel to the new underworld king of Chicago.

From across the packed dance floor, Eddie noticed a stern-faced man sidling up to the bar. Maybe it was just his discount-store haircut, but he didn't seem to fit in with the festivities. Then another oddball joined him, and this one definitely had *Johnny Law* written all over his ugly face. It was beginning to seem like a real good time to be somewhere else.

Eddie leaned to his girl and whispered, "Do you want to get out of here?"

"Where to?"

"Across town," he said, giving her a sly, suggestive smile. "Come on, I want to show you around my office."

It was a quick drive to Cicero, and when they'd climbed the stairs to Eddie's private haunt he could tell that she was impressed.

That corner office where he and Capone had first met three years ago was now Eddie's opulent base of operations. It was stocked full of things he'd always dreamed of one day owning: art, sculptures, handmade furnishings, and all the rarities and luxuries that dirty money could buy. The massive leather divan alone was worth more than Mayor Kelly's touring car.

Hundreds of impressive cloth-bound volumes crowded his floor-to-ceiling shelves: casebooks and federal statutes, precedent opinions, lofty treatises, and details of many tens of thousands of regulations.

These books made for a classy backdrop, but they had a practical use as well. Unlike most attorneys, who used these books as a guide to the narrow letter of the law, Easy Eddie used them as a vast encyclopedia of loopholes, exploits, and artful legal dodges.

While others in his profession might advise their clients from the top floors of a high-rise building downtown, Eddie's one-man firm overlooked the homestretch of the dog track at Sportsman's Park.

Eddie had been told that many doors would open for him when he became a big-city lawyer. It was true; some of these doors led to politics, some to corporate power, some to a judge's seat, and others down troubled streets and the never-ending fight for the rights of the common man.

But there's one more door, an old, dark one, way down near the end of the hallway. That's the one Eddie found, standing open just a crack, when he'd first hung out his shingle. He knew damn well he shouldn't look at it, much less swing it wide and walk right through—but he'd done it anyway.

"Hey, Eddie?"

"Yeah, sweetheart."

"I never get out to the track and I love it here. Do you mind if I go down and make a bet?"

"Don't mind at all." He walked over and handed her a hundred, then gave her a pat on the bottom. "I've got a box right on the finish line. Just tell the boys you're with me and they'll get you whatever you want. Go on, I'll join you in a few."

When she was gone he sat at his desk. There were things to be done, as always, but he had no desire to do them at the moment. He poured himself a drink from the flask in his top drawer and before long he was lost in his thoughts again.

With Eddie's growing wealth had come the free time he'd always wanted. But, by the time 1927 rolled around, it was far too late to save his status as a family man. All his business travels, along with his wandering eye, had finally run his marriage into the rocks. But, despite the rifts his choices had created, Eddie continued to provide for his kids, and held out hope that he could be a positive presence in their lives, however small that might be.

He'd bought his soon-to-be ex-wife and the kids a fine new home and tried to make up for the neglect of his fatherly duties through financial support. The girls, he was convinced, would be fine; their mother had raised them right. It was his son who'd proven to be a cause for concern.

Eddie saw a lot of himself in the boy. And that wasn't a good thing.

Eddie had tried to teach his son the right things; things that a normal, at-home dad would be there to pass along. He taught him to play fair, to stand up to bullies, and to protect those unable to protect themselves. He taught him how to box and wrestle, and he took him to the shooting range until the boy had become an outstanding marksman. He took him flying, often talking their way into the cockpit so his son could try his hand at the controls. He'd tried his best—at least that's what he told himself—but on one recent visit, he realized that his best hadn't been good enough.

His son was also called Eddie, in honor of his wayward dad, but around the neighborhood he'd been picking up nicknames better suited to the billiard hall or the jailhouse than the Harvard Club. The kid was becoming lazy and spoiled as well, acting as if a cushy address on Easy Street were the only place he ever dreamed of living.

These early warning signs were enough to convince the elder Eddie that it was past time for a major change. Last month he'd put his foot down: the boy would leave St. Louis immediately and enroll in the Western Military Academy in Alton, Illinois—far from the ne'er-do-wells he'd begun to associate with, and near enough to his father's

Chicago home that the remainder of his youth could still be well supervised.

Eddie finished his drink, stood, and gave himself an approving once-over in the mirror by the coatrack. As he walked downstairs to join his girlfriend in the stands, he quietly hoped that, for the first time in a long time, he'd made the right decision.

It may have been too late for Eddie to pick the right door in life, but his son still had a chance.

Sportsman's Park
Cicero, Illinois
Early June 1930

Whether or not Eddie's concerns for his son had been justified, a few years later it seemed that his efforts had paid off. One of those early nicknames had unfortunately stuck, but other than that, young Eddie Jr. had grown into a confident, disciplined, square-shouldered cadet, ready to graduate with honors and set out on his own path. Where his ambitions had once involved a couch and a comic book, the boy now wanted to make it to the United States Naval Academy.

At last, things seemed to be looking up.

But, as so often happens to those who boldly stray to the wrong side of the law, just when things look their brightest, the devil is coming for his due.

Eddie arrived at his office on this warm June morning to find the feds waiting. That seductive door he'd opened long ago had slammed shut behind him. The good cop sat him down and brought him a coffee, and then the bad cop laid out their ironclad case. He was to be arrested on an old bootlegging rap, and the G-men were confident that a number of serious tax irregularities would surface in the run-up to the trial. When it was over Eddie had little hope of ever seeing daylight again.

Unless.

Naturally, it wasn't just a crooked Chicago lawyer they were after; the going price for those was a dime a dozen. No, J. Edgar Hoover wanted Al Capone and he wanted him bad. He'd sent his men to talk to the one insider who could finally help them put him away.

In return for information, Eddie would dodge the current charges and be assured of leniency toward any minor crimes that might come to the government's attention in the future. Then they told him about the icing on the cake: despite his father's sullied reputation, it would be arranged that his son would receive the necessary congressional nod to be approved and admitted to Annapolis. Without their influence, they assured him, the son of a gangster would never have a snowball's chance in hell of getting into the U.S. Naval Academy.

In truth, even without the threat of prosecution, Eddie had been considering making such a move on his own for quite some time. From a business standpoint, Capone had become a major liability and a constant thorn in his side, leaving no room for any legitimate enterprises. The offer to get his son into Annapolis was appealing, but he wasn't even sure if these guys could actually pull it off. On the other hand, they could definitely sling enough mud to keep his son *out* of the academy if they didn't get what they wanted.

It didn't take long for him to consider his options. After only a moment or two, Easy Eddie nodded and smiled, and did what he did best.

He made a deal.

Sportsman's Park
Cicero, Illinois
November 8, 1939

By the clock on the wall, Eddie had been lost in his memories for quite a while. He blinked a time or two, and the past faded away.

The waning daylight through his tall windows had grown dim and warm, and the hallway outside his office was still. In fact, it was so damned still it seemed that every last employee must have gotten a whispered word to go home early and avoid the line of fire.

Eddie knew there was no doubt that he'd done what he set out to do. In the end, however, he had to admit there wasn't a lot to be proud of. Over the years he'd lied and swindled nearly every working day. He'd

kept ruthless criminals on the streets and let innocent men be sent to
rot behind bars. He'd been an accessory to felonies and even murder—
though he'd never actually pulled the trigger himself—many times over.
He'd lost his wife, neglected his children, and nearly watched his boy
drift into a lowlife existence of sloth and ill-repute.

Eddie was too much of a realist to accept the idea of redemption,
especially for the kind of man he'd become. The best he could hope for
was that he'd soon be forgotten, and that, for the sake of his son, the
name they shared wouldn't forever be synonymous with infamy and
shame.

The newspaper lay open on his desk, and the headlines spoke of
dark days to come. It was an uncertain world he'd be leaving behind.
Hitler was consolidating Poland and turning his eyes toward new
conquests. President Franklin Roosevelt had just declared the United
States to be resolutely neutral in the war that was surely on the way,
but that position couldn't last much longer. Eddie knew as well as anyone the workings of the criminal mind: some madmen will never stop
unless someone stops them; sooner or later the United States would be
drawn in. As a sailor, his son would no doubt be a part of whatever terrible battles were in store.

But whatever was coming, Eddie knew he wouldn't be around to see
it. His partner had a special knack for dealing with his enemies. Ten
years before, Capone had invited the North Siders to a Tommy-gun
party down on North Clark Street. It had been a St. Valentine's Day
that Bugs Moran and the rest of Chicago would never forget.

That was it, then. All his memories had been revisited and nothing
was left to do but stand up and face the music.

He walked to the sideboard, poured and downed a last short scotch
and water, and felt once more for the pistol under his overcoat. As he
walked out through his office door he paused and smiled. The irony
was not lost on him: This door, the one that he'd walked through and
changed his life, was also the one he'd walk through to end it.

Eddie was pleasantly surprised when he opened the back exit and
wasn't immediately cut down by machine-gun fire. As he started his
car there was a moment of relief when the bench seat didn't instantly

explode beneath him. But then, about halfway home, he saw the dark sedan approaching from behind.

It was hopeless, he knew, but as that car slipped closer he stepped on the gas and decided to give them a good run for their money.

Traffic ahead was stop-and-go, but Eddie flashed his lights and laid on the horn and people seemed to get the message. He pumped the clutch and downshifted and heard his tires squeal as he rocketed through a space so tight he clipped off his outside mirror. Unfortunately the car behind matched every dodge he made, and more than once they got close enough to bump him good and hard from behind.

After a high-speed mile or two up Ogden Avenue the sedan managed to pull up alongside him. He was hemmed in with nowhere left to turn and no way to go any faster.

He looked to the side, straight into the barrel of a shotgun, and saw behind it a face that he recognized from his many years on the wrong side of the law. He wasn't surprised. That's the way they do it; they take care of their own. And then there was a double-barreled flash, a spray of glass and metal, and far less pain than he imagined. He was already dead when, seconds later, his car slammed into a trolley pole by the side of the road.

Aboard the USS *Lexington* with Task Force 11,
far into enemy waters
Two and a half years later: February 20, 1942

Butch lay in his bunk, still in his flight suit, flipping playing cards into the hat of his dress uniform across the small sleeping room. He had a championship run going, forty-four cards without a single miss. The unofficial all-time wardroom record was in sight.

He paused his target practice as the ship listed slightly to starboard, and he felt the rumble of the carrier's engines as they labored to turn the *Lexington* into the wind for another launch.

He sighed, flipped another card into the hat, and recalled a phrase he'd heard a thousand damned times from his instructors.

A lot of war is waiting.

All through the Academy, and then later on in flight school in

Pensacola, Florida, that was the wet blanket some old-timer would toss out whenever a rookie was overheard fantasizing about the exciting life of a navy flyer.

No, the wise guy would say, that's not the way it is. There would be hours and days and even months of tense anticipation followed quickly by a few terrifying minutes of heart-stopping, blood-curdling, adrenaline-pumping chaos. If you were brave and prepared and skilled and exceptionally lucky, that flash of chaos could be kept just barely under your control. You might even live to tell your grandkids about it all.

Butch's father had once said that if you ever want to hear God laugh, all you've got to do is make a plan. At the time, his dad's comment concerned his own struggles to build a business and support his family through the depths of the Great Depression, but his admonition was as true in battle as anywhere else. The military brass often spent weeks on their brilliant strategies and tactics, only to see the tables turned in a last-minute frenzy when the enemy failed to behave as expected.

The day's plan, for example, was set to be supervised from the flag bridge by Vice Admiral Wilson Brown. Before it all blew up it had probably looked just swell on paper.

The USS *Lexington* and the rest of Task Force 11 had been ordered to attack the enemy base at Rabaul, a major strategic prize off the coast of New Guinea that had recently been overtaken by the Japanese. The loss of this base was a major blow to the Allies. As the enemy ramped up air and sea forces there it would become a huge threat to vital shipping lanes.

While this small task force didn't pack nearly enough muscle to actually retake the base, their job was to throw a monkey wrench into the machine and cause as much damage as they could. Butch's air division had been chosen to lead the assault—bombing runways, sinking ships in the harbor, destroying as many hangar-bound Japanese Zeroes as possible. Down the road, a larger Allied operation would follow up, conquer the base, and send the Japs packing.

The battle plan hardly had a chance to get going, before a long-range enemy scouted the American ships. Butch had just returned from his morning patrol by then and could only watch as other fighter pilots from the *Lexington* took off and went after the airborne spy.

Butch's shipmates had taken the scout, but before he was shot down the sneaky bastard had almost certainly radioed his position and sent a warning to his distant commanders.

And that changed everything. A surprise attack by a minor strike force was one thing, but without that element of surprise, Task Force 11 was just a slow-moving target, a sitting duck in the middle of some very hostile waters. Another enemy reconnaissance flight soon followed, another Japanese spotter plane was splashed, and that was all the convincing required to turn the whole mission into a bust.

But at this point, even running away wasn't going to be a walk in the park.

TF 11 had already made it to a waypoint a little over 450 miles from Rabaul, and now the enemy was alerted. By this time Admiral Aritomo Goto had likely cooked up a surprise of his own for the discovered Americans—one involving a swift and overwhelming retaliation with a squadron or two of his long-range bombers and torpedo planes.

Though the American attack was off, an official retreat hadn't yet been ordered. Admiral Brown was famously reluctant to give up on a strategic goal, so for the moment all the task force could do was stay the dangerous course toward Rabaul, keep a sharp eye on the skies, and wait.

Butch wondered how he might stack up in an all-out, life-or-death dogfight like the one that might be coming soon. That was one test he hadn't faced so far.

According to his reviews, he was an exceptional pilot, and since he was a boy he'd been an excellent marksman. Putting those two skills together, though, had proven to be the biggest challenge of his twenty-eight years. He'd flown plenty of missions, but he still hadn't had the opportunity to fire a single shot in battle.

Butch flipped one card and then another for two more direct hits.

In the calm before the storm, he thought about his father.

The last letter he'd written to him a few years ago had been dashed off and routine, nothing like the note he would have written if he'd known there'd never be another. He'd let an awful lot go unsaid over the years, but *thank you* was the one sentiment that Butch had probably neglected the most. And when his father was murdered—gangland-style, no less—a number of unpleasant things that had gone unspoken were confirmed.

A busload of reporters and photographers had nearly ruined the funeral. But, after a few ugly days of lurid headlines—CAR CRASH KILLS CAPONE CANARY, SHOTGUN JUSTICE FOR UNDERWORLD SNITCH—the stories shrank and slipped to the back pages and were gradually forgotten.

Mother said that's what his father would have wanted in the end: to be forgotten by all except his family. Whatever his failings, Dad had been proud of his boy and girls. Flaws and all, he'd done the best he could for them, and he had hoped that the tarnish on their family name would fade with time.

But his bad choices had left quite a dubious legacy. Easy Eddie was survived by a criminal record, a broken marriage, a young trophy girlfriend, two fine daughters who'd grown up mostly without him, and a fairly shy, slightly overweight, navy pilot son who was pushing thirty years old and still waiting to prove himself among his peers.

Butch drew in a deep breath, took aim past the brim of the hat, and flipped the last card that would tie his personal best.

The door to the cabin banged open, swatting the flying queen of diamonds cleanly into the trash can. His friend and wingman, Marion "Duff" Dufilho, stood there, trying to catch his breath.

"C'mon, Butch, we're up!"

Out in the hall a loud Klaxon had begun to wail. As the two men clattered up the stairs toward the flight deck they felt the big ship beginning to maneuver and accelerate, and heard the repeating action order booming over the horns from high on the bridge:

Battle stations!

Battle stations!

Battle stations!

No need for a stop by the ready room; they got their mission briefing on the run.

Radar had picked up what looked like a jagged V about seventy-five miles west. As it disappeared and reappeared among the shifting storms the operator soon realized what he was seeing: a large contact that wasn't one of us, inbound at eight thousand feet and making 150 knots. A patrol was scrambled and launched to investigate.

Meanwhile, an earlier air patrol was returning, low on fuel and ready to land, but the remaining idle planes on the deck had been cleared and stacked astern to allow the just-departed squadron to take off. Now all those planes had to be moved to the bow again so the returning out-of-fuel patrol could be recovered before they started dropping dead-stick into the drink.

The flight deck was helter-skelter and crowded wingtip to wingtip. All available hands were occupied with respotting the planes, fore and then aft again. Aircraft were being fueled and rearmed, and the air boss was bullhorning and directing it all like a mad orchestra conductor.

"Pilots, man your planes! Thach, take thirteen, Sellstrom in number two, O'Hare in fifteen, and Dufilho in four!"

The microphones from the radar room and the tower had been routed directly to the topside loudspeakers, and an operator's voice blared out:

"Contact! I've got a contact! Bogies inbound, forty-seven miles west!"

Butch and Duff had been ordered to man the last two F4F Wildcats on the deck and given call-signs of Raven 5 and 6. After a last confirmation of orders both men were soon squeezing into their narrow cockpits.

"That contact," Butch shouted back over the rising noise, "is that the same one our boys have already gone after? Or another one?"

"Do I look like I know?" Duff yelled forward. "Just strap in, cross your fingers, and get her ready to roll!"

The last plane from the previous patrol had finally caught a cable and was down, and the desperate front-to-back respotting began again. Butch looked to the storm-darkened sky and saw a stuttering exchange of tracers from machine-gun fire lighting up the distant clouds.

He put on his headset, got the signal, and called out ahead to clear the nearby crew. As he started up his engine and ticked through his preflight checklist, the radio told him what was happening up there: A formation of nine Japanese bombers had been found heading straight for Task Force 11. The latest patrol was doing all they could to shoot them down before they got close enough to drop their deadly load.

That created another emergency. The deck of the *Lexington* was crowded with fully fueled aircraft, a prime target for incoming bombers. The planes on the deck were the scouts, torpedo planes, and land attack craft meant for the raid on Rabaul. But they were useless now; the only thing needed in the air right then were fighters.

And there were only two of them left. Butch and Duff were sitting in those fighters, last in line to depart. They could only sweat it out and wait their turn as the rest of the vulnerable inventory was launched, one by one, into the relative safety of the open air.

The action in the sky was now close enough to see with the naked eye. A couple of enemy bombers had already spiraled into the sea, and now another one, the lead plane of the Japanese formation, was on fire and badly disabled—but it was still homing in on the carrier.

Thundering anti-aircraft guns cut loose from the *Lex* and the surrounding cruisers and destroyers, filling the attacker's flight path with flak and blooming black bursts of shrapnel. But the plane kept coming. There was nothing left to do but watch as the flaming twin-engine bomber leveled, descended, and approached with suicidal intent, its pilot obviously struggling to hold his course on a kamikaze run toward the carrier deck.

At last focused gunfire tore through the cockpit and destroyed some final, vital system. The shredded enemy bomber lurched and snap-rolled into a screaming, careening, knife-edge pass and disappeared just shy of the hull of the carrier. It had only missed its mark by a stone's throw as it crashed into the churning water beside the vessel.

Butch looked back to the runway. There was only one departing plane left in front of him, and Duff, in the last ready fighter, was the only backup behind him. He tuned his engine and ran it up to begin his taxi, pulling the canopy forward and closed. Soon the flag dropped to send him barreling down the white line behind 1,200 horsepower, and he was off like a homesick angel.

As soon as airspeed allowed, he banked into a climb toward his hastily assigned coordinates, fighting against buffeting winds as he cranked the heavy handle beside his leg thirty-two times in order to pull up the landing gear.

Manual retracts were one of the many pains-in-the-butt of this aging airframe. But what the Wildcat lacked in other areas, it made up for in pure iron guts and toughness. Butch had seen one of these birds come back from a sortie with more than five hundred bullet holes, perforated from end to end, and it was still out fighting again the next day.

By the time the wheels were up and locked Butch was nearly at altitude. He banked again onto a heading toward the aerial battle, which was now taking place well within sight of the American ships.

As his wingman joined alongside, Butch saw more enemy planes going down in the distance. Some of the survivors had dropped their bombs even as they struggled to evade the fleet's defenders. So far those falling salvos were missing their targets by a comfortable margin.

Within seconds the few remaining Japanese bombers were breaking formation and scattering. Those that were able were bugging out and heading home defeated, with American fighters hot on their tails.

Butch keyed the radio.

"Raven Six, this is Raven Five. Duff, let's have a gun check."

"Roger that, though I don't know why the hell we'd go to the trouble. Looks like we missed the party again."

"Always a bridesmaid, never a bride," Butch replied. Duff was right; by then the sky was empty and the high-speed chases had already disappeared from view. Nevertheless, procedure was procedure. He flipped on his illuminated sights, charged his guns, and fired a quick test burst from the four .50-caliber cannons mounted on his wings.

"Hey, Butch," Duff radioed, forgoing the call-signs. "I've got a little problem over here—"

His wingman's voice was abruptly cut off by a shouted transmission from the *Lexington*'s tower.

"Raven Five and Six and all available, we have bogies inbound, repeat, bogies are inbound from the east at—" The remaining words were obscured by a sharp crackle of static, maybe the interference of a stroke of lightning from one of the surrounding storms.

"Lexington, this is Raven Five," Butch answered. "Say again, say again from 'inbound.' Did you say fifty miles out?"

"Raven Five, I said *fifteen miles*, one-five, large radar contact at your three o'clock low. Check that range, now twelve miles, twelve miles, it looks like a second damned full formation and she's right on top of us, inbound dead astern at angels niner and descending!"

Twelve miles.

Butch checked his own coordinates as he did the math. Whatever was there was only a couple of minutes from the undefended flank of the task force—and, by his rough calculations, only a few thousand feet directly below his current position.

He pushed the nose down, Duff still on his wing, and soon, as he settled through a thick bank of haze and rainclouds, there they were.

Six—no, *eight* Japanese twin-engine land attack bombers—"Bettys," as they were called in the briefings—were lined up on Task Force 11 in a tight formation, clearly on the final leg of an uncontested bombing run.

In the flurry of radio traffic during his descent, one thing became clear as a heart attack: No other fighters were anywhere near close enough to help in time. And while Duff was still with him, that problem he'd mentioned before was a fatal one: His guns were all jammed and he couldn't fire a shot.

Butch was flying the only armed plane left in the sky—with a mere thirty-four seconds of live ammunition—the last man standing between that squadron of enemy bombers and the thousands of sailors and airmen below.

If this had been the Japanese plan all along, they'd executed it perfectly. They'd taken some losses, but they'd also drawn away every defending aircraft from Task Force 11 and left the door wide open for a devastating strike that could send several ships, including a U.S. carrier, straight to the bottom. Their victory was just ahead, and there was nothing the Americans could do to stop it.

Like hell, Butch thought.

He keyed the mic and looked over to his right. The two planes were close enough that he could see the grim expression on his wingman's face.

"Duff, you stay clear, now."

"What the hell are you going to do, Butch?"

"The same thing you'd do, buddy: whatever I can."

• • •

If Butch had any advantages, they were raw speed and surprise. He rolled hard left and then pitched his Wildcat into a screaming descent, setting his sights on the trailing bomber on the right-hand side of the V formation. He streaked in from the high side and stayed off his guns until the Betty's starboard engine crept into the crosshairs. When he fired, it was with a rifleman's precision.

Those first few precious bullets tore through the enemy's cowling and a cloud of black smoke and flames burst forth as a second careful volley pierced the wing tanks. Target number one dropped out of formation, badly disabled and barely under control.

Butch's dad had taught him to shoot long ago and, so far, he would have been proud. The score was one down and seven to go, but from here on out it would be different. They knew he was there.

Butch jinked and evaded but held his heading as the Japanese tail-gunners swung their own cannons around and began returning fire. He took three quick shots at the next bomber up the line, and then, as Butch leveled off and rocketed through the crumbling formation, another Betty dropped out and spun downward in flames.

He pulled up and rolled out to set up for another run—this next one surely doomed to fail—and caught a brief glimpse of another lone Wildcat weaving its way through the bright tracers of the enemy defenses. It was Duff, dead guns and all, flying like a man possessed, trying his level best to distract their adversaries and draw their fire.

The second pass began just like the first, but things changed fast. As Butch pulled the trigger on the left-rear bomber he felt several heavy impacts thudding through his airframe. The Wildcat absorbed its punishment without a hitch. Meanwhile, Butch's latest target had taken critical damage. The big plane banked to flee the fight, one engine afire, and dropped his bombs into the empty ocean below as he made a limping turn away.

Butch was amazed when he came around for his third high-side pass and saw only four bombers left in formation. The *Lexington* was now clearly in sight down below. Fierce anti-aircraft fire began to fill the air ahead. He dove in again, but this time there was nearly as much danger from the flak of the ship's response as from the guns of the Japanese.

By the count in his head, his guns were running low. He again fired in metered bursts toward the most vulnerable points on the enemy planes. Through the crosshairs he watched one of the engines on the nearest Betty burst into flames, then he shifted toward the head of the V, scoring yet another direct hit on the leader that sent his port-side radial engine exploding out of its nacelle.

Between Butch's one-man assault and the anti-aircraft fire from the task force, the remaining planes were bracketed and their formation nearly broken up.

On his fourth and final shooting pass, as those last bombers prepared to let loose their loads, Butch felt his guns finally run dry and silent. He banked and then leveled off with a seat-of-the-pants plan to run his plane into the side of one of the Bettys if need be.

But then, streaking in from behind and overhead, the cavalry arrived.

Led by Lieutenant Commander John "Jimmy" Thach, several fighters had just returned from their pursuit of the survivors of the first wave. The sight of them evidently convinced this tattered second formation of Bettys to give it up and flee. They dropped their bombs well short of the ships of the task force and split off to run for clear air with the Americans closing in for the kill.

One of the casualties of Butch's run had been his radio, so he could neither transmit nor receive as he waited his turn for a landing on the *Lex*. It hadn't hit him quite yet, what he'd done; all he felt was anxious to get the wheels back on the runway.

But his anxiousness didn't last long. After rolling to a stop on the deck, Butch pulled back the canopy and stood up in his seat to a ship-wide cheer so loud and long, it sounded like the Cubs had finally won the Series at Wrigley Field.

Aboard the USS *Enterprise*, Central Pacific,
near the enemy-controlled Gilbert Islands
Twenty-two months later: November 26, 1943

With time and experience he'd grown accustomed to the rigors and
chaos of battle. Every engagement was unique, of course, but that
evening, as Butch sat in his cockpit—now in command of his own
squadron—the scene outside looked strangely familiar. It was almost as
though he'd lived this moment before.

Just like that long-ago day aboard the *Lexington*, the flight deck of the
Enterprise was well-controlled mayhem. And, just like that day, a score
of Japanese bombers had been detected on radar, heading in for blood.
The Allies were preparing to go up to try to bring them down—but,
unlike that first dogfight, this would be a rare nighttime engagement, a
daring mission planned by Butch himself.

He completed his preflight checks and his eyes soon found the picture of his wife, Rita, that he'd clipped near the altimeter. Right beside
it was another photo—his father and mother on one of their happier
days, twenty years earlier. It was cracked and fading from time and
much thoughtful handling.

In the end, it seemed as though Easy Eddie had been granted his
final wish: He was already forgotten by most, but not by those he'd
done his best to protect and care for.

Butch thought for a moment about his father and about everything
that had brought him to the deck of this carrier. Two months after his
incredible mission to save the *Lexington*, Butch had returned to the
States on extended leave. With his wife by his side, he was escorted
to the White House, where FDR himself promoted him to lieutenant
commander. He was then presented with the first Medal of Honor
awarded to a navy man in World War II.

The citation was for conspicuous gallantry and intrepidity in aerial
combat, but later in the text it was stated more simply: In the course of
saving his carrier and countless lives, Butch had performed the most
daring single action in the history of combat aviation.

When he'd returned to his native St. Louis, sixty thousand people
turned out for the parade that was held in his honor. The event was

compared to the celebration of Lindbergh's homecoming after his pio-
neering solo flight across the Atlantic.

The war effort needed heroes in the conflict's earlier years, and Butch
could very well have parlayed his well-earned fame into a safe, extended
stateside public relations tour. But that wasn't him. Before long he was
back on active duty, first as a trainer and then in combat again.

Now, as Butch peered out his cockpit window and watched the busy
deck of the USS *Enterprise*, he realized he'd been right: this was where
he belonged. He took a last quiet moment to give thanks for everything
and everyone who'd helped him get there, including a flawed man
who'd no doubt be the first to admit he'd been far from the perfect dad.

The deck boss gave him the sign, the flag dropped, the engine
roared, and Edward Henry "Butch" O'Hare tore down the runway and
took off into the sky, never to return again.

Six years after being killed in combat and four years after the end of the
war he'd helped the Allies win, Chicago's Orchard Depot was renamed
in Butch's honor: O'Hare International Airport.

8

The Saboteurs:
In a Time of War, the Laws Are Silent

The Farm
West of Berlin, Germany
April 14, 1942

The Farm looked like every other large villa in the serene countryside near Berlin. Once owned by wealthy Jewish industrialists, most of these estates were now the property of the Third Reich and had become uniform in their operation and appearance.

But this particular estate was different.

As the sun rose over the center of a million square miles of Nazi-occupied Europe, George Dasch—thirty-nine years old, with long, lanky arms, and a streak of silver through the center of his dark hair—sat through another class on bomb-making. Well-trained German shepherds patrolled the perimeter of the estate, just beyond a large stone wall.

Each student at the Farm had been specifically chosen for a special mission based on their ability to blend into ordinary American communities. All of them had spent time in the United States, most having left only after failing in a string of professional pursuits.

As George watched the instructor demonstrate the bomb assembly for what seemed like the five hundredth time, he looked around the classroom and began to wonder about his classmates. None of them, to his knowledge, had demonstrated any real loyalty to the Nazis or hatred toward the United States. He had neither. Worse, none of them had experience in espionage or military tactics or any of the other skills that might make someone a useful candidate for this kind of mission.

It was all pretty surreal, George thought, and so atypical of the way the Nazis normally operated. Loyalty and allegiance to the Third Reich were everything to them. He'd expected to be interrogated, maybe even tortured, in an attempt to break him. He'd prepared for the inevitable pain that was to come; worked to control his heart rate and breathing, and he thought carefully about how he would answer questions about his time in the United States. How would he fake the animosity they would so desperately want to see? He worried that he'd never be able to pull it off. He worried that he'd be labeled a sympathizer of the enemy and executed, his body thrown in some shallow grave outside the Farm.

But George didn't need to worry about any of that, because the interrogation never came.

There were no questions, no torture, and no threats against his family.

Now he and his classmates were inside the Farm, training for an incredibly difficult and important mission—and none of them had the slightest idea how they'd gotten there.

New York City
Monday, December 8, 1941

John Cullen thought he was minutes away from becoming a U.S. Marine.

That morning he, along with hundreds of other tall, blue-eyed twenty-one-year-olds, set out for the New York City Armed Services recruiting station. He wanted to hit back against the Japanese personally, violently, and immediately.

Well, not quite *immediately*. After all, Christmas was just over two weeks away. He figured he could sign up now, spend one more Christmas with his family, and then ship out right afterward.

John entered the recruiting station, waited in line, and eventually reached a Marine sergeant who looked to be straight out of Hollywood central casting. "We're here to sign up," he said, pointing to the friend he'd brought along.

"If you fellas are ready to ship out tonight, we will take you," snapped the sergeant. "If not, leave now. Don't have no time for those who prioritize holidays over freedom."

John and his friend looked at each other. Neither of them wanted to be the first to say what they were thinking—but, to the sergeant, the look on their faces was obvious.

They left the Marine recruiting station and joined the Coast Guard instead.

The Farm
Wednesday, April 29, 1942
5:30 P.M.

George carefully mixed the chemicals and prepared the detonator as he was taught—but he knew it was hopeless. Remembering details was not his strength. That might be okay when it came to names and dates and places, but when those details meant life or death, bad things were bound to happen.

Would the bomb explode? At the right time? With enough power?

Creeping through the darkness, looking in every direction for anything out of place, George attached the bomb to the fuel tank and turned to leave. As he did, a series of explosions stopped him dead in his tracks. The noise was incredible. George covered his head with his arms, his ears ringing, eyes burning from the smoke and legs singed by sparks.

Then it all stopped just as quickly as it had started. The fireworks were done; the drill was over. George had failed.

That night, every student at the Farm took a version of the same final exam. Every student failed.

The next day, they received their assignments.

They were headed for America.

The Farm
Thursday, April 30, 1942
9:15 A.M.

"There will be two teams of four men," the heavyset instructor told his students. "U-202 will take Team One to New York's Long Island. U-584 will take Team Two to the east coast of Florida. The subs will get as close to shore as possible, surface briefly, and then each team will take a small rubber boat to the shore."

George and his seven classmates stared incredulously at the instructor. If the bomb-making classes had seemed surreal, this plan—or whatever it could be called—seemed downright absurd.

"Your first task will be to bury the TNT crates on the beach—you'll retrieve these later, right before the attacks are set to begin. In the meantime, you'll go out and find lodging and clothing and begin to blend back into the American society. This should not be difficult; you've all done it before."

The instructor, sweat dampening his forehead and cheeks, then began to explain the carefully selected targets designed to cripple American morale and frustrate industrial production.

"This bridge is called the Hell Gate Bridge. It connects Queens to the Bronx. Team One is going to blow it up.

"This bridge crosses Horseshoe Curve. It's critical to the Pennsylvania Railroad. . . .

"These two factories in Pennsylvania process cryolite, which is needed for aluminum production. . . ."

He continued down the list, explaining the need for each operative to memorize the targets, which included bridges, railroads, canals, factories, and, most important of all, he said, a series of aluminum factories in east Tennessee.

"You can't make a war plane without aluminum," he said. "And every blue cross you see on this map is a factory that produces it." Many of the crosses were dotted around a small town, just south of Knoxville, called Alcoa.

"Team One"—he looked at George, who had been selected as its leader—"your job is to blow out the electricity at these power plants for eight hours. Eight hours. That's all it takes. After eight hours of no electricity, the metals will harden. If the metals harden, the stoves break. If the stoves break, the factory dies. If the factory dies, the aluminum supply dries up. If the aluminum dries up, there are no new planes."

He paused to dramatize the moment, as though some of the students might not be taking it seriously enough.

"And if there are no more American planes, we win the war."

Long Island, New York
Saturday, June 13, 1942
12:25 A.M.

Coastguard Seaman Second Class John Cullen was just beginning his midnight patrol. Dressed in his standard Coast Guard uniform, he walked along the beach through the Long Island fog, quietly singing to himself "I've Got a Girl in Kalamazoo."

Some days he regretted turning down the Marines in favor of the Coast Guard. He imagined himself training for the upcoming invasion of Guadalcanal and taking the fight to the enemy. Instead he was pounding sand on beaches nine thousand miles away, patrolling a dark and quiet coastline from . . . what, exactly?

The good news was that he felt safe; the bad news was that he felt very alone.

In reality, he was neither.

Fifteen minutes into his patrol, John saw the most unlikely of sights: people. The fog was too thick to be sure of it, but it looked like they were pulling a dinghy out of the surf and onto the beach. Shining his flashlight toward them, its light doing nothing but illuminating the fog, he called out, "U.S. Coast Guard. Who are you?"

"Coast Guard?" shouted back one of the strangers. He had dropped the dinghy and was walking toward John.

Cullen could barely make out in the darkness the other three strangers busying themselves unloading materials of some kind out of the dinghy and onto various points along the beach.

"Yes. Who are you?" John asked.

"Fishermen. From East Hampton," the man replied.

The man bore no resemblance to a fisherman. He wore a red woolen sweater, tennis shoes, a dark fedora hat, and pants that had been soaked through. Besides, he had no fishing supplies.

"We were trying to get to Montauk Point, but our boat ran aground," he said, his long, lanky arms flailing. "We're waiting for the sunrise to continue." He was a thin man, shorter than average, with a streak of silver running through the middle of his jet-black hair.

"What do you mean, East Hampton or Montauk Point?" asked John. The two locations were twenty miles from each other, and these supposed fishermen were only five miles from where they said they'd started. *Fog or no fog*, John thought, *who misses their landing spot by fifteen miles?*

"Do you know where you are?" he asked the man in the odd clothes, with the odd accent and even odder story.

"I don't believe I know where we landed," he replied. "But you should know."

"You're in Amagansett. That's my station over there," John said, pointing up the beach to a building that was barely discernible through the fog. "Why don't you come up to the station and stay the night?"

"All right," the stranger said. But then, after a few steps, he stopped.

John's suspicions grew. The bizarre stranger seemed even more nervous than before. If he were truly a lost fisherman, he would have no reason not to come to the Coast Guard station.

But John was now quite sure that this was no fisherman. And so the mysterious man's next statement confirmed what John already knew.

"I'm not going with you."

Shangri-La
Catoctin Mountain Park, Maryland
Saturday, June 13, 1942
12:30 A.M.

In a large house set inside the most isolated of country estates, the President of the United States slept alone and undisturbed, his face a picture of a man at peace. The fate of his republic, and perhaps a few others as well, hinged on the choices he made during the day—but the night was his. He slept soundly at this weekend retreat in the mountains north of Washington, this place he had repurposed as a retreat and named Shangri-La after the fictional Himalayan utopia.

Yes, it was true that his nation and its allies were losing a war in which the very freedom of mankind was at stake. And yes, MacArthur was trapped in the Philippines, while Rommel was racking up victories in North Africa and half of America's fleet lay useless at the bottom of Pearl Harbor. But Franklin Delano Roosevelt had carried the nation through a depression. There was nothing, he believed, he could not bend to his iron will—and that included the Nazis.

Amagansett, Long Island
Saturday, June 13, 1942
12:35 A.M.

"What do you mean you're not coming with me?" John Cullen asked.

"I have no identification card, and no permit to fish."

"That's all right. We'll sort it all out."

"No, I won't go."

"You have to come," Cullen said, grabbing for the man's arm.

"Now listen," the man replied, his tone suddenly changing, his hands trembling, his eyes narrowing, his accent becoming clearer. "How old are you, son?"

"Twenty-one," replied John.

"You have a mother?"

"Yes."

"A father?"

"Yes."

"Look, you have no idea what this is all about. I don't want to kill you. Forget about this and I'll give you some money and you can go have a good time."

"I don't want your money," John said, his heart beginning to race.

A second man was now visible through the fog, coming closer and dragging a large canvas bag. He started speaking in German to the man John had been questioning.

"Shut up," the man called out in English, looking mortified. "Go back to the other guys."

The other man did as he was told and retreated.

"Take a good look at my face," the man said as he removed his dark fedora, reached into a tobacco pouch, and stuffed a wad of money into Cullen's hand. "Look into my eyes. Would you recognize me if you saw me again?"

"No, sir," John lied. He knew he would never forget the odd streak of silver hair through the middle of the stranger's head, but the time for honesty had passed. He was unarmed and powerless over these men, whoever they were. "I never saw you before."

"You might see me in East Hampton sometime. Would you know me?"

"No, I never saw you before in my life."

"You might hear from me again. My name is George John Davis. What's your name, boy?"

"Frank Collins, sir," he lied again—now even more nervous after hearing the man say his name. *Why is he telling me these things?* he thought.

Cullen slowly took a step back. Then another. And another. After a few more paces the man had disappeared into the fog.

Cullen ran.

New York City
Saturday, June 13, 1942
7:30 P.M.

The Governor Clinton Hotel was among New York's ritziest, and its restaurant, the Coral Room, among the city's most elegant. As George sat down for dinner, he thought of all the other times he'd been in places like this, as a waiter, never as a customer. Now, far from his old life, and far from the scarcity of war-torn Germany, George sat in the Coral Room with a fine linen napkin across his lap and eighty thousand dollars in cash strapped around his waist. It was more money than the president of the United States made in a year.

After his encounter with the boy from the Coast Guard this morning, George and his three teammates—Peter Burger, Richard Quirin, and Henry Heinck—had found their way to the Amagansett train station. There they'd boarded an early morning Long Island Rail Road train headed for Queens. George and Peter had checked into the Governor Clinton while suggesting to the team's other two members that it would be safer if they found a different hotel.

Across the table was Peter Burger, a toolmaker by trade. But neither Pete nor George looked liked a tradesman tonight. After treating themselves to a shave and a shopping spree in Queens, they'd made it to Manhattan and headed straight for Macy's. There they bought more shirts, trousers, underwear, ties, handkerchiefs, and suits—plus new watches and three suitcases to carry it all in.

George was smart enough to know that shopping sprees and steak dinners were not exactly the best way to stay inconspicuous—but at that moment he didn't really care. This was a celebration. After all, they'd somehow convinced their own government not only to let them leave the country, but to send them back on their own private U-boats.

"My sister's father-in-law was seventy-three, a fine man," George said to Peter once they'd finished talking about their early morning escape. "The Nazis threw him into a concentration camp. Nine months. Because he was too Catholic. While he was in there, his wife died."

Pete, perhaps buoyed by the wine, perhaps emboldened by George's criticism of the Nazis, talked about his own seventeen months in prison. How he'd written a paper critical of the Gestapo. How he'd been held with sixty other prisoners in a windowless cell. And how his pregnant wife had been harassed, pressured to divorce him, and shaken down by the Gestapo. When she miscarried, Pete knew whom to blame.

"I have a lot to talk to you about," George said. It was, by any measure, an understatement.

"I know what you are going to tell me," said Pete. "I am quite sure that our intentions are very similar."

George looked around. He badly wanted to talk with Peter now—but there were too many people sitting around them, too many prying ears. George knew that he'd been sloppy up until this point—he was an untrained, unmotivated, unsympathetic German. His carelessness and erratic nature were among the reasons he'd failed in most of his professional pursuits, none of which—from waiting tables, to clerking at a soda fountain, to managing a brothel—had prepared him for international espionage.

But he would not be sloppy anymore. He didn't care about his mission, but he had no idea if the Nazis had sent others to watch him and his team. *Be patient*, George told himself.

"In the morning," he said.

New York City
Sunday, June 14, 1942
8:30 A.M.

"I want the truth, nothing else—regardless of what it is," George said. Looking Pete in the eye, pointing to the window across the hotel room, he added, "If we can't agree, either I go out the window or you do."

"There is no need for that. I think we feel very much the same," Pete replied. "Let's get on with it."

But George was in no hurry. Instead of getting right to the reason the two of them were there, he instead started telling Pete about his life.

He explained how he'd left Germany in 1922 at age nineteen for America. That another nineteen years later he'd retreated back to his home country, looking for a new start.

He knew almost instantly that it had been a mistake. It was 1941 and, as George explained, "There was too much terror and too much want, not enough food and not enough fun."

His next stop was the Farm—and then right back here, to America.

Pete told a story not altogether different: a childhood in Germany, an emigration to America, and a return home that he quickly regretted. "I never intended to carry out the orders," he said, beginning to cry. "And when I got to the beach yesterday, I started sabotaging the mission right away."

"When you were talking with the Coast Guardsman, I dropped a pack of German cigarettes," Pete continued, "and a vest. And some socks and swimming trunks. Then I dragged the crates of TNT along the beach. I could have carried them. They were light enough. But I knew dragging them would leave marks leading right to where we buried them. The fog obscured what I was doing from the others—they had no idea."

Smiling, and sure he'd found an ally, George gripped Pete's shoulder with his trembling hand. "Kid, I think God brought us together. We are going to make a great team."

New York City
Sunday, June 14, 1942
7:51 P.M.

The FBI received a lot of phone calls. Some of them were taken seriously, and the rest were routed to an agent who sat at a "nutter's desk."

"Can you spell that, sir?" asked the agent who was, at the moment, listening to a caller who claimed to have arrived from Germany the prior morning.

"Franz. F-R-A-N-Z. Daniel. D-A-N-I-E-L. Pastorius. P-A-S-T-O-R-I-U-S."

The agent wrote down "Postorius."

"And what type of information do you want to give?"

He told the agent that he would be traveling to Washington to report something "big." Once there, he wanted to speak directly to J. Edgar Hoover. "He is the person who should hear it first."

"Mr. Hoover is a busy man—"

"Take down this message," the caller demanded. "I, Franz Daniel Pastorius, shall try to get in touch with your Washington office this coming week, either Thursday or Friday, and you should notify the Washington office of this fact."

Before hanging up, George added, "Tell them I am about forty years old, and have a streak of silver in my hair."

From the nutter's desk, the FBI agent typed a memo for the file. Neither it, nor George's message, ever left New York.

Washington, D.C.
Friday, June 19, to Wednesday, June 24, 1942

It was Friday morning when George dialed the operator at the Mayflower Hotel in Washington, D.C. His message to the FBI may not have made it to the capital, but he had. "Room service, please."

Peter Burger knew that George was in D.C. to turn himself in to the

FBI and expose the entire operation, but the other two team members had no idea. Peter had told them that George was leaving New York for a few days to get in touch with some Nazi sympathizers living in America, hopeful that they could help with logistics.

George was finally beginning to feel like himself again. It had been a long time. But now, between the great food, seeing old friends, and playing marathon games of pinochle, he was starting to realize that his future was bright. His next step, which would be to explain the entire German plot to the American government, would finally set him free.

George had spent a lot of time over the past few days thinking about what he'd do with his life once the Americans had labeled him a hero. Maybe he could help the U.S. war effort by improving their propaganda. Or maybe the government would have its own ideas. Whatever the case, as long as he was helping to bring down the Nazis, he'd be happy.

Picking up the phone to call the FBI, George had a moment of doubt—not about whether to call, but about whom to call. It suddenly occurred to him that maybe the Secret Service was the proper agency. Unsure, he dialed the U.S. Government Information Service and told the woman who answered that he had "a statement of military as well as political value." She suggested trying the colonel in charge of Military Intelligence at the War Department. George hung up, called the colonel, and left a message.

Undeterred, and in something of a hurry for a change, George reverted to his original plan: He called the FBI and asked to speak to J. Edgar Hoover.

The operator transferred him to a second office; which sent him to a third office. That office connected him to Duane Traynor, the agent in charge of the FBI's anti-sabotage unit.

If George couldn't talk directly to Hoover, he figured Traynor would have to do. "Did New York tell you I was on my way?"

Of course, New York had not told him anything. But, intrigued, Traynor sent a car to the Mayflower to pick George up and bring him in. While he waited, George wrote a letter to Pete:

Got safely into town last night and contacted the responsible parties. At present I'm waiting to be brought over to the right man by one of his

agents. I had a good night's rest, feel fine physically as well as mentally
and believe that I will accomplish the part of our participation. It will
take lots of time and talking but please don't worry, have faith and
courage. I try hard to do the right thing.

After arriving at the Justice Department, George sat down with Agent Traynor. "I have a long story to tell," he said, "but I want to tell it my own way."

For twelve hours, George told Traynor about the Farm and the U-boats, about the second team sent to Florida and about the targets they were ordered to hit. Of course, he also treated Traynor to a healthy dose of his life story as a team of six stenographers worked in one-hour shifts to record every word that came out of his mouth. Finally, perhaps for the first time in his life, George had a receptive audience willing to sit and listen to anything that popped into his head.

As midnight approached, George was beginning to lose his voice. Accompanied by Traynor, he returned to the Mayflower, where the FBI agent slept in a spare bed. It was all going according to plan, George thought. It was exciting. And even though it was exhausting, and a little scary, he was having fun. It felt good to be a hero.

On Saturday, Traynor asked, "Is there any way you can get in touch with the leader of the other group?"

"Well, yes," George said. "I had him write the name of somebody on a handkerchief." If they found that man whose name was on the handkerchief—a friend of the other group's leader, Edward Kerling—they would probably find Edward himself.

George reached into his pocket and took out the handkerchief. It was blank. "Well, how do you develop it?" asked Traynor.

"I can't remember." George paused, squeezed his eyes, and put his index finger to the top of nose, thinking hard. "You use some kind of smelly stuff."

A day later, the name of the "smelly stuff" finally came to George. "Ammonia!" he exclaimed. "I passed the handkerchief over a bottle of ammonia. It shows red until it dries. You read it slowly and then it goes away again."

• • •

Four days later George signed each of the 254 single-spaced typewritten pages that made up his statement. "My mind is all upside down," he told Traynor, but George expected the next steps to be much easier: a prominent government job helping in the fight against Hitler. At the very least he'd keep the eighty thousand dollars and start a new life.

But after six days of talking and thinking about all of the places where this new life might lead him, George had never stopped to consider the one place that it actually would: prison.

Washington, D.C.
Monday, June 22, 1942

"Take this down," J. Edgar Hoover told his secretary. "To President Franklin Delano Roosevelt. Regarding Nazi spies. The FBI has apprehended all members of the group which landed on Long Island. They are being held secretly and incommunicado. I have taken detailed statements from each of the persons arrested and the story is a startling and shocking one. Long and extensive training is being given by the German authorities to specially selected men who in turn are being placed on board German submarines to be landed on the shores of the United States. I expect to be able to have in custody all members of the second group."

Hoover hadn't risen to the top of the FBI—and stayed there—by sharing credit. Almost every sentence in his memo included the word *I*. Not once did it mention that George Dasch had turned himself in or that his initial call to the New York field office had been referred to the "nutter's desk."

Washington, D.C.
Thursday, June 25, 1942

A few minutes past noon on June 25, Duane Traynor explained to George Dasch that he was under arrest and that he would be stripped of his personal belongings, from his gold watch to his eighty thousand dollars. And that he would be spending the night in jail.

Recording the saboteurs' every move, a jailer noted in an official logbook: "G. Dasch. Urinated at 11:40 p.m. Appears a little depressed."

New York City
Saturday, June 27, to Sunday, June 28, 1942

"I have a very important statement to make," Director Hoover told the reporters he'd assembled in the FBI's New York office. "I want you to listen carefully; this is a serious business."

The next morning, Hoover picked up the Sunday edition of the *New York Times* and cracked a rare smile. The headline was huge; it was as big as the headline that had announced the attack on Pearl Harbor: "FBI SEIZES 8 SABOTEURS LANDED BY U-BOATS."

"Before the men could begin carrying out their orders," reported the *Times*, "the FBI was on their trail and the round-up began. One after another, they fell into the special agents' nets."

The story was perfect. Hoover only needed to make sure the public never heard the truth from George John Dasch.

Hyde Park, Washington, D.C.
Saturday, June 27, to Tuesday, June 30, 1942

Smiles were rare for J. Edgar Hoover. But not for Franklin Roosevelt. Along with his cigarette holder and fireside chats, his smile was something of a trademark. And for one of the first times since the war began, the president had a lot to smile about.

"Eight spies and one hundred seventy-five thousand dollars in cash," Attorney General Francis Biddle called Hyde Park to report.

The president loved a good spy story. And a good joke.

"Not enough, Francis," he said. "Let's make real money out of them. Sell the rights to Barnum and Bailey for a million and a half—the rights to take them around the country in lion cages at so much a head."

Biddle was sure he was kidding, but the memo FDR dictated to him three days later was no joke. "The two American citizens," said Roosevelt—referring to Herbie Haupt, who was a naturalized citizen, and to Burger, whose American citizenship was questionable—"are guilty of high treason. This being wartime, it is my inclination to try them by court martial." Not that a trial, in Roosevelt's mind, was necessary to determine their guilt.

"I do not see how they can offer any adequate defense. Surely they are just as guilty as it is possible to be and it seems to me that the death penalty is almost obligatory."

In that regard, the American people, regardless of their politics, were in complete agreement. An editorial by the *Detroit Free Press* read, "Realism calls for a stone wall and a firing squad, and not a holier-than-thou eyewash about extending the protection of civil rights to a group that came among us to blast, burn, and kill."

Others were more succinct. "Shoot them," said the *New Orleans State*. "Give them death," demanded the *El Paso Times*. The *New York Times* reported that "Americans want to hear the roar of rifles in the hands of a firing squad." And *LIFE* magazine's headline bluntly declared, "The Eight Nazi Spies Should Die."

Moving on to the "six who I take it are German citizens," Roosevelt said, "They were apprehended in civilian clothes. This is an absolute parallel of the case of Major Andre in the Revolution and of Nathan Hale. Both of them were hanged."

The president, impatient with civil liberties even in peacetime, was not about to deny America "the roar of rifles in the hands of a firing squad" that so many demanded. Americans were sacrificing their lives and loved ones in a war for the nation's survival—a war that was not going well. The navy was waging a war on two oceans with just half the fleet that had been sailing on December 6, 1941. General MacArthur, the country's most beloved general, was trapped in the Philippines, his invincibility shattered, his army starving. *Americans deserve a victory*, Roosevelt thought.

And he was going to give it to them.

"Here again it is my inclination that they be tried by court martial as were Andre and Hale. Without splitting hairs, I can see no difference."

Of course, Roosevelt knew that the Supreme Court might try to interfere and decide the case belonged in a civil court. What would he do if the men in black robes said the Constitution required a trial by jury, guilt beyond reasonable doubt, individual counsel for every defendant, the right to exclude coerced confessions, and a sentence in accord with civil laws? After all, under civil law, their sentences would likely not exceed two years in prison.

Roosevelt wouldn't hear of it. "I want one thing clearly understood, Francis," he told Biddle. "I won't give them up. I won't hand them over to any United States marshal armed with a writ of habeas corpus. Understand?"

Biddle nodded, thinking that the president, though never boring, could be a bit boorish.

United States Department of Justice
Washington, D.C.
Wednesday, July 8, 1942

Unsure how his plan had gone so wrong, and unclear about why he was even under arrest, George was once again on his way to the Justice Department. But this time, his ride to the corner of Ninth and Constitution did not begin at the Mayflower, and what awaited him was not a tribe of stenographers hanging on his every word but a military commission—a tribunal of seven officers who would decide whether he lived or died.

The caravan that carried him included six police motorcycles, an army truck packed with machine-gun-bearing soldiers, two vans with soldiers on the running boards, another truck, and more motorcycles. Along the procession, thousands of onlookers shouted lines like "there go the spies" and "Nazi rats."

When George walked into Room 5235, where he would be tried for war crimes, he expected to find something that looked like a courtroom. Instead, he found a long and narrow area of bland office space that had once been a classroom. It sat along a hallway easily closed off from the rest of the building. Glass doors connecting other corridors were boarded up and watched by armed guards. The room's windows were covered in black curtains to preserve secrecy, and as George looked around, he was surprised to see that there were no members of the press. He badly wanted to tell his story to the public, but he was beginning to wonder if powerful people in the U.S. government had something else in mind.

No sooner had the commission begun to swear in the officers of the court than a six-foot, five-inch-tall colonel rose to speak. He wore a green, loose-fitting Class A uniform and spoke with a soft country drawl. The colonel had a Harvard law degree and a skillful courtroom manner. He was George's best hope.

"This entire proceeding is invalid and unconstitutional," said Colonel Kenneth Royall, who also represented the other seven defendants. "In 1866, the Supreme Court was clear. Civil courts have jurisdiction when they are open in the territory in which we are now located."

George, for the first time since his arrest, began to get his hopes up. Perhaps, he thought, the commission would be dissolved on its very first day.

After a lengthy discussion and a short recess, the general in charge of the commission ruled on his attorney's plea: "The commission does not sustain the objection of the defense. Proceed."

The general then read the charges against them—espionage and sabotage—and when his name was called, George stood up, looked at the presiding general, and answered the charges with the same plea as the other defendants.

"Not guilty."

Hyde Park, New York
Sunday, July 12, 1942

"What should be done with them?" the president asked his aide. The tribunal had not yet decided the saboteurs' guilt or sentences, but the president was thinking ahead.

His aide wondered, but only for a moment, if the president was considering clemency.

FDR turned back to his aide and clarified his question. "Should they be shot or hanged?"

United States Supreme Court
Washington, D.C.
Wednesday, July 29, to Thursday, July 30, 1942

The spectators in the packed impromptu courtroom sat in rapt silence as Colonel Royall rose before them. Like the colonel, everyone there—including J. Edgar Hoover, and the gentleman beside him, the associate director of the FBI, Clyde Tolson—believed the argument that Colonel Royall was about to make would be the difference between life and death for his clients.

"Mr. Chief Justice," Royall began, "and may it please the court."

Royall had challenged the authority of the military tribunal, which had not yet rendered its verdict, all the way to the Supreme Court of the United States. For three days, Royall quoted from the court's precedents and appealed to its highest ideals. Citing a seventy-six-year-old case called *Ex Parte Milligan*, Royall explained to the justices that Abraham Lincoln had attempted to try a southern sympathizer in a military tribunal. The defendant had been arrested in Indiana in 1864, and the Supreme Court had ruled it was unconstitutional to convene a military tribunal in a territory where the civil courts were open.

When it was the prosecution's turn, Attorney General Biddle approached the podium. "The United States and the German Reich are now at war," he told the Court. "That seems to be the essential fact on which this case turns and to which all our arguments will be addressed." He argued that the "Indiana of 1864" bore no resemblance to the "East Coast of today." Modern war is "fought on the total front, on the battlefields of joined armies, on the battlefields of production, and on the battlefields of transportation and morale, by bombing, the sinking of ships, sabotage, spying, and propaganda."

Speaking on behalf of the commander in chief, Biddle told the court, "Our whole East Coast is a theater of operations in substantially the same sense as the North Atlantic or the British Isles."

Countering that Biddle's notion of "total war" was broad enough to cover any crime by any person committed anywhere in wartime, Royall did his best to fight back. There must be some limit to Biddle's theory, he said, "or we have very few constitutional guarantees left when we go to war."

Royall could tell from the justices' cold reception and hostile questions that he was losing. But he was unaware of something even more dismal: Some of them had already made up their minds. As Justice Felix Frankfurter told his colleagues behind closed doors, Royall's clients were "damned scoundrels" and "low-down, ordinary, enemy spies who, as

enemy soldiers, have invaded our country and therefore could immediately have been shot by the military when caught in the act of invasion."

Justice Frankfurter did not plan to tie the president's hands. This
was war.

Washington, D.C., Jail
Saturday, August 8, 1942
9:00 A.M.

The clanging of the keys woke George up from a nap. He hadn't been
sleeping well at night ever since the Supreme Court had publicly denied his appeal and sent the case back to the military tribunal. Brief,
restless naps were his best chance to sleep.

The provost marshal entered his cell—with a stern look on his face.
Despite all of the disappointments and betrayals he'd experienced over
the previous months, George still expected to be told that he was a free
man; that the tribunal and, in fact, the country, had come to its senses
and realized that he was not a spy or a saboteur; he was a hero.

"George John Dasch," the marshal began, "I am here on behalf of
the government of the United States of America to inform you that you
have been found guilty of espionage and sabotage and sentenced to
thirty years in prison."

George, arms flailing, began rambling about his family, words sputtering out of his mouth faster than he could control them. The provost
marshal turned and left. He couldn't understand what the convicted
spy was saying and, like many before him, he really didn't care.

The provost marshal preferred the reaction of Peter Burger, whom he
found lying in bed reading a magazine. When told he would spend the
rest of his life in prison, Pete looked up, said, "Yes, sir," and went back
to reading the *Saturday Evening Post*.

The other six defendants were not so lucky. The provost marshal
entered each of their cells and recited the same line: "You have been
found guilty of espionage and sabotage and your sentence is death.
Your execution is scheduled for later today."

Among the six who received that news was Herbie Haupt, a twenty-two-year-old American citizen, who had recently written a letter from prison to his parents in Chicago.

Please don't judge me too hard.

While I was in Germany I worried night and day wondering how you were getting along. I tried to get work in Germany but I could not, and when they told me that they had chosen me to go back to the United States you don't know how happy I was. I counted the days and hours until I could see you again and probably help you.

Dear Mother, I never had any bad intentions. I did not know what a grave offense it is to come here the way I did in wartime. They are treating me very well here, as good as can be expected.

Dear Mother and Father, whatever happens to me, always remember that I love you more than anything in the world. May God protect you, my loved ones, until we see each other again, wherever that may be.

Love, your son, Herbie.

Washington, D.C., Jail
Saturday, August 8, 1942
3:30 P.M.

Guards strapped Herbie Haupt's hands and feet to the electric chair and attached electrodes to his head and leg. A switch was flipped. His body tightened, trembled, and, sixty seconds later, relaxed.

Washington, D.C., Jail
Wednesday, August 12, 1942

When FBI agent Duane Traynor walked into George's cell, he saw a thinning, pale man—a shell of the excitable and talkative optimist he'd met a month earlier.

For a moment George's eyes sparkled at the sight of the confidant he had once trusted, the partner he had once believed to be his friend. *They've finally come to let me out.*

Those sparkles turned to tears when he realized that Traynor was only there to say good-bye.

New Hampshire
August–October 1942

The Supreme Court's decision had been announced in July, but the more complicated task of explaining in a written opinion why the president had not violated the Constitution still lay ahead. It would not suffice to simply quote the old Latin maxim *Inter Arma Silent Leges*: In a time of war, the laws are silent.

Alone at his summer home in New Hampshire, Chief Justice Harlan Stone was rereading the attorney general's legal brief. He was searching for sound legal reasoning to support the court's decision. But Stone wasn't finding what he wanted. "I certainly hope," he told his clerk, "the military is better equipped to fight the war than it is to fight its legal battles."

Finally, though regretting that "the opinion was not good literature," Stone sent a draft to his colleagues, who unanimously signed onto it.

But what other choice did they have? By then, four of the justices had doubts about their decision, but six men had already been executed as a result of it.

Atlanta
Wednesday, November 3, 1943

The psychiatrist typed his report slowly. "The prisoner has an obsessive, compulsive, neurotic personality type. He complains of depressive trends, nervousness, insomnia, and vague pains. He repeatedly stated that he did not mind being in prison but that he was hurt by the way it was done; that he has terrific prejudice and anger and that he feels he cannot go on long this way."

A few miles away, the prisoner—the one with a silver streak running through his black hair—wept quietly to himself.

Washington, D.C.
December 1971

J. Edgar Hoover sat down at the large desk in his dark office. It was just over a week before Christmas, his fifty-second at the FBI. It would be his last.

On his desk were two stacks of Christmas cards, one with the notes he would read, and one, a much larger stack, with the notes his secretary assured him he could ignore.

Near the bottom of the larger stack was a holiday card that had come virtually every year since 1948, when Peter Burger and George Dasch were granted executive clemency by President Harry Truman and deported back to Germany.

"Merry Christmas," it said. "Yours, Peter Burger."

EPILOGUE

2001–2004

Just a few months before the attacks of September 11, 2001, a twenty-year-old American citizen named Yasir Hamdi ran away from home. A devout Muslim, he had been told wonderful things about the Taliban from his friends and religious leaders, but when he'd arrived at a Taliban training camp in Afghanistan that summer, he quickly realized it had all been lies. He soon became disillusioned and, after just a few weeks, left the camp.

On his way home, Hamdi was arrested by Afghan warlords, who told their American allies that he was a Taliban fighter. The American military labeled Yasir Hamdi an unlawful enemy combatant and detained him: first in Afghanistan, then in Guantanamo Bay, next in Norfolk, Virginia, and finally on a naval base off the coast of South Carolina.

Hamdi told his captors that he was not an enemy of the United States and believed that a trial would exonerate him. For years the United States held him without charge, arguing that, as an enemy combatant, he was not entitled to due process.

Finally, in 2004, his case made it to the U.S. Supreme Court, where his attorney argued that, as a U.S. citizen, his right to a jury trial was guaranteed by the Constitution.

The government's case was made by the Solicitor General of the United States. He reminded the justices of an obscure legal precedent decided in 1942, when eight Nazi saboteurs had tried to make a similar argument. The government's brief was forty-one pages long and referred to the saboteurs' case thirty times.

In 2004, not many people seemed to care that the 1942 decision had been made hastily in the midst of a world war, or that four of the justices regretted their decision before the official opinion had even been released. It didn't matter because the passage of time destroys context and circumstance the way termites destroy wood: slowly, steadily, and completely.

Yasir Hamdi, thanks in large part to a decision made sixty years earlier, lost his case. He was stripped of his U.S. citizenship and deported to Saudi Arabia in 2004.

9

Who Is Tokyo Rose?

San Francisco, California
July 6, 1949

The courtroom was a marble masterpiece. It covered the walls, the floor, and the round columns that stretched the length of its preposterously tall ceiling. Plump cherubim stared down from the tops of those columns and a gaudy mosaic behind the judge's desk faced enormous, gilded doors.

Under dim lights that did little to brighten the solemn and austere setting, the only empty seat belonged to Thomas DeWolfe, the tall, balding special prosecutor. As he began his opening statement, he could feel the eyes of the judge, jurors, lawyers, and all 110 spectators boring into him. He could also feel the eyes of the defendant, a plain-faced, simply dressed, thirty-three-year-old woman on trial for treason against the United States of America.

DeWolfe's voice was strong and confident and echoed off the marble, giving it a larger-than-life feel. "We will show," he said, "that in one broadcast after the Battle of Leyte Gulf, the defendant told American troops: 'Now, you boys really have lost all your ships. You really are orphans now. How do you think you will ever get home?' "

DeWolfe spoke slowly and methodically, in keeping with his

personality. The middle-aged lawyer's style was as modest as the room he worked in was ornate. DeWolfe rarely took time away from work, and on the rare occasions he did take a vacation, he preferred to be alone. His work was his life, and his trial skills were second to none. What Thomas DeWolfe lacked in charisma he more than made up for with clarity and credibility.

"We will show that the defendant told American troops that their wives and sweethearts were unfaithful," he continued. "That they were out with shipyard workers with wallets bulging with money. That she told them to lay down their arms. And that the Japanese would never give up and had the will to win."

DeWolfe paused to look at the defendant. Her tan plaid suit was old and out of style. Her face was pale and expressionless. He wondered if the jury would ever believe that the petite woman before them was the infamous Tokyo Rose. She didn't look much like the woman whose seductive voice had been broadcast by Radio Tokyo all across the Pacific, hypnotizing the minds of Allied troops with Japanese propaganda, making them homesick, telling them that defeat was inevitable, and sometimes driving them to desertion or suicide.

"We will show that she talked about the mosquitoes and the jungles, and when she heard some troops were short of food, she told them they should go home where they could get steak and French-fried potatoes."

With every new accusation, DeWolfe's tone became sharper, giving the impression of increasingly greater disgust and outrage. He never raised his voice; that was not his style. But he wanted—he *needed*—the jury to hate this woman. They had to see her as a California-born Benedict Arnold who verbally tortured and tormented America's brave sons and husbands who were off fighting for their freedom. He needed them to see that words could be just as savage and destructive as guns and bombs.

Only then would they convict Iva Toguri.

Only then would they convict a woman who Thomas DeWolfe knew was innocent.

New York Times, February 14, 1943

The men often tune in on Radio Tokyo to hear the cultured, accentless English of a woman announcer they have nicknamed Tokyo Rose. Tokyo Rose pours it on so thick that the little company of Americans in a submarine far from shore who hear her usually get a lot of humor out of her broadcasts.

Tokyo, Japan
August 25, 1943

The English-born major was tall and, despite the hunger that had left him ill and emaciated, still remarkably handsome. He had been the Edward R. Murrow of Australian radio before the war began, but he'd been captured in Singapore after volunteering to leave the broadcast booth in favor of combat.

After a Japanese officer inferred that he could choose between being executed or working for Radio Tokyo, Major Charles Cousens agreed to write the script for an evening show called *Zero Hour*.

That didn't mean, however, that he would write it the way they wanted. Even with his life on the line, Cousens was not about to be a pawn for the enemy. He tried his best to keep the program free of propaganda while undermining the Japanese war effort by using the English-language show to entertain Allied troops.

So far, it was working. The two POW hosts of Cousens's *Zero Hour*—an American named Wallace "Ted" Ince and a Filipino named Norman Reyes—read the "news" they were given by the Japanese so fast that it couldn't be understood. They repeated inside jokes that the Japanese didn't understand and that brought laughter rather than fear to Allied listeners. They filled most of the program with lively music—peppy marches and fun, popular songs—while telling their Japanese overseers that the music would demoralize Allied soldiers by making them homesick. Inexperienced in American media, unable to understand the subtleties of the English language, and willing to defer to Cousens's talent for attracting an audience, the Japanese staff at Radio Tokyo did not interfere much with *Zero Hour*'s programming.

As Cousens sat in the POW's small common room at Radio Tokyo putting the finishing touches on that evening's script, he heard a friendly, upbeat voice from the doorway.

"Hey, boys," the stranger said. "How ya doin'?"

The smiling woman at the door appeared to be Japanese, although her accent was definitely American. She was short and wore glasses and looked almost as malnourished as the POWs, yet her voice exhibited an energy that was missing among the Americans. She was looking at them like they were the first friendly faces she'd seen in years.

"My name's Iva," she said, shaking Cousens's hand, and then the hands of the two show hosts.

Cousens introduced himself but was careful not to say too much in the presence of a Japanese stranger. His caution, however, did nothing to slow the conversation, because the newcomer was more than happy to do all the talking.

"I was born in Los Angeles and I only ended up here by accident. See, my mother asked me to go to Tokyo to visit my aunt Shizuko, who was sick. But I hated it here right away. I tried to find a way home to L.A., but the government kept asking me for more and more paperwork and then they took forever to approve it. Once Pearl Harbor happened it was too late—and so here I am."

Cousens and his two hosts stared at her blankly. It was as though she'd kept all of this information bottled up inside her and it was now all spilling out. They offered little encouragement, no nonverbal feedback like smiles or nods of the head, but Iva kept talking anyway. She told them about the life she missed in America, the postgraduate classes she'd taken at the University of California, Los Angeles, and how she passed the time watching college football and horse racing at Santa Anita. But now, she explained, her life in Japan was completely different.

"One time the secret police knocked on my door at three in the morning. Scared me half to death! They told me how I would be so much safer if I dropped my American citizenship. See, my parents were born in Japan, and so I'm entitled to be a citizen here as well. But, honestly, I'd rather be interned as an enemy here than be a subject of the emperor. That's exactly what I told them."

Iva explained that she'd moved into a boardinghouse so that her aunt would not be subjected to the suspicions and harassment that came with sheltering an American citizen. Since she refused to renounce her American citizenship, the Japanese had also taken away her ration card, forcing her to share the meager provisions of other boarders. Needing a job to survive on her own, she'd found work two days ago as an English-language typist at Radio Tokyo.

Then, as quickly as she'd arrived to spill out her life story, she was walking back out the door.

"You look hungry," she said to Cousens. Then she smiled and whispered, "Tomorrow I will bring you some apples."

Tokyo
Three months later: October 25, 1943

"This week it's apples, eggs, some flour, and a bushel of vegetables!"

Every weekend, Iva walked more than ten miles to buy and barter for food and medicine at farms in the countryside. She was particularly proud of the haul she'd just acquired.

"Any medicine?" asked Cousens. Iva's pro-American attitude and willingness to smuggle things into Radio Tokyo had eventually won Cousens's trust. He regularly took some of the provisions back to Camp Bunka, where he lived with twenty-six other POWs, many of them sick and starving.

"Some quinine and aspirin," she said. "And a few vitamin pills."

"You're a lifesaver, Iva. And I don't just mean that as an expression."

Cousens had spent the last few months admiring Iva's willingness to risk her own safety to smuggle food and supplies for others. Over time he had grown to trust her enough to explain to her their ongoing scheme to sabotage the Japanese propaganda.

"Why not share the plan with her?" he'd said to his skeptical cohosts at the time. "She's one of us."

Tokyo
November 12, 1943

"You have to bring in another announcer for a new 'homesicky' segment," George Mitsushio told Charles Cousens.

Mitsushio was a fat thirty-six-year-old who'd been born in San
Francisco but had chafed at the discrimination he'd encountered. In
the 1930s he had immigrated to Japan and, after Pearl Harbor, chose
his adopted country over the United States. He had officially become a
Japanese national seven months earlier.

Given the circumstances, Mitsushio was, at least according to
American law, a traitor for having served the Japanese government in
various attempts at propaganda for seventeen months before renounc-
ing his American citizenship. He was also, at least nominally, Charles
Cousens's boss, although he generally let the Aussie do anything he
wanted when it came to *Zero Hour*.

"This is an Imperial Order," Mitsushio persisted. "It has got to be
done." Slicing his hand across his throat, he added, "If not, it is my
neck as well as yours."

"All right," said Cousens, who was already formulating a plan. "We'll
see what we can do."

As soon as Mitsushio left, *Zero Hour* announcer Ted Ince turned on
Cousens. "What the hell do you mean, 'we'?" Ince said. "I want no part
of this!"

"Hold your horses," Cousens calmly assured him. "This is our
chance to make a complete joke of *Zero Hour*." Cousens knew the Japanese wanted a segment that would make Americans miss all the things
they loved most about America. He knew he'd have to come up with
something that would sound authentic to the Japanese while making
American troops laugh. The idea he was about to let Ince in on had
come to him a few nights earlier.

"How?" Ince asked.

Cousens smiled. "Sex." Other radio shows at the time used a sultry
woman to make the troops miss their wives and girlfriends back home.
Cousens planned to do the same, but with a very different result. "We'll
use a woman."

He knew it could not just be any woman; it had to be someone with exactly the right kind of voice. The Japanese would mistake her banter for flirting, but the Americans would clearly recognize it as over-the-top comedy.

"Who?" asked Ince.

"The only woman we can trust," said Cousens, who was enjoying the little resistance effort he'd been waging behind enemy lines. "Iva."

Tokyo
November 13, 1943

"This is crazy!"

Iva had just performed the first script Cousens had written for her. She knew there were at least six other women who broadcasted to Allied troops in English over Japanese radio stations, but she didn't own a radio so she'd never actually heard their shows.

"I can't do this! I'm no good at it," she said.

"You are exactly what we want," Cousens promised. "We're not looking for an experienced announcer and we don't want a sweet, gentle voice. We want a Yankee voice with a certain personality to it—a little touch of a WAC officer and a lot of cheer."

Iva still looked dubious. "I'll coach you to read the scripts the way I want them," Cousens said, "so don't worry."

Iva liked the idea of being needed by the handsome, charming Aussie, even if it was only in a professional sense. She may have had serious doubts about her own broadcasting talent, but she had no doubts about the coaching abilities of Major Charles Cousens.

"How long will you stay with the show?" she asked.

"Until we've defeated Japan," he told her. He had no desire to leave so long as the show was accomplishing his purposes, but it was kind of a moot point anyway. The Japanese weren't letting him go anywhere until the war was over.

That was good enough for Iva. She smiled and nodded.

"Me too."

New York Times Trivia Quiz, December 19, 1943

Question: Who is Tokyo Rose?
*Answer: Tokyo Rose delivers Japanese propaganda broadcasts—in
cultured English accents—directed to American fighting men in the
Pacific. The men are amused by Japan's exaggeration of American losses.*

Tokyo
April 21, 1944

"Greetings, everybody!" Iva said into her radio microphone. "This is
Ann back at the microphone and presiding over Radio Tokyo's special
program for listeners in Australia and the South Pacific."

Cousens had chosen the name "Ann" as Iva's radio alter ego because
it was an abbreviation for *announcer.*

"How's my orphan family? Have you been good boys?"

There were other female disc jockeys, Cousens had explained to Iva,
who might have asked this question in a sultry, sexy way. But he wanted
her to sound jolly, like a happy sister or an old friend. He'd coached her
through every word.

"All right, then, we'll have some music. A tango to start with. 'I Kiss
Your Hand, Madam.' "

As the record played, Iva sat back in her chair and closed her eyes.
She thought of her old life in California—a life full of friends and movies and dancing. She desperately wished she was back there, but she
was also happy to have found a way to serve a purpose in the war. The
thought that she might be helping the Allies in some small way made
her get out of bed each morning with a smile.

"Thank you, thank you, thank you," Iva said as the tango faded.
"Any latecomers listening? Well, you're sharing Radio Tokyo's regular
program for Australia and the South Pacific. Dangerous enemy propaganda, so beware! Our next propagandist is Arthur Fiedler with the
Boston Pops Orchestra playing Ketèlbey's 'In a Persian Market.' "

After a few more songs, interspersed with some brief chatter scripted
by Cousens, Iva's twenty minutes on *Zero Hour* were up. She turned
the microphone over to Ted Ince and headed out the door, singing the

UCLA football fight song, Gershwin's "Strike Up the Band," in her head. At her request, Cousens had made it a regular on the program, knowing that any homesickness it might induce would be trumped by the song's timely and inspiring lyrics.

There is work to be done, to be done.
There's a war to be won, to be won.
Come, you son of a, son of a gun.
Take your stand. Fall in line. Yea a bow.
Come along. Let's go. Hey, leader. Strike up the band!

Iva Toguri smiled. *When the war is won,* she thought, *maybe I'll make a career of this radio stuff.*

Time, April 10, 1944

No one knows for sure who Tokyo Rose really is. [Listeners] are inclined to think she is a Japanese, born on the island of Maui, Hawaii, and educated there. Her voice is cultured, with a touch of Boston.

Tokyo
March 19, 1945

"Will you marry me, Iva?"

Iva liked Felipe d'Aquino, a bony, kindhearted twenty-five-year-old Portuguese-Japanese pacifist known as "Phil" to his friends. They had bonded at work over their shared opposition to the Japanese war effort. In a city with few American-sympathizers, Iva did not have a lot of people with whom to celebrate her little victories over Radio Tokyo.

"Yes!" responded Iva, feigning some of the excitement she'd seen from newly engaged girls in movies by wrapping her arms around Phil. He deserved that much at least.

He is kind and loyal and in love with me, Iva told herself. *He will make a very good husband.*

Okinawa, Japan
August 30, 1945

Clark Lee was one of the most famous war correspondents in America. Six feet tall, with smooth dark hair and tanned skin, the thirty-eight-year-old had just been through an exciting four years. Trapped on Corregidor with MacArthur, he had escaped on the last submarine off the besieged island, then published a book titled *They Call It Pacific*, covering the European Theater. Lee returned to the Pacific in time to hear the Japanese emperor's surrender statement live on Radio Tokyo. Tomorrow morning, he and a small group of reporters were scheduled to fly to the Japanese mainland. Now that combat had ended, General MacArthur was planning to touch down at the Atsugi Naval Air Facility, forty miles from Tokyo. It would be a historic day.

As Lee relaxed on a stone wall by an ancient Japanese burial tomb, he looked at his old friend and fellow reporter, Harry Brundidge. Short and balding, Brundidge was twenty years past his prime—which had come with a series of stories he'd written about organized crime in St. Louis. Since then, alcohol and aging had taken their toll and Brundidge looked every bit of his forty-eight years. He was still as brash and daring as ever; he just wasn't as good.

"Want to make a deal?" Brundidge asked Lee.

"What kind of deal?" Lee liked Brundidge, but he wasn't about to follow him blindly.

"Well, we've both lived in Japan," he replied. "So we know something about the Japanese people that others don't: when Hirohito told them to quit, they quit. I'm willing to bet that, despite our orders to stay out of Tokyo until the Allied occupation force gets there, it's perfectly safe. I say we make a break for the capital the minute we land."

Lee nodded. The military was concerned about guerrilla attacks so reporters had been ordered to stay out of Tokyo until they were given a green light that it was safe. But Lee loved the big scoop and knew they only came to those willing to take a few risks.

"Suppose I agree," Lee said. "What's our story when we get there? Seems like everyone already knows the war is over."

Brundidge smiled. "Tokyo Rose. The whole world wants to know who she is. Our Japanese friends will help us find her."

Lee was intrigued. The mystery of Tokyo Rose was one of the hottest stories around. If they found her and got her to talk, then Brundidge and Lee could write the first articles about her—Brundidge for *Cosmopolitan* and Lee for the *International News Service*. It was a potentially career-making scoop.

Lee pictured the large-type, front-page headline and then shook Brundidge's meaty palm. "I'm in."

Tokyo
August 31, 1945

Iva was ecstatic.

Leslie Nakashima, a Japanese newsman, had just called and asked if she'd be willing to tell two American reporters about her experience as Tokyo Rose in exchange for two thousand dollars. Iva replied she'd never heard of "Tokyo Rose," but Nakashima explained that it was simply the name Allied soldiers had given to English-language radio hosts in the Pacific and Iva certainly qualified.

Between needing the money and wanting Americans to know how her and Cousens had foiled Japanese propaganda efforts with *Zero Hour*, her answer came fast.

"Tell me where and when to meet them."

Tokyo
Morning, September 1, 1945

Iva Toguri walked into room 312 of the Imperial Hotel with Leslie Nakashima and her husband, Phil d'Aquino, without a care in the world. The war was over, the Allies had won, and now she was about to make seven times more money in a single morning than she'd made during her entire time in Tokyo.

Casting her eyes on a short man pouring a glass of bourbon, and then on his taller, fitter colleague, Iva was happy to finally have a chance to talk about her small role in helping the American war effort. She knew these men would help bring that part of the story back to the United States.

"Good morning," said the taller man. "I'm Clark Lee from the *International News Service* and this is Harry Brundidge from *Cosmopolitan* magazine."

Iva shook hands with the men and they all sat down. Brundidge got right to the point. "So, you are Tokyo Rose?"

Iva detected a little hostility in his voice. "Mr. Brundidge," she replied politely, "there are five or six girls to whom that name should apply. I am just one of them."

"You worked at Radio Tokyo," Brundidge replied. "You announced introductions to records. You were a sort of disc jockey, weren't you?"

"Yes," said Iva.

Lee turned to Nakashima. "You told us that you went to Radio Tokyo and someone there gave you her name?"

Nakashima nodded. Iva had no idea Nakashima had been paid $250 by Lee and Brundidge for identifying "Tokyo Rose."

"Then she will do!" said Lee, grinning. "Now, let's get to her story."

With that, Clark Lee unpacked his typewriter, and Harry Brundidge, for reasons that Iva did not yet fully understand, locked the hotel room's door.

Tokyo
Afternoon, September 1, 1945

After everyone had left his hotel room, Clark Lee fed a blank piece of paper into his typewriter and stared at it. The interview that had just concluded had not gone according to plan. For starters, he'd expected someone who looked, or at least *sounded*, like a femme fatale. This Iva woman didn't fit the bill. More important, Iva had denied broadcasting any propaganda: Nothing about unfaithful wives, the horrors of warfare, or the fictitious sinking of American ships.

Nevertheless, and despite her protests that she was just one of many hosts, Iva had eventually agreed to sign a paper saying she was "the one and original Tokyo Rose." That should have been good enough, but now, as Lee stared at the blank white paper in his typewriter, he was starting to have second thoughts.

Part of Lee's hesitation was that he had personally heard a broadcast by a woman whom the troops had called "Tokyo Rose" in 1942—a year *before* Iva said she'd began working at Radio Tokyo. That got his mind running. *How many Tokyo Roses were out there? And which of them had actually broadcast propaganda?*

Clark Lee stared for a while longer. He knew that if Iva hadn't committed treason against her country, then he had no scoop. On the other hand, she had signed the statement.

Finally, he made up his mind and his fingers began pecking away at the keys.

TRAITOR'S PAY: TOKYO ROSE GOT 100 YEN A MONTH...$6.60.

In an exclusive interview with this correspondent...

Tokyo
October 17, 1945

As Iva finished washing her hair, she heard a knock on the door. *Another reporter*, she thought to herself.

After the publication of Clark Lee's article—which, to Iva's shock and horror, had portrayed her as a traitor to her country—the media had gone into a feeding frenzy. Interviews had been followed by a press conference, which was followed by intensive questioning by investigators from the Eighth Army's Counter Intelligence Corps. Through it all, Iva had answered every question asked of her. She knew that she had nothing to hide and was convinced that no one would believe her to be a traitor once they'd heard the full story about her time on the radio.

Iva opened the door, her dark hair still wet. Three officers and a master sergeant from the Army Counter Intelligence Corps stood on her front porch.

Iva Toguri was under arrest.

Tokyo
July 4, 1946

It was her birthday, but after spending the last eight months in prison, Iva Toguri was not in a celebratory mood. Showering at Tokyo's Sugamo prison, where many Japanese war criminals were also being held, Iva felt sad and alone. She missed her husband, whom she was only allowed to see for twenty minutes a month. She missed Charles Cousens, who had been sent back to Australia, where he told military authorities that Iva was innocent of any wrongdoing. She missed her father and siblings, whom she'd not seen in five years. And, most of all, she grieved for her mother, who, unbeknownst to Iva until now, had died three years earlier in a Japanese-American internment camp.

As Iva emerged from the shower stall, she stopped suddenly and screamed. She had been through a lot of surreal experiences in recent years, but this was the most bizarre of all. Peering through a window and into the foggy bathroom like they were viewing a circus act were sixteen well-dressed men.

She did not know it, but they were all United States congressmen.

Tokyo
October 25, 1946

Amid the popping of reporters' flashbulbs and the shouting of questions, Iva Toguri ran through the lobby of Sugamo prison and into the arms of her smiling husband. After a year behind bars, Iva was being unconditionally released by the United States military due to lack of evidence.

She took the bouquet of flowers that Phil had brought for her and smiled. It was a new beginning, a chance to put this nightmare behind her and return to her life in California.

Or so she thought.

Tokyo
January 5, 1948

Iva had cried for so long that her eyes had run dry. It was hard not to think of everything that had brought her to this point and wonder if it all would have been different had she not been so naïve.

It had now been over a year since the U.S. State Department told her that she was in a line of ten thousand second-generation Americans stranded in Japan waiting for approval to return to America. Now she wondered if that was just another lie.

Cynicism did not suit Iva well, but she'd come a long way since she'd accepted that interview with Clark Lee and Harry Brundidge three years earlier. She knew that if she'd been less naïve back then, she would probably be back at home in Los Angeles right now nursing her and Phil's first child.

Instead, she lay in her bed in Tokyo, her husband holding her tight as her body shook and heaved uncontrollably.

Their baby had died that morning.

Washington, D.C.
May 25, 1948

Thomas DeWolfe sat at his small desk, dictating a memo to the un-luckiest secretary at the Department of Justice. She was the only assistant in the building still working this late at night and DeWolfe was, as usual, the only attorney.

DeWolfe knew his bosses, especially Attorney General Tom Clark, did not want to hear what this memo had to say: Iva Toguri was innocent.

That same conclusion had been reached almost two years earlier by lots of others, including the Counter Intelligence Corps's legal section, its intelligence division, the U.S. attorney in Los Angeles, and the assistant attorney general in charge of the Justice Department's Criminal Division, Theron L. Caudle.

After Toguri was released, the American press had gone crazy. Walter Winchell, the most powerful gossip columnist in America, waged a personal crusade against her. Furious that Iva was trying to return to the United States, Winchell labeled her a traitor in his syndicated columns, which were read by seven million Americans, as well as on his Sunday night radio broadcasts, heard by twenty million listeners. He wanted the government to re-arrest Iva and prosecute her for treason. At the very least, he wanted to make sure that Iva never set foot on American soil—unless, of course, it was in handcuffs.

"Good evening, Mr. and Mrs. America, and all the ships at sea!" he began every radio show. It was great entertainment, delivered with the panache of the vaudevillian he once was. The information that followed it, however, like the "news" in his columns, was usually wrong.

According to Winchell, the lawyers at the Justice Department who were blocking Iva Toguri's re-arrest and prosecution were "emperor-lovers and friends of the Zaibatsu." He also told his audience that Clark Lee had turned the original typewritten copy of Toguri's eighteen-page confession over to FBI agents. In it, according to Winchell, she had named two witnesses against her, both of whom were available to testify if she was brought to trial.

Thomas DeWolfe knew that almost everything in Winchell's reporting on Iva was wrong: there were no "emperor-lovers" in the Justice Department; Iva's "confession" was nothing more than Clark Lee's notes from his interview—where she had unequivocally denied any wrongdoing; and the "two witnesses against her" were Charles Cousens and Ted Ince. DeWolfe knew these two men would actually *confirm* Iva's innocence if they were called to testify. Cousens, in fact, had written to the Justice Department saying as much.

The career federal prosecutor understood Washington well enough to know that a memo from him concluding that Iva Toguri should not be re-arrested would win him few friends in the Truman administration. But DeWolfe also knew that it was his job to tell his bosses the facts. It was *their* job to decide whether to listen to them.

"There is insufficient evidence to make out a *prima facie* case," he dictated to his tired secretary. "Don't forget that *facie* is f-a-c-i-e, and that last sentence should be in all capital letters."

"Thank you, Mr. DeWolfe." Debbie had worked with him for a dozen years and not once had she ever called him "Tom."

"The government witnesses, almost to a man, will testify to facts which show that the subject was pro-American, wished to return to the United States and tried to do so prior to Pearl Harbor, attempted, again, unsuccessfully to return to the United States in 1942, and beamed to American troops only the introduction to innocuous musical recordings."

DeWolfe had no doubt that other female disc jockeys, other "Tokyo Roses," had broadcast propaganda that was far from innocuous. Nor did he doubt why the American government was not interested in prosecuting any of them: The press had not appointed itself as judge, jury, and executioner of *those* women; Clark Lee and Harry Brundidge had not labeled *those* women as "Tokyo Rose"; and Walter Winchell had not publicly directed his wrath and vitriol toward *those* women.

DeWolfe continued dictating: "The government's evidence likewise will show that subject was a trusted and selected agent of the Allied prisoners of war, who selected her as the one they could trust not to sabotage their efforts against the success of the Japanese propaganda machine."

When it was complete, DeWolfe's memo totaled approximately 2,500 words. Not one of them indicated that he had any doubt about Iva Toguri's innocence.

Washington, D.C.
August 16, 1948

The presidential election was only months away. President Truman, feeling pressure from the public over Tokyo Rose—pressure that was fueled almost daily by Walter Winchell—and sick of being labeled by the media as "soft on communism" and "soft on spies," ordered Attorney General Tom Clark to make a case against Iva Toguri.

Clark ordered that Toguri be arrested in Japan and brought to California to stand trial for treason. He appointed Thomas DeWolfe, the government's best trial attorney, especially when it came to cases involving treason, as her prosecutor.

San Francisco
One year later: August 12, 1949

Thomas DeWolfe was having trouble sleeping. In fact, he hadn't slept well from the moment he gave his opening statement in *United States v. Iva Toguri* to the day he questioned the last of his forty-six witnesses—a period of five weeks.

He tried to pass the insomnia off as simple nervousness about the trial, but deep down he suspected it was something else: an uneasy conscience. DeWolfe knew he was a compartmentalizer, and he comforted himself in the belief that the decision to prosecute an innocent woman was not his to make. His only job was to follow orders and to give the Department of Justice his absolute best effort.

In the past five weeks, that best effort had included ensuring an all-white jury through peremptory strikes of African and Asian Americans during jury selection. It had also included calling to the witness stand American GIs who remembered hearing a female disc jockey broadcasting Japanese propaganda, even though these witnesses had trouble remembering key details—like the dates of broadcasts, times of day, and the sounds of the voices they heard—that would help distinguish Iva from other announcers.

Despite those weaknesses in his case, DeWolfe's direct examination of two men from Radio Tokyo had gone exceedingly well. George Mitsushio, the American who'd renounced his citizenship, and his sidekick Kenkichi Oki had perjured themselves after being solicited by none other than Harry Brundidge, whom the Department of Justice had sent to Japan as an agent of the government to find and interview witnesses for the prosecution.

DeWolfe knew that, four years after Brundidge had first interviewed Iva, he was still more interested in making a name for himself than in finding the truth. The yellow-journalist-turned-government-investigator had threatened former American citizens like Mitsushio and Oki with treason charges if they didn't testify against Iva.

As DeWolfe lay in bed, staring at the ceiling for the fifth straight hour, he tried to quell his uneasiness with the idea of putting witnesses on the stand who were very likely lying. *Not your job, Thomas*, he said to himself. *These are the witnesses your bosses want you to call. It's not your job to question their decisions.*

It's your job to win.

San Francisco
August 14–17, 1949

The day before Charles Cousens was scheduled to testify, Iva Toguri ran into his arms and cried tears of joy.

Part of the reason Iva was so happy to see Cousens was that she knew he could rebut all the lies told by Mitsushio and Oki. The other part was that she had simply missed him. His confidence and determination, his talent for writing and comedy, and his interest in coaching and leading Iva in a secret mission against the Japanese had been important to her during the war.

Several days later, on Cousens's third day of testimony in Iva's defense, she had something else to smile about. DeWolfe had asked him, "Did any other Japanese bring you food besides the defendant?"

Cousens did not miss a beat. "The defendant was not Japanese," he replied. "She was an American."

San Francisco
September 7–15, 1949

On the forty-sixth day of what had become the most expensive prosecution in American history, Iva Toguri raised her right hand and, with an American flag standing behind her, took the witness stand and swore to tell the truth.

As she looked out at her husband, father, and siblings in the row behind the defense table, she knew they were worried about the decision she'd made to testify. But she didn't share their fears. Iva understood what was at stake in this trial, but she was sure that if she took the stand and was honest, then the truth would prevail. *This is America*, she told herself. *The system works.*

Over four days of direct examination Toguri described her entire life, from her childhood in California through her broadcasts at Radio

Tokyo and her interview with Clark Lee and Harry Brundidge. At the end, her attorney, Wayne Collins, finally asked her, "Did you do anything whatsoever with intent to undermine or lower American or Allied military morale?"

"Never," she replied.

"Did you do anything with intent to create nostalgia in the mind of Americans or Allied armed forces?"

"Never."

"Did you do any act whatsoever with the intention of betraying the United States?"

"Never."

"Did you at any time whatsoever commit treason against the United States?"

There it was, the word that had haunted her since Clark Lee's "Traitor's Pay" article; the word that had been flung around recklessly by Walter Winchell and Harry Brundidge for the past two years: *traitor*.

Iva's anger and outrage were boiling inside her, but she kept her emotions in check, offering only the slightest glimpse of them by the forcefulness with which she replied to Collins's last question.

"Never."

San Francisco
September 29, 1949

Rising to her feet as the judge and jurors entered the courtroom, Iva stared down at her tan plaid skirt, the same unflattering, out-of-style one she'd ironed in her jail cell every night and worn to her trial every day.

"Has the jury arrived at a verdict?" asked Michael Roche, the seventy-two-year-old federal judge who had issued jury instructions that were extremely detrimental to the defense. Roche had told the jurors that they were not to consider Iva's giving of food and medicine when judging her intentions. They were also forbidden to consider her refusal, even in the face of constant intimidation from the secret police, to renounce her American citizenship.

It was 6:04 P.M. on the fourth day of jury deliberations and it seemed that another full day and night was about to pass with no resolution in sight. No one in the courtroom expected that a verdict had been reached.

The judge didn't expect it. He had recently suggested to the jurors that they take a break for dinner.

The spectators didn't expect it. If a verdict had been likely at this hour, there would have been more than forty people in the largely empty courtroom.

The press didn't expect it. Only ten journalists were milling around the courtroom at this late hour.

And Iva certainly didn't expect it—though by this point she had pretty much lost all faith in her ability to predict events. She once thought that after the jurors heard the defense witnesses and her own testimony, an acquittal would come quickly. But her confidence had been shaken by the four days of jury deliberations. "If they go more than a day," her attorney had told her, "it's not a good sign."

In response to Judge Roche's question of whether the jury had reached a verdict, John Mann, the pleasant bookkeeper acting as jury foreman, replied, "We have, Your Honor."

The court clerk took the verdict form from Mann. He passed it to the judge, who read it in silence, before returning it to the clerk, who broke the silence with a single word.

"Guilty."

EPILOGUE

Chicago, Illinois
Forty years later: January 13, 1989

The Toguri Mercantile shop on North Clark Street was closed for the evening. Iva sat at her small desk in the back room, reviewing the day's receipts and filling out quarterly tax forms. For more than three decades, she had worked at the store her father founded. Now, at seventy-three years old, she was the store's owner, manager, accountant, and primary salesperson.

Most of the store's customers had no idea that the petite shopkeeper had once been convicted of treason. Or that she had lost her American citizenship upon her conviction, had served more than six years in federal prison, and had then barely escaped deportation when her enemies tried to expel her from the country as an "undesirable alien" after her release. They certainly did not know that the government had destroyed her marriage by barring her husband from entering the country.

These customers also did not know that John Mann, the jury foreman, had quickly come to regret the verdict he and two other holdouts had begrudgingly been persuaded by the other nine jurors to approve. They could not have known that Thomas DeWolfe, who had been instrumental in taking six years of Iva's life, had taken his own just three years earlier.

And they had no idea that the owner of the Toguri Mercantile shop had received a full, unconditional pardon from the president of the United States in 1977. In doing so, Gerald Ford had finally returned to Iva Toguri the one thing she had so defiantly clung to for so many years: her American citizenship.

As Iva closed the account books, marking the end of another fourteen-hour workday, she glanced at the photograph on her desk of a distinguished-looking man with a confident, charming smile.

And after all these years, she was still comforted by Charles Cousens.

Seventeen years later: January 16, 2006

Iva had tried to keep her emotions bottled up inside her during the trial. But now, at a solemn ceremony in downtown Chicago, the eighty-nine-year-old saw no reason to hold them back any longer.

"Throughout an ordeal that has lasted decades," declared a broad-shouldered, aging World War II veteran, who was more than a head taller than the ceremony's guest of honor, "Iva Toguri has endured her fate with dignity, courage, and a deep faith in God and in the essential fairness of the American system."

As Iva wiped tears from her face, the veteran continued: "For her indomitable spirit, her love of country, and the example of courage she has given her fellow Americans, the World War II Veterans Committee proudly bestows the 2005 Edward J. Herlihy Citizenship Award on Iva Toguri."

During the same time that Iva was trying to cheer up American soldiers and sailors in the Pacific, Edward Herlihy had become so famous announcing newsreels that he had been called "The Voice of World War II." After being the object of a media witch hunt, it was one of life's great ironies that Iva was now about to accept an award named after an American journalist.

As the veteran draped the medal around her neck, Iva thought of how much her reputation had changed in sixty years, but how little her patriotism and idealism had. She had regrets but no bitterness. She still loved America, despite what its press and government had done to her.

Facing the standing crowd and its thunderous applause, she thought back to the first time she'd seen the malnourished Charles Cousens. She thought of the first lines she'd spoken into a microphone at Radio Tokyo. And, finally, she thought of her father's first words to her when she'd returned to California to stand trial for treason.

"I'm proud of you, girl. You didn't change your stripes."

10

The Battle of Athens:
Repeated Petitions, Repeated Injuries

Athens, Tennessee
August 3, 1936

On the outskirts of a small mountain town in east Tennessee, twelve-year-old Bill White picked berries. By force of habit, he walked on the inner sides of his soles. The outer sides had begun to wear out, and his parents wouldn't have money for another pair until Christmas. Not that he was complaining. He earned a dime a day for picking his neighbor's blackberries from sunup to sundown. He could have saved up for some new clothes if he cared to.

Instead, the dime always went toward a movie ticket. On a good day, one of the two theaters in town was showing a western. Bill loved John Wayne. His cause was always just, his aim always true. The *Daily Post-Athenian* called the young actor's early films B-movies, but Bill didn't pay much attention to the newspaper. He could neither afford a copy nor read much of it. There were schools in McMinn County, but not good ones.

After about twenty minutes, a voice from the distance called, "Billy! Dinner!"

The broad-shouldered boy kept picking the berries.

"Billy!"

It had become a familiar routine for Ma White, who had already walked a quarter of a mile to call him home. She knew he liked to daydream, and she didn't mind hiking all the way past the outhouse and past the neighbor's barn with the "Paul Cantrell for Sheriff" sign on it to shake her son back into the here and now.

"Billy!" she tried one last time. But there was no response. The music of *The Lone Ranger* was playing in his head, and scenes from last night's radio show were flashing through his imagination: The hero's galloping horse, the silver bullets flying through the air, and the victory over a brutal band of cutthroats who had been terrorizing a small town. "I believe," said the Lone Ranger's creed, "in being prepared physically, mentally, and morally to fight when necessary for that which is right."

It was Bill White's creed, too.

Five years later: December 8, 1941

Clifford "Windy" Wise opened the door of the Dixie Café and strolled confidently to the soda counter. Lunch was over, and the restaurant was closed to customers. But the bagmen for the current three-term sheriff Paul Cantrell's political machine were no ordinary customers. The rules—be they store hours, or the county's sundry prohibitions on liquor, gambling, and prostitution—did not apply to them.

"You fellas are like clockwork, ain't ya," said the café's skinny, gray-haired owner, pulling a bottle of Jack Daniel's from under the counter and pouring Wise a shot. "Here we are, under attack from the Japs. Whole country is signing up to fight. And here *you* are, collecting Cantrell's kickback."

Wise drank the shot of whiskey in a single gulp. Without looking up, he tapped his finger next to the empty glass. It was filled, and then gulped down again.

"Let me ask you a question," Wise said, finally deigning to look up at the restaurant owner. "It's about that back room. Behind that closed door. Now, I'm not sayin' there's ever any drinkin' back there. I'm not sayin' there's ever any whorin' back there. And I'm not sayin' there's ever been a single one-armed bandit back there. But supposin' there was." He tapped the bar, and the shot glass was refilled. "My question is: Are you plannin' to put an end to it, just because there's a war on?"

The café owner said nothing. He simply reached for the floor and pulled up a small satchel of cash.

Wise took another drink.

"I didn't think so," the deputy sheriff said, grabbing the satchel and turning to leave. "See you next month."

Tarawa, Central Pacific
November 20, 1943

Bill White was floating in the ocean, a hundred yards from shore. He wasn't dead, but he was pretending to be. All around him were angry splashes of bullets from Japanese machine guns, along with hundreds of American Marines, bleeding and lifeless, bumping into him. The explosions of artillery launched from the shore punctuated the relentless pounding of the machine guns. Strangely absent was the barking of orders heard at the Marines' prior amphibious landings, where Americans had faced no serious opposition.

After what seemed like an eternity, Bill finally floated his way to within a few yards of the shoreline. He sprang out of the water and raced for the four-foot seawall that separated land from water. Beyond it were the Japanese snipers and pillboxes, the low concrete structures that protected the Japanese machine gunners responsible for the carnage that extended several hundred yards into the sea. So long as Bill stayed crouched behind the wall, he was safe—at least for the moment.

Bill scanned up and down the shoreline. He expected to find at least a few of his fellow Marines alive. He didn't.

My God, he thought, *there ain't none of them gonna get in here. I'm all alone.*

Bill had been in tough scrapes before. One night, after a shell from a Japanese destroyer had knocked him out of his small Higgins boat, a rescue ship had to be called to save him from the sharks that had already started to prey on his comrades. He had also managed to survive six months of hell on Guadalcanal. But never before had things looked so desperate.

Finally, through the smoke and bullets, he saw a figure dashing out of the ocean. Another Marine, who had also survived by pretending to be dead, was running through waist-deep water, his back bent forward and his hands covering his head. And he was not the only one. Bill watched more Marines emerge until an even dozen had made it to the protection of the seawall.

By this time, Bill was furious at the Japanese. "We can stay here and die," he shouted above the din of gunfire to the dozen Marines crouched behind the wall with him, "or we can move out and die. But let's move out and take these damn sons of bitches with us!"

Without waiting for a response, Bill jumped up on the seawall. The others weren't sure why this crazy squad leader with a strong country accent had chosen to expose himself on a spot that was, at that moment, the most dangerous place in the most deadly war in the history of human conflict. Bill wasn't sure, either. But when he jumped back down—just moments before machine-gun fire laced his section of the wall—he had a plan.

"Start shooting them trees and knock some of them snipers out of them trees up there." No one moved. The stunned Marines just stared at him as though he were insane.

"Start throwing grenades at these pillboxes in front of us here." Again, no reaction.

"Listen, if we don't knock these pillboxes out then no other troops gonna be able to get in here to help us!"

Bill pulled the pin from his grenade and heaved it toward the closest pillbox. Then he crouched behind the wall—not on top of it this time, as there were some limits to his madness—and fired at the pillbox directly in front of them. Others followed his lead and the first fortification was soon destroyed. The dozen Marines then leapt over the wall and knocked out two more.

When the third pillbox was cleared of enemy gunners, Bill looked back to the sea. It was chaotic, and the newly arriving Americans were still taking heavy casualties, but something about the scene had changed. Bill saw Marines running down the front ramps of Alligator boats and splashing through the football-field length of ocean that separated them from the beach. There were hundreds of them, hundreds of American boys who would have been dead if those pillboxes had still been in place.

Athens
November 16, 1945

As the bus climbed over mountain roads, it passed signs saying "Jesus Is Coming Soon!" and "Prepare to Meet God!" But when it stopped that evening in Athens, it wasn't God standing there to meet the passengers. It was Windy Wise and three of his fellow deputy sheriffs.

Friday nights were big for the Cantrell machine. Buses coming through town were packed, and every tourist was a ripe target for arrest in this dry county. If they had a bottle of beer on them, and sometimes even when they didn't, they were arrestable. It made no difference in Athens. The county paid the sheriff "expenses" for each day that someone was held in jail. Whereas weekend arrests should normally have topped out at about fifteen, arrests in recent years had averaged 115. Over the last decade, Paul Cantrell's fee grabbers had collected about $300,000 in county expenses, much of it from returning GIs, who were frequent targets of the unfair arrests. Cantrell himself was now a state senator, but the official salary of his crony, sheriff Pat Mansfield, by contrast, was $5,000 per year.

Most of the passengers, many bound for Atlanta, were asleep when their bus stopped in Athens. But not Bill White. The twenty-two-year-old was much too excited to sleep. He had trained in California, fought in the Pacific, and been honorably discharged in South Carolina. But now he was coming home.

As soon as Bill's bus pulled into the station, Windy Wise bounded up the steps, followed by three other deputies.

"You're under arrest," he said. "All you folks is under arrest."

"Under arrest?" asked a half-awake passenger. "What for?"

"Drunkenness!" shot back Wise. "Don't worry. A night in jail won't do you no harm. And you can just pay a lil' fine in the mornin'."

"But," Wise added, turning to the tourist with the gumption to ask the reason for his arrest, "if I hear any more lip outta you, I'll give you the biggest beatin' you ever seen. And then I'll add resistin' arrest and obstruction and the fine won't be so lil'—"

"Bullshit!" shouted a young GI, standing up in the back the bus.

The four deputies marched toward the soldier, their hands on their metal batons and their eyes on the boy with the big mouth.

Without the weapons, and without the three extra deputies, a brawl between Windy Wise and this GI might have been a pretty fair fight. Both were big men, not so much in their height as in their build. Both were good athletes. And both had been in a lot of brawls.

But Windy Wise was not without his police baton or his three allies. And the melee that ensued was not a fair fight at all.

March 24, 1946

"Hello?" said Bill, as he picked up the phone in his parents' kitchen.

"Bill, it's Jim Buttram. How you doing?"

"Fine, I s'pose," Bill replied, curious about the local grocer's reason for calling. "Are you lookin' for my pa?"

"No, Bill. Looking for you. Some of the GIs are pretty fed up with Paul Cantrell and his gang. They've been out of control for a while, but ever since GIs started coming home, Mansfield and his deputies have really had a field day arresting us and beating us for no reason. They've even shot a couple boys. So when I heard about your run-in with Windy Wise back in the fall, I thought you might be with us."

"Hell, yes," said Bill, recalling the pain he felt from the pounding of Windy Wise's baton. "But there ain't nothin' you or me or no one can do about it."

"Well, we'll see about that. There's a meeting tomorrow night—a secret one. We're putting together a nonpartisan ticket to run against them in the five races up for election in August."

"What kind of nonpartisan ticket?" asked Bill.

"An all-GI ticket. You know Knox Henry? Fought in the North African campaign."

" 'Course I do," Bill said. "Everyone knows Knox."

"Good," Jim Buttram replied, "because he's going to be our new sheriff."

July 3, 1946

It was past midnight when the phone rang at the Whites' farmhouse. It woke Bill on the first ring, and he bounded toward the kitchen, hoping to catch it before it woke his parents.

"Hello," he said, slightly out of breath, not so much from the run to the kitchen but from being startled by the unexpected noise in the night.

There was silence on the other end.

"Hello?" he asked. "Hello!" he tried again, angrier. "Who the hell is this?"

The silence continued until Bill hung up. He started walking back toward his bedroom, but before he had made three steps, the phone rang again.

"Now listen, here, you son of a bitch," Bill said into the receiver, before he was cut off by a deep, purposely disguised voice on the other end of the line.

"No, Bill." A pause. "*You* listen here." The speaker was going out of his way to enunciate every syllable, talking so slowly it sounded like a recording being played at three-quarters speed.

"You have a nice family and a nice future," the voice continued. "It would be a shame if something happened to them."

It all clicked together in Bill's brain the second that last word oozed out of the caller's mouth: the campaign. Cantrell's machine was ramping up.

"Stay. Away. From tomorrow's rally."

Bill slammed down the phone. He returned to bed and stared at the ceiling, thinking about the voice. But he did not for a moment, that night or any other, think about quitting the campaign.

July 4, 1946

Flags flew from every shop surrounding the green lawn of the town square, and the white courthouse at the end of the block was covered in patriotic bunting. As soon as the sun set, fireworks lit up the night sky.

Bill White was excited, although he wasn't exactly enjoying the fireworks. Ever since the Pacific, he flinched at loud noises, and tonight he had an additional reason to feel nervous. This farmer's son, who had known nothing of politics when he left for war, was about to make his first public speech.

After the fireworks' grand finale—accompanied by a small local brass band playing "When Johnny Comes Marching Home"—Bill walked to the front of the county courthouse. Standing behind the microphone, he said, "And now it's time for the real fireworks!"

The crowd of more than a thousand supporters politely applauded as the young war hero looked out over the densely packed town square. The bankers and lawyers wore ties. The farmers and mechanics wore overalls. And behind them, in the distance, stood deputy sheriffs in broad-brimmed hats with folded arms and arrogant glares.

"You know, folks, there's an election coming up August first. And I reckon we seen a lot of elections 'round here. And every damn one of 'em's been stolen right out from under us!"

Paul Cantrell had been "elected" sheriff in 1936, when just enough mysterious votes had materialized at the last minute to give him the victory. He had been reelected through similar election-day shenanigans in 1938 and 1940, and, after being elected to the state senate in 1942 and 1944, he had decided to run for sheriff again this year, after it became apparent just how angry the county was with Cantrell's crony, Sheriff Pat Mansfield.

The crowd clapped in agreement. Bill reminded himself to keep his language in check. He didn't want to embarrass the political ticket hosting the rally.

"But this election is gonna be different." He told the crowd the story of a secret meeting of veterans in March in the basement of a

Studebaker dealership. He explained how they had decided to run a nonpartisan ticket of GIs, including Knox Henry, against Cantrell's Democrats and of how word had been spread throughout the county's three thousand GIs, risking the wrath of the Cantrell machine.

"It ain't been easy," he continued. "I've gotten them phone calls in the middle of the night. Threatenin' me. Threatenin' my folks." Heads nodded among men, women, and even children who had received the same calls.

"I've opened my mail. Seen them nasty postcards. Tryin' to intimidate us." The crowd murmured its agreement.

"Those sons-a-bitches even arrested a boy who was puttin' up a Knox sign on that tree right over there," he bellowed, pointing toward one of the many maple trees lining the town square, "even though they would have just torn the sign right down anyway!" There was more nodding and clapping.

"Well, I say the hell with all of 'em!" Bill shouted, pointing his thumb over his shoulder like an umpire calling a runner out. "We went over there to fight for American freedom. But when we came back to Athens, it was like Nazi Germany right here in Tennessee!"

Now the applause really began to build. There were three thousand veterans in McMinn County, and many of them were in the audience, growing angrier with every word Bill said.

"Our county is controlled by a damn bunch of Gestapo thugs, beatin' up GIs! Drunk as skunks most of the time!" The crowd's applause continued to grow louder, as did Bill.

"And then there's our very own Hitler, Mr. Paul Cantrell!"

The group roared even louder at the first mention of Cantrell's name, and by now the cheering was almost louder than the words coming from the loudspeaker by Bill's side.

"He's so used to money and power. That's all he cares about. And I say it's high time we clean out the kickbacks, and the phony arrests! I say it's high time we throw these gangsters right out of office, once and for all!"

There would be other speakers that night, many of them more eloquent than Bill White. But all of them—candidates and supporters, young and old, rich and poor—ended with the same promise: *We will not allow another stolen election! Your vote will be counted as cast!*

From the back of the town square, at every repetition of the GIs' promise of a fair election, Windy Wise smirked. He knew all the tricks: how to put phony ballots for the Cantrell ticket in the ballot box before the first vote was ever cast; how to intimidate voters with armed guards; and, most important, how to take the ballot boxes from the key precincts to the county jail, a place where only Cantrell supporters could watch the counting. The square, redbrick building on White Street had been built to keep law-breaking people in. But on Election Day, it served as the perfect place to keep law-abiding people out.

July 25, 1946

"Dear Director Hoover," the letter from the people of Athens began. "We are writing to request FBI observers to ensure an honest and fair election on August 1.

"Every recent election has been stolen by ward-heelers, ringsters, and the boss of the county, Mr. Paul Cantrell. They and their supporters have flagrantly voted minors, voted more than once, bought votes, stuffed ballot boxes, blocked poll watchers, and excluded opponents from buildings where the votes were counted.

"We complained of fraud in 1940, 1942, and 1944, but the Department of Justice never responded. We challenged elections in court, but the local judges are part of the Cantrell machine. This year, we are hoping you will take action ahead of time, before it is too late."

One hundred fifty-nine GIs signed the petition.

A similar plea was sent to both the attorney general of the United States and the governor of Tennessee.

Bill White, well aware of the governor's loyalties and the federal government's indifference, did not expect to receive a response.

Election Day: August 1, 1946
8:20 A.M.

Downtown Athens was only about nine square blocks, but that was plenty big enough for the city's seven thousand residents, many of whom farmed and lived on the outskirts of town. In the town center, things seemed to come in twos: two banks, two movie theaters, two Methodist churches. And in the summer, the city was always green— green bushes in front of local stores, green trees along the streets, green grass on the town square.

As Bill White walked toward the town square he passed the marquee for the Athens Theater, which advertised a Gary Cooper western called *Along Came Jones*. He'd been too busy with the election to watch any movies recently, but he put it on his to-do list. After today, his schedule would change.

After today, he told himself, *a lot of things will change.*

Bill passed Woolworth's and caught up with his friend Fred Boone, who delivered orders for Athens Hardware. "Big day," said Bill.

"Absolutely," Fred replied. "I'll sure be glad when it's over. For two weeks, I've been running all over the county." He stopped walking. His voice became a little quieter. "Everybody's stockin' up on ammo, Bill. Shotgun shells. Rifle cartridges. Even some bullets for pistols. People can't get enough."

He added, laughing, "One feller told me, 'Got some big huntin' to do—some *big* huntin'.' But nobody's foolin' nobody. I don't have to tell you. You of all people know best. You GIs are expectin' trouble from Cantrell today, aren't ya?"

Bill's eyes narrowed. There was nothing he wanted more than a peaceful, fair election, but he doubted it was possible with Cantrell involved.

"Stay tuned," said Bill, before walking ahead, aware that no one from the government had bothered to respond to their petitions for neutral election monitors.

When Bill came to the corner of Washington and Jackson streets, his hopes and fears for the day were both confirmed simultaneously. To his left was a line of voters stretching for half a block out of the Eleventh Precinct—the City Waterworks. The polls were not even open yet, but Athens was a town of early risers. Bill looked at the white-haired old-timers, the farmers in blue denim, and the mothers holding the hands of their children, and he knew at least two out of every three were there to vote for the Knox Henry/GI ticket. There weren't many se-crets in a town as small as Athens, and the GIs knew who their friends were.

They also knew who their enemies were, and when Bill looked to his right, he saw a pack of forty out-of-towners marching toward the Waterworks, swaggering with every step. Most of them carried a rifle or shotgun, and all of them had obvious bulges in their coats where sidearms were holstered. They were silent, but their faces—especially their eyes—did plenty of talking. These were cold men—cold and cocky. They were the last battalion to arrive, the final troops in the two-hundred-man army Paul Cantrell was assembling to intimidate voters. Their purpose, Bill knew from previous elections, was to block the view of election monitors, and, most important, keep GI supporters out of the jail, where key ballot boxes could be "counted" in secret.

Bill stared at the oncoming horde and thought, *I reckon it looked some-thin' like this, in all them little towns, when the Nazis first arrived.*

But Bill wasn't scared. He and his fellow GIs had something the unarmed townspeople of Europe never did. *There's more of us than them*, said Bill to himself.

And we've got more guns.

3:00 P.M.

Tom Gillespie walked by Windy Wise and up to the ballot box at the City Waterworks. He was a quiet man, a hardworking farmer who had lived most of his life in Athens. There were many southern towns where a man with Tom Gillespie's skin color wouldn't be allowed near a ballot box, but Athens was different. It had always played by its own rules— like siding with the Union during the Civil War and declaring war on Spain in 1898, two weeks before Congress did. And even though white supremacy ran deep in Athens, it wasn't pervasive enough to keep Tom Gillespie from voting. But things were different this year.

Windy Wise watched Gillespie with a growing fear. He wasn't scared of Gillespie necessarily, but of the GI supporters he represented. Wise was hot—there was no air-conditioning on this steamy August day— and tired. The tension had been rising throughout the day right along with the temperature. GI election monitors had already been beaten and arrested and the whole city felt like a tinderbox. Wise started developing a fierce headache when he began to worry that the quantity and enthusiasm of GI supporters was going to make stealing this election far trickier than expected.

Just as Gillespie was about to place his ballot in the box, the deputy sheriff grabbed his wrist and snatched the paper from his hand.

"You can't vote," Wise said. He sounded relatively calm, despite his growing fears.

"He can too!" shouted a GI supporter, who knew Gillespie was on their side.

For a moment everyone froze. The silence was finally broken when Tom Gillespie quietly asked Wise, "Why's that, Mr. Wise?"

The "Mr." part of his question was calculated. Blacks did not ask whites "why" very often in the American South, and Athens wasn't progressive enough for Tom Gillespie to do so without showing as much deference as possible.

"Boy," said Wise, his volume increasing, "you can't vote here today!"

Gillespie opened his mouth to protest, but Windy Wise had heard enough. He reached into his pocket, slipped brass knuckles onto his right hand, and slammed his fist into the left cheekbone of Tom Gillespie's face.

Gillespie fell to the ground, his face bleeding from where the metal on Wise's knuckles had cut through flesh and chipped away bone. Suddenly his head jerked back, propelled by the force of Windy Wise's boot, which sent Gillespie rolling out the door.

The stunned crowd outside the Waterworks, which had been gathering by the hundreds in the streets all afternoon, assumed Gillespie would remain on the ground, or at least outside the polling station.

But Tom Gillespie had worked hard for the respectability he'd earned over a lifetime. He believed he deserved the right to vote for the men his conscience compelled him to support. He wasn't finished fighting for that right.

It had been shocking when Gillespie talked back to a white man— especially to a Cantrell man. But what he did next was even more stunning. The proud, bleeding farmer stood up, wiped the dust off his denim overalls, and walked back into the Waterworks.

And that's when Windy Wise grabbed his pistol and shot the defiant, would-be voter who was walking past him right in the back.

7 :oo P.M.

All day, vast crowds had gathered in downtown Athens, hoping to show the Cantrell machine that this election would not be stolen while they sat idly by. Many were GIs, but some were simply supporters and patriotic Americans who believed in clean government and honest elections. Others were people who had been shaken down by the Cantrell machine over the years and were sick and tired of it.

The largest of the crowds gathered outside a local garage and tire shop called the Essankay, across the street from the GIs' campaign headquarters. It was this crowd, which included Bill White, that Jim Buttram, the GIs' campaign manager, reported to on the events of the day.

"Early this morning, at the courthouse precinct, Walter Ellis asked to look inside a ballot box before the voting began, just to make sure it was empty," said Buttram, standing on an oversized tire. "Now, that was Walt's right under Tennessee law, but Cantrell's boys beat him up and arrested him. He's still locked up in the county jail."

Bill White liked Buttram, the tall grocer with the big jaw, who was wounded twice in a war that took him all the way from Tunisia, to Sicily, to Normandy. Buttram had a just-the-facts style to his speaking that Bill appreciated.

"Throughout the day, we've seen repeat voters for them," Buttram continued. "And intimidated voters for us. And I don't have to tell you what happened at the Eleventh to Tom Gillespie. He's recovering from his bullet wound at Foree's clinic now."

The crowd broke into a brief moment of conversation, partly in anger at the reminder of Gillespie's shooting and partly in relief at the good news that he would likely survive.

"Then, at the Twelfth Precinct, Bob Hairrell protested when a young girl tried to vote. He'd made challenges to those kinds of stunts all day. He'd been ignored every time, but this time Bob knew she was seventeen. She even admitted she was seventeen. That's when Minus Wilburn just hit him across the skull with a blackjack! Then he kicked Bob in the face and let the girl vote!" Bill White had had a few run-ins with Wilburn, and he knew more than enough about the deputy sheriff's baton and boot.

"Now, the good news is that we've won by a three-to-one margin in precincts where the vote's been counted honestly, in the open." The crowd applauded tentatively, knowing there was more to come.

"But the bad news," said Buttram, waving his hands to quiet the crowd, "and it's *very* bad news, is that Cantrell's got most of the rest of the ballot boxes locked up in that jail." The crowd booed.

"He can count them behind closed doors however he wants, and he's got his cronies on the election board inside there to certify it. Once that happens there's no court around here that's gonna change it. We've been down this road before and we know where it leads. The question is, what are we gonna do about it this time?"

Bill White had heard just about enough. He didn't know what the crowd intended to do, but he had a pretty good idea what they *should* do. Bill thought back to everything he'd been through: killer sharks; months of starvation; the Imperial Army of Japan. He saw the faces of all the dead Marines he'd buried with his own hands and the enemy troops he'd killed in the name of freedom. It all boiled over.

"Listen!" Bill yelled over the noise of the crowd, which had taken Buttram's last question as an invitation to argue over an answer.

"Listen to me, dammit!" He didn't have Jim Buttram's natural talent for projecting his voice, but Bill White could be heard when he wanted to be.

"I fought with the bravest of the brave and the best of the best."

His voice softened, just a bit. "Nobody could have been any better or braver." Bill had never talked about the war before.

"They fought for democracy," he said. "All of us fought for democracy. And I'll be damned if I can figure out why you'd fight for it over there, and *not* over here!"

Bill wasn't sure whether he was moving the crowd, but he could feel his own emotions building.

"You call yourselves GIs?" He looked his fellow veterans in the eyes, repeating the question he'd asked a smaller group earlier in the day. "You go over there and fight two or three years, but you are gonna let a bunch of yellow-bellied draft dodgers push you around? A bunch of hoodlums who stayed here while we watched our friends die?"

By now the applause had begun, and Bill was fighting to be heard over the "Hell no's!" of an increasingly animated crowd.

"If you people don't stop this, and now is the time and place," shouted Bill, "you wouldn't make a pimple on a fightin' GI's ass!"

As the crowd accepted the challenge with a thunderous roar of applause, Bill ordered his friends and neighbors to exercise one of the rights they had all fought so hard to protect.

"Get your guns, boys!" ordered Bill White. "And then meet me at the jail."

9 :00 P.M.

The common law of Tennessee provides that every citizen has the right to stop a criminal in the act of committing a felony. In a similar spirit, the state constitution's Declaration of Rights says: "That government, being instituted for the common benefit, the doctrine of nonresistance against arbitrary power and oppression is absurd, slavish, and destructive of the good and happiness of mankind."

These abstract doctrines, however, were as far from Bill White's mind that night as they had been at Guadalcanal and Tarawa. He was no lawyer or philosopher; Bill White was a fighter, and he didn't need anyone or anything to tell him whether to fight for the things he believed to be right.

Bill stood across the street from the McMinn County Jail and shouted, "We've come for the ballot boxes!" The redbrick fortress now protected Paul Cantrell, Windy Wise, sixty deputies, and the ballot boxes that, if counted fairly, would hand the Cantrell machine its first political defeat.

Behind Bill White, in the darkness, was a semicircle of five hundred armed veterans and GI supporters. Farmers held shotguns that had hung peacefully above their fireplaces for decades. Hunters carried their .22s and veterans their .45s. There was even a contingent of skinny, baby-faced teenagers who'd come with BB guns and visions of glory. More ominous for the Cantrell machine was the collection of military rifles taken from the local armory and divvied among men who had last used them in places like Bastogne and Iwo Jima.

"Bring out those damn ballot boxes!" Bill called again.

Perhaps because of the darkness, Windy Wise didn't realize the size of the force opposing him, or perhaps he was simply so accustomed to having his way that it never occurred to him to hold his tongue. He had earned his nickname, after all, for being long-winded as a boy. Whatever the reason, Wise's next words made it clear that those in the jail were not taking the situation as seriously as they should have.

"Why don't you call the law?" Wise called out a second-story window as the "law" inside the jail laughed along with his joke.

"There ain't no law in McMinn County!" Bill fired back, not amused.

A brief silence followed, broken by the unmistakable locking sound of a shotgun's barrel snapping into its handle.

"Aw, go to hell!" shouted the deputy who had loaded the weapon. Bill had only a moment to wonder which deputy it was before the man aimed into the crowd of GIs and pulled the trigger.

The blast echoed down White Street, past the Dixie Café and the county courthouse beyond. Fifteen of the pellets found GI supporter Edgar Miller's shoulder and eight more lodged into supporter Harold Powers's neck. Like Tom Gillespie's, their wounds were not fatal.

Powers refused to leave the jail, but he did take cover, as did Bill White and the hundreds of men around him. Several dozen ran into a boardinghouse directly opposite the jail, where the windows of guest rooms provided the perfect cover from which to fire back at the thieves and bullies across the street.

Before those running for the boardinghouse could make it up the stairs, a barrage of gunfire rang out from those on their side who had found protection outdoors, behind cars and trees and the short walls of a nearby hillside. Glass windows shattered, and sparks punctuated the darkness.

Bill White fired both cartridges from his double-barreled shotgun, emptied the rounds in his rifle, and then shot his pistol until no bullets remained.

Then he reloaded all three weapons and repeated the cycle.

One more time, he thought to himself. *One last fight for what's right.*

The battle for Athens had begun.

August 2, 1946
1:15 A.M.

Windy Wise had seen Paul Cantrell many times, but never like this. On a normal day, Cantrell strode down the streets of Athens with the most confident of airs and the most distinguished of looks. This look featured a walking cane that he did not need, rimless glasses and suspenders, and the hat of a southern gentleman, always tipped off to the side just so. The political boss had been so sure of his position, so invincible in his own mind, that he'd named his prize bird dog "Lady Feegrabber."

But four hours into the Battle of Athens, with bullet holes in the walls and several deputies on the floor bleeding and dying, Paul Cantrell was feeling something he hadn't felt in more than a decade: fear. The hat and cane were gone, the fidgety twitch he'd tried to suppress since childhood had returned, and sweat was streaming down his large head and onto his small neck.

"Any word from the governor?" asked Wise, walking into Cantrell's makeshift office, where torn and crumpled ballots lay strewn across the floor. Their markings were irrelevant to the vote count Cantrell would report if he could survive the siege.

"Don't know," Cantrell said in his slow southern drawl. "The GI boys shot out the phone lines fifteen minutes ago." He wiped a stream of sweat from his forehead. "Last we heard, the National Guard was on its way."

Since their first volley, the GIs had kept up periodic barrages of fire. Their ammunition, which they'd retrieved from homes, hardware stores, and the local armory, seemed endless. In contrast, Cantrell's men had spent most of their bullets in the first half hour of gunplay. They needed to save the rest to defend against what they believed to be an inevitable storming of the jail.

The state guard, which was under the command of a politically loyal governor, was the Cantrell machine's best hope, though many in the jail doubted whether the governor in Nashville would risk his reputation to save a mountain county boss fighting a band of popular and heroic war veterans.

"Think they'll come?" asked Wise.

Cantrell wiped his forehead again and fidgeted with a pipe.

When he finally looked Wise in the eye, he looked as afraid as his deputies cowering in the jailhouse.

"No."

2:45 A.M.

Crouched behind a copse of trees he had been using all night for cover, Bill White knew that time was not on his side. The GIs had been winning the battle, but the siege could only last so long. How many armed supporters, brave enough to stand by him in darkness, would cautiously melt away at dawn? And what about the rumors of the National Guard coming to Cantrell's rescue?

"There's an old saying," Jim Buttram said to Bill. "If you're gonna shoot at the king . . ." Buttram paused. "Don't miss."

Bill knew he was right. If reinforcements from the governor arrived before Cantrell surrendered the ballot boxes, his regime would somehow survive. And if it did, his vengeance would be sure and swift. Bill White knew that he would likely be the first to experience it.

"I had a few boys go out and get some dynamite," Bill said, pulling a couple of sticks of the explosives from his jacket pocket. Then, for the first time that night, he flashed a wide smile. "I think it's time we end this thing."

Buttram nodded in agreement, and within minutes Bill had taped three sticks of dynamite together and heaved the first bundle toward the jail.

As soon as the dynamite left Bill's hand, he knew it was going to land short of the jail. It did, sliding under a deputy sheriff's Chrysler in the no-man's-land of parked cars separating the jail from the GIs. The massive car lifted into the air, turned over, and crashed back to the pavement, its windows shattering.

Before the wheels on the upside-down sedan had stopped spinning, White reared back and heaved another bundle of dynamite toward the jail.

There was another earsplitting explosion, but once again, the dynamite had landed too far short of the jail to seriously damage it.

"We're going to have to get some charges up there on the building," Bill said to Buttram. Both men knew the risks inherent in that proposition. The last time any GIs had exposed themselves in the area near the jail, a single shotgun blast had taken out Edgar Miller and Harold Powers. But compared to what he'd faced in the jungles of Guadalcanal and the beaches of Tarawa, this current mission seemed almost safe.

Bill put together another bundle and crawled under the cover of the earlier explosions' smoke. He slid right up to the overturned cars, lit a fuse, and pitched the dynamite onto the jail's front porch. This time he was plenty close enough. The blast shook the jail to its foundation and wooden porch planks flew into the night sky. Windows in neighboring stores rattled.

With the floors beneath them shaking and the ceiling above them trembling, the jail's defenders, except for Sheriff Mansfield, who had previously managed to sneak into an ambulance that had come to carry away wounded deputies, came rushing out of the battered building they had once been so confident would protect them. With smoke in their eyes and white handkerchiefs held high, the once-arrogant group of deputies tumbled out into the street.

5:45 A.M.

It would be a day before Paul Cantrell, who skipped town in disguise, conceded defeat. And it would be longer than that before Windy Wise felt safe showing his face again in Athens. Not that he had much choice. Wise was tried and sentenced to one to three years in prison for the shooting of Tom Gillespie.

It had taken several hours to deal with the other Cantrell deputies who surrendered to Athens's GIs that morning. Largely for their own protection, the men, most of whom were out-of-towners, had been returned to the jail they'd fled and locked away until it was safe for them to go home.

Somehow, in a six-hour gunfight involving hundreds of people, no one had died, and in the predawn hours after the shooting stopped, the mature and less vindictive of the GIs made sure it stayed that way.

Bill White finally headed from the city center to his parents' farm, past the old sign that read "Welcome to Athens, the Friendly City." He moved at a slightly quicker pace than normal, even though his body ached from almost twenty-four hours on his feet. Some of the speed came from the adrenaline that still flowed through his body. War was hell, but it also provided an unparalleled rush.

As the sun rose over the Smoky Mountains and Bill rounded the bend toward home, the tired young man slowed just a bit. He began to wonder what he would do with his life now that the campaign was over. He'd tried the GI Bill for a few months, but college wasn't for him. He wanted to find something else like the campaign, a corner of the world where he could right wrongs and stand up to crooks and thugs. He wanted a job that came not just with a paycheck, but also with a purpose.

There was a familiar tune playing in his head as he pondered his prospects; the same melody that had kept coming to mind throughout the night's battle. It was a song he had heard many times, but one whose title, the "William Tell Overture," he would never have been able to identify if asked.

"Maybe I'll be a lawman," Bill said to himself, holding his shotgun over one shoulder and resting his rifle on the other. "With a silver star on my shirt and a loaded gun in my holster."

He stopped and looked back toward the town he loved.

After all, Bill thought with a smile, *Athens is gonna need some new deputy sheriffs.*

11

The My Lai Massacre:
A Light in the Darkness

Tuttle-Woods Convalescent Home
Camden, New Jersey
March 15, 2008

Close to midnight, a commotion started halfway down the D-Ward corridor. Though outbursts weren't all that unusual, this one was different: unceasingly shrill and somewhat violent, like some old codger was trying to raise the dead.

Sticking to unofficial procedure, Everly Davison ignored the rising clatter and pressed on with his crossword puzzle.

Everly, who was better known as *E-bomb* among his off-duty circle of friends, was head of the security shift that night. This temporary promotion had been awarded by default, not by merit. All three of his useless superiors had called in sick on this cold, rainy, late winter evening.

Not that Everly was complaining. He so rarely got the chance to be the boss that he was making the most of it: feet up on the desk, microwaved hot chocolate with hazelnut Coffee Mate and a secret splash of Jim Beam, and the keys to all the snack machines on his utility belt. Hell, if this was work, he couldn't wait to see vacation.

That one disturbed resident down the hall was the only thing keeping this from being a great night. *No need to make an issue of it,* Everly thought. Not just yet. Even crazy people have to blow off a little steam once in a while. Waiting out his outburst would be safer and simpler for all concerned—and keeping things simple was what Everly did best.

Following his early release from Riverfront State Prison, Everly had swabbed out a few thousand of the world's nastiest porta-johns, manned a medical waste incinerator, delivered pizzas on foot through the worst gang-war hot zones of Newark, washed a nightly truckload of dishes in an institutional kitchen, and spent three bloody weeks as an apprentice on the kill-floor at a slaughterhouse. After all that, he'd finally stuffed enough padding into his ex-con's résumé to land his first real, full-time job: janitor at Tuttle-Woods.

Everly was perfectly happy with the work—climate control was a wonderful thing—but a few months later things got even better when he was promoted to security guard. To most people, walking the halls of an old folks' home on the graveyard shift might not seem that glamorous, but to Everly Davison it was like winning the lottery—even though he knew that lottery ticket was being cashed at someone else's expense.

A couple of weeks earlier, one of the guards had called the home's outside security contractor for help with an elderly lady who'd gotten it into her head that her daughter-in-law was coming to kill her and steal all her money. She'd taken a swing at the doctor who was trying to bring her meds, then she grabbed some silverware and holed up in the public bathroom. The rulebook says to call in reinforcements, so to speak, when things get out of hand, and that's what the guard on duty had done.

The rent-a-cops arrived at the home in riot gear and cleared out the regular workers. They hit the old woman with a Taser and a twelve-gauge beanbag gun, and she died right where she fell.

The security contractors later issued a report saying that the woman had come at them with a butcher knife. The guard who'd called for reinforcements was quickly fired for making noise about what he'd seen, and with nobody else alive willing to say otherwise, that was the end of it. Everly Davison happily accepted his promotion from the janitorial department into his new cushy security job.

The lady from Human Resources had laid out the requirements for the promotion, adding at the very end that she was specifically looking for someone who understood that discretion was the better part of valor. Whatever that phrase had meant when it was first written down, Everly knew what she was getting at. *See nothing; say nothing.* He nodded his head in agreement and that was that—Everly Davison was officially a security guard.

The yelling on D-Ward hadn't stopped and now it sounded to Everly like somebody down there had started throwing furniture around. A number of orderlies were in sight and Everly motioned for them to handle the disturbance while he went to the front entrance to answer the shrill buzzing of the doorbell.

The young woman standing outside was not unattractive, though she looked like a drowned rat in the driving rain. She was dressed for business and had an official-looking clipboard in her hand. Everly's first thought was that she was some kind of a state inspector, which wouldn't be good at all, but when she pressed her ID against the glass it said she was from the newspaper.

"Thanks," she said, after he'd let her inside the foyer. "I'm Julia Geller, from the *Courier-Post*. I made an appointment a couple of days ago. I'm here to interview one of your residents."

"Really?"

"Really."

"Because nobody told me."

"Sorry to hear that, mister . . ." She wiped the rainwater from her glasses, and squinted at his name tag. "Mr. Davison." She replaced her spectacles and made a note on her pad. "Should we call up your boss, because—"

"No, no," Everly said. "I believe you, let's not make any waves. Come on with me, we'll find whoever you want to talk to."

She told him to call her Julie and relayed the name of the resident she'd come to see. When Everly checked the room assignments it was clear that this was more bad news for the trouble-free evening he'd planned. This reporter wanted to talk to that man on D-Ward, the very one who was still down there raging like a lunatic.

"Do you mind if I slip back there so I can see your screen?" Julie asked, edging past him without really waiting for his answer.

"I don't think I'm supposed to—"

"It's okay, thanks." She sat at the computer and started typing and clicking.

"I don't want to lose my job," Everly said quietly.

"Neither do I." In a few seconds she'd found the records for room D-31. "Tell you what, there's a hundred dollars cash in it for you, if I get what I need for my story. How does that grab you?"

He gave a look around the security station to make sure the coast was clear. "Sounds fine to me, I guess. Just—"

"Good." After a bit more searching she seemed to find what she was looking for. "Morgan Campbell, age fifty-nine," she said to herself, and she began writing again on her pad. "No next of kin . . . VA transfer, diabetes, emphysema, cancer survivor, diagnosed in '01 with early-onset Alzheimer's. . . ."

"Alzheimer's," Everly repeated. "So how're you going to interview him if he can't remember anything?"

"Memory's strange in these patients," she said, still scrolling through the screens of confidential data. "It's first-in, last-out. He might not know who the president is, or what day it is, he might not even remember his breakfast this morning. But I'm betting he can tell me all about what happened forty years ago. Tomorrow's the anniversary."

She'd said this as though Everly might know what she meant. "Anniversary of what?" he asked.

In the silence that followed, Julie looked up from the computer. "Ever met a mass murderer, Mr. Davison?"

His checkered past being what it was, he had to think about that for a moment. "What do you mean, like three or four people?"

"Like three or four *hundred*. Maybe more."

The lights flickered for a second as thunder rolled outside, and right then Everly Davison felt the full weight of the gold plastic badge pinned on his chest.

"No," he said, "I never have."

She nodded. "Then come with me."

•   •   •

When they got to Morgan Campbell's room, the old guy was strapped down hand-and-foot and the safety rails on the bed were lifted and locked in place like sideways prison bars. All in all, he didn't look like much of a threat.

Campbell watched them intently as they stood in his doorway. Everly had quite an array of guard's accessories dangling from his belt, but much like his badge, they were largely for show. The most serious weapon allowed in his possession was a sample-size tube of pepper spray, its contents probably about as potent as the hot sauce at Taco Bell.

"Who is this guy?" Everly whispered.

"Ever hear of My Lai?"

"Me lie?"

"My Lai, Quang Ngai Province, Vietnam. It's a little town in a region the Americans called Pinkville during the war. That's where Mr. Campbell was, forty years ago tomorrow."

"What did he do?"

"That's what I'm here to find out." She stepped to the side of the bed with Everly behind her. She raised her voice a bit; it had said in his record that he was somewhat hard of hearing. "Mr. Morgan Campbell?"

The man nodded, his eyes locked on hers. He reached out, to the extent that the straps would allow. There was a tremor in his right hand, and the skin of his palm looked like it had been ravaged by an old burn that had never fully healed.

"My name is Julia. I'm a reporter. I'd like you to tell me what you remember about March 16, 1968."

"Pinkville," he whispered.

"That's right." She had her pad and pen ready, resting on the bedrail. "I want you to tell me all about it."

"Why?" The old man looked at Everly, and then back at the reporter again.

"Why not?" she replied.

"Because once you've been there," Morgan Campbell said, "you don't ever come all the way back."

June 1967

Morgan Campbell was nineteen years old when his number came up in the draft. He knew boys who'd dodged their service one way or another, but that kind of thing wasn't for him. His dad had been a bombardier in World War II, so going overseas to fight for freedom and stop the spread of communism seemed like the right and natural thing to do.

Before Morgan knew it he had become a soldier. He was too young to buy a six-pack of beer, but after nine weeks of basic the army suited him up, gave him an M60 machine gun, and put him on a transport bound for the last phase of preparation before their first tour in the Vietnam War.

The troops of Charlie Company trained in Hawaii for a time, learning guerrilla tactics and how to survive in jungle terrain. Those were grueling weeks, but Morgan and his squad had made it through with honors. Under the hard and watchful eye of Captain Ernest "Mad Dog" Medina they'd posted some of the highest marks on record. By the time their training was over they were tough as nails and had bonded like brothers, all 140 of them.

Four men stood out to Morgan Campbell in those early days, all for different reasons.

The first was Captain Medina. War truly is hell, Medina reminded them, and so the highest goal must be to win as soon as possible. He told them the only proven way for a fighting force to win was simple: You kill people and break things, better and faster than the other side. He called his men "death dealers" and handed out packs of cards that were all aces of spades. One of those cards was to be left on every dead gook body, to let others know that Charlie Company had been there. Medina hated the enemy, loved his country, was admired by most, and respected by all.

The second memorable man was Lieutenant William Calley. The soldiers of his First Platoon saw him as something of a blowhard and a bungler, and from what the men could tell he was little more than a butt-kissing yes-man to his superiors. Medina had nothing but scorn for Calley, but that just made the lieutenant try all the harder to impress him.

The third man was Billy Weber, whom everyone genuinely liked and vice versa. Billy may have been the only soldier in the U.S. armed forces whom Lieutenant Calley could call a friend.

The last man was Warrant Officer Hugh Thompson Jr. Thompson flew a little OH-23 helicopter on recon and rescue missions, risking his life every day and night, flying low cover and drawing enemy fire so the troops on the ground could get early warning of any ambush up ahead. He saved a lot of men with the risks he took. Life expectancy was short for such pilots and their crews, but he was damned good at what he did and as brave as they came. No one ever saw Hugh Thompson sweat.

Morgan Campbell's first month in Vietnam passed with almost no fighting at all.

When Charlie Company visited villages on their patrols, the troops were welcomed by the Vietnamese locals. The infantry would march in and establish a safe perimeter, give some candy to the kids, and help old ladies with their chores. It was Boy Scout–type stuff, building goodwill and winning hearts and minds.

Where's the war? That's what the men asked themselves on the long hikes back to base. It was a good time, if any time spent in a war can be called that. Between hitting the bars and beaches off duty it felt more like their training stint in Hawaii than a battle zone, but the peace was deceptive. They all knew it couldn't last.

And it didn't.

Tet Offensive
January 31, 1968

The widespread violence came without warning, in the midst of a mutual cease-fire agreed to in observance of the Vietnamese New Year's celebrations. In the largest coordinated enemy campaign to date, eighty thousand communist troops stormed into more than one hundred cities and vital strategic targets across South Vietnam.

The Americans and their allies were taken completely by surprise.

While some of the lost territory was quickly regained, the war had suddenly and permanently been redefined. The Vietcong and the North Vietnamese Army had made it clear to the world that they were more than a match for any invading force, superpower or not, and they were in it for the long haul.

A few days earlier, Charlie Company had been reassigned to Task Force Barker. This battalion-sized unit was stationed along the coast in the central region and their circle of operations included a particular stronghold of enemy activity. The place was called Pinkville because of the odd color that was used to label it on their tactical maps.

On the second night of the Tet Offensive, Morgan Campbell and Charlie Company were camped close enough to Quang Ngai City to see in the distance the very forces they'd soon be fighting. It was the Vietcong Forty-Eighth Battalion—the VC equivalent of the Green Berets—rumored to be the most elite and organized unit the enemy possessed, and Quang Ngai was thought to be their home turf.

It would be Charlie Company's job to go out, meet the Forty-Eighth Battalion head-on, and destroy them.

Pinkville
February–March 1968

In a daily briefing before a routine patrol, one of the brass actually had the stones to quote Chairman Mao with a straight face.

The enemy is the fish, he'd said, *and the civilians are the sea*.

Mao had been preaching the gospel of guerrilla warfare when he said something similar, but now his saying was being repurposed as warning to the troops. The major's point was that you can't always tell who's who, so you can no longer trust anybody Vietnamese. There were stories of old ladies and even little kids walking up to a sentry, giving him a big hug, and then pulling the pin on a grenade hidden under their smock.

Over the weeks since Tet, something fundamental had shifted in the atmosphere.

As the fighting had intensified, the locals started to change. Before the offensive they'd welcomed the Americans into their villages. Now that Quang Ngai was a free-fire zone, and regular bombing and shelling had begun across the region, honest friendliness was replaced with tight-lipped suspicion and distrust. The soldiers could feel themselves being watched from every shadow.

The locals knew where the minefields and booby traps were set, and where the snipers of the Forty-Eighth were hiding—but they didn't tell. They'd prefer to keep their silence and let a man walk right into a trap and lose his leg or his life.

As time went on, and reports of daily casualties mounted, there was a growing feeling among the American troops that if the civilians were aiding and abetting the enemy, then weren't *they* the enemy as well?

The war that Morgan Campbell and Charlie Company had trained for was different than the one that was closing in all around them. There were no uniformed opponents and few, if any, solid strategic goals. They'd go out on patrol every day, waiting for the inevitable attack and hoping the odds would be with them. The VC Forty-Eighth was fighting a war of attrition, picking off their enemies man by man and then retreating into the impenetrable jungle, knowing that the Americans couldn't fight what they couldn't see.

Yet even with those strategies in play, and entire villages of locals working against them, Charlie Company still hadn't taken any major losses as the war escalated. But that changed fast.

One morning, a patrol led by Lieutenant Calley was ambushed by sniper fire down by the river. No sooner had they dived for cover when Calley ordered the platoon to get up and cross the river, right out in the open, and go after the sniper nest dug in on the other side. The men knew it would be slow and dangerous wading through the water, but they followed their orders. They'd hardly taken one step forward when a well-placed bullet hit Billy Weber in the side.

It didn't look so bad at first. He was shot through the kidney, though, the organ was shattered, and the guy who got him must have known that his target would die slowly and in a lot of pain. The field medic did what he could, but nothing outside of morphine was going to help. It took almost an hour before Billy Weber finally died.

Throughout the ordeal some of the men were firing back, just shooting randomly up into the hills, yelling for the enemy to come out and fight. But that sniper had already done his job and had slipped back into hiding again.

With Weber's death, the men of Charlie Company knew that their charmed existence in this war was finally over. Throughout February, they lost a man almost every day, yet it still seemed like there was nobody out there to fight. The VC were ghosts. They would hit hard and then melt back into the jungle and the villages around Quang Ngai.

Somewhere close to the middle of March, the First and Second Platoons were out on patrol when they walked into different minefields at the same time. The first one blew, *boom*, and as men went in to help the injured they'd step on another mine, and then another, and another. Through it all, Captain Medina ran with his troops right among the worst of it, shouting orders, pulling soldiers to safety, leading as though he were invincible.

Charlie Company had started out with 140 able soldiers. Now they were down to 105.

What Charlie Company lacked was a crystal-clear military objective and an enemy they could face and fight. Brigade commander Colonel Oran Henderson arrived on the scene and, with Captain Medina by his side, delivered both at a March 15 mission briefing.

The new intelligence, Henderson told Charlie Company, was rock solid: the Forty-Eighth Vietcong Battalion was using a nearby group of villages called My Lai as a base of operations from which to launch attacks against the American forces. If Charlie Company struck fast and hard, Medina and his death-dealers could take them out once and for all. The mission would take place the following day.

After Colonel Henderson left on a reconnaissance flight with the other unit commanders, Captain Medina stepped up to add his own perspective to the briefing. The Americans would be outnumbered two or three to one, but the good news was that almost all of the civilians in the area had already fled the zone. Anyone they encountered, he told them, was to be considered a combatant, either VC or VC sympathizers.

Lieutenant Calley chimed in here and there like a teacher's pet, and the room soon became electric, taking on the tone of a pep rally rather than a mission briefing.

Every soldier was told to pack three times the ammunition that would be carried on a normal raid. They would go in strong and blow away everything that moved, laying waste to the crops and the live-stock, fouling the wells, and burning the place to ashes so that the vil-lage would be useless to any surviving enemy.

Medina implored Charlie Company to remember who and what they'd lost so far: Billy Weber and all the others. They were to gut up and go in with one stone-cold intent: to kill people and break things, to search and destroy until not even a stick was left standing. This was their chance to even the score.

My Lai, Vietnam
Early morning, March 16, 1968

As Morgan Campbell and the rest of Charlie Company strapped into the transport helicopters they heard Warrant Officer Hugh Thompson, the recon pilot, reporting over the radio. He'd flown in first, as usual, braving enemy fire so the infantry could get a picture of what they were about to face. His door-gunners had strafed the tree line on either side of the target village and, according to Thompson, theirs was the only gunfire to be seen or heard. There wasn't an enemy in sight. Then again, there was nothing so unusual about that.

They were almost to the landing zone when Medina gave his last orders.

"I don't give a damn what recon says, this is a hot zone we're landing in. Maybe the hottest you've seen so far. The colonel's in the command craft up above us, and believe me, he knows what's what. You hesitate and you'll get us pinned down in there, understand? Remember your orders! This is your fight to win! You've heard the old-timers talk about Iwo Jima? Well, this is yours, boys, right here today!"

The helos had barely touched grass when Morgan Campbell and all the others jumped out and hit the ground running. There was spo-radic gunfire as the men fanned out and headed in toward the hamlet.

Campbell saw movement among the trees and fired into them before moving on while others backed him up and laid down heavy suppression fire so they wouldn't get flanked in the advance.

Somebody ran past the window of a hut and Campbell swung his M60 around and cut the place up. Every fifth round was a tracer, and that allowed him to shoot from the hip with enough accuracy to hit what he was aiming at. Fleeing the hail of lead, two people burst through the door and Campbell shot them down just as his first ammo belt ran out.

As Campbell knelt and reloaded, he saw the rest of his company moving into the hamlet. There were people running away from them, some with hands in the air, and they were easily killed as the troops went house to house and cleared each dwelling of danger.

Campbell turned and saw a soldier he'd had dinner with the night before. The man walked up behind a young Vietnamese woman with an infant in her arms and shot her point-blank through the chest.

By then, some of the huts were burning. The helicopters overhead whipped up the smoke, hurting visibility and casting a dark, eerie shadow over the village. Campbell thought back to what he'd just seen. Or, more precisely, what he *thought* he'd seen. He couldn't be so sure anymore.

Campbell stood up and felt the deadly hesitation that Captain Medina had warned them about. He shook it off, assessed the scene again, and continued his advance. The sound of gunfire was dying down, but intermittent shots still echoed throughout the village.

By the time he reached the center of the village it looked like their orders had changed. With Lieutenant Calley directing, a few hundred people had been rounded up and were being marched to the east, toward a long drainage ditch that ran the length of the clearing. When they got there the scene grew still. The Vietnamese stood with their backs to the ditch and a line of soldiers facing them. Morgan Campbell walked over and joined his friends in that line.

Some of the wounded Vietnamese were being dragged to the edge and tossed into the ditch by other soldiers. As those bodies began to stack up, an OH-23 landed nearby, and seconds later, Hugh Thompson walked up in his flight suit and got right into Calley's face.

"What the hell's going on here, Lieutenant?" Thompson shouted. Calley outranked him but it looked to Campbell as though military hierarchy was not on Thompson's mind just then. "These are unarmed civilians; you can see that, can't you?"

"This is my business," Calley said. "We've got our orders."

"Orders? Whose orders?"

"I've got my orders, Thompson, and you've got yours. Intel tags all these people as the enemy—"

"Intel? Tell me, Lieutenant, have you never known intel to be dead wrong before?"

"I told you, I've got my orders! Now get the hell out of here so we can damn well do our job!"

"You ain't heard the last of this," Thompson spat, heading back for the radio in his aircraft.

When the helicopter had taken off again, Calley walked up to Campbell and the others, and he said, "Now, men, let's do what we came here to do."

More than any other detail in those next minutes, Campbell remembered the feel of pulling the trigger—the unholy *ease* of it. He hadn't been the first to start shooting all those people—grandmothers and grandfathers, women and boys and girls, almost no one of fighting age at all—but once he'd brought himself to make that one small motion with his right-hand index finger, the hardest part was behind him. From then on he killed efficiently and without hesitation.

As people died and fell to the ground there was nowhere for the others to run. Many began to jump down into the drainage ditch, some shielding their children with their own bodies. A few started forward, pleading, their arms outstretched as if they could stop the bullets with their hands. They were cut down like all the others.

When his ammo ran out, Campbell knelt to reload, then stood again and stepped to the edge of the ditch to scan for survivors. Each time he saw movement, he fired.

At last the ditch grew quiet; a still sea of arms and legs and bodies and faces with empty, staring eyes. Morgan Campbell looked around when it seemed like it was over and realized he was the only soldier remaining at his post and ready to fire.

It appeared that some of the men had put down their weapons and refused Calley's orders. Others seemed to have simply fled the area. Another dozen or so were following the lieutenant as he chased a small group of villagers that had somehow been missed in the sweep of the town.

Campbell followed them, watching the pursuit. The survivors ran toward a bunker with the small contingent of Charlie Company in hot pursuit.

Campbell caught up just as the Vietnamese disappeared underground. Calley called out for his grenadiers to advance on the bunker, and that's when Hugh Thompson landed his helicopter again, right between the soldiers and their unarmed, fleeing prey.

Thompson's door-gunners unharnessed their machine guns and stepped out, facing their fellow Americans. It was a standoff; neither side took aim, but neither side looked like it was going to back down, either. And then the unarmed pilot walked out between all those guns and made an announcement.

"I'm going to go over to that bunker, now," Thompson shouted, so all the soldiers could hear him clearly, "and I'm going to fly those civilians out of here myself. And Lieutenant, if you make a move to shoot them or me, by God you'd better be ready to take the consequences!"

Campbell continued to watch as three, then seven, then maybe fifteen people were brought out of the bunker. It was far too many to fit into his helo, but Hugh Thompson wasn't going to leave anyone behind. He called down a pair of gunships to help ferry the group away.

Then, as he was departing, Thompson made one last pass over the drainage ditch. He hovered low, and Morgan Campbell saw the gunners jump down and wade into all that death and gore to pull a small boy, alive, from the depths of the mountain of bodies.

It wasn't until that moment that he understood what he had done. What they'd all done.

Campbell dropped to his knees, numb from the realization, gritted his teeth, and grabbed the barrel of his M60 with his bare right hand.

The metal was still hot as a branding iron from all the killing he'd done. He held on tight, his skin burning to the bone, until the pain overcame him and finally swept his consciousness away.

Tuttle-Woods Convalescent Home
Camden, New Jersey
March 16, 2008

Except for the storm outside, the room was quiet again. Morgan Campbell had stopped talking, as though he'd reached a moment in the retelling of his past that he didn't wish to venture beyond.

"And what happened next?" Julia Geller asked.

Campbell blinked a time or two.

"Next?"

"Yes. What happened to everyone?"

The old man answered slowly, as though each detail required a deeper search of his failing memory.

"They covered it up, that's what happened next. They told us to shut up about My Lai, and then they sent all of us up into the highlands, the real dangerous country. We were up there, cut off from civilization, for fifty-eight days. I don't think they wanted any of us who'd been part of the mission to ever come back.

"Same for Hugh Thompson. After they debriefed him they sent him out to one of the worst hellholes possible. He was shot down five times. The last crash broke his back. But Hugh had already raised such a stink that they had to investigate. Colonel Henderson handled the job himself. Surprise, surprise, it was a total whitewash. After a month his people issued their verdict: Only twenty civilians had been killed in My Lai that day, not four or five hundred. All twenty had apparently died by accident.

"It took more than a year before the American press got enough real information to take notice, and then the military finally had to take some real action. The first truth to come out was that our intel for that day had been completely wrong. The morning we came into My Lai the entire Forty-Eighth VC Battalion that we were supposed to wipe out was camped one hundred and fifty miles away."

"There were trials and convictions," Julia said. "I remember that much. What happened to everyone?"

"Captain Medina was brought up on charges," Campbell said, "but F. Lee Bailey did for him what he later helped do for O. J. Simpson, and he got off with hardly a hitch. The heart of his defense was that he'd never given any orders to kill civilians.

"Calley was found guilty on twenty-two counts of premeditated murder and it caused an uproar among some. Jimmy Carter was the governor of Georgia at the time and he asked people to drive with their lights on for a week in protest of the verdict. George Wallace flew up from Alabama to visit Calley in the stockade and petition for a presidential pardon. State legislatures across the country made resolutions and requests for clemency.

"They handed down a life sentence for Calley, but a few days later Nixon intervened on his behalf and had him transferred to Fort Benning for a term of house arrest in a two-bedroom apartment. Three years later he was released for time served.

"I'm not sure if anyone was ever punished, not really—except for Hugh Thompson. Some congressman tried to get him court-martialed. He held a press conference and said that Hugh Thompson was the only one at My Lai that day who should be charged with a crime. Hugh got death threats and hate mail, and people drove by and threw dead animals onto his front porch.

It was thirty years before anyone in power ever bothered to officially call Hugh Thompson a hero and a patriot for what he did. In 1998 they gave him and his crew the Soldier's Medal. That's the highest award the U.S. Army can give for bravery in action not involving direct contact with the enemy."

"And what about you?" Julia asked quietly.

"What about me?" Campbell repeated. His voice was weak; it was like he was fading away from where he'd been.

"Yes, Mr. Campbell. What happened to you?"

"I got off, all right." He struggled against his restraints. "But don't you see? I never really got away."

•   •   •

Later that night, Everly Davison hung up his uniform, walked out, and never came into work again.

He watched the newspaper for days afterward, but Julia Geller's story never appeared. When he called her up to ask about it, she told him that her editor had turned it down, saying there was nothing new in Morgan Campbell's story, and certainly nothing that the paper's dwindling audience would be very interested in reading about. In its place they ran a puff piece about some local beauty pageant for rich little girls and their pampered mothers.

That should have been the end of it, but something was sticking in Everly's mind.

He kept thinking about Hugh Thompson, and the truth, and about doing the right thing, no matter if it meant you might never live it down. He thought of that old woman who'd died at the hands of those storm troopers for hire, of the guard who'd spoken up and been fired, and of the promotion he'd taken as a result.

Everly Davison picked the phone back up and called Julia Geller. He told her that he had an idea for another story, one that, if there was any justice left in this world, might just make the front page.

12

The Missing 9/11 Terrorist:
The Power of Everyday Heroes

Orlando International Airport
August 4, 2001

Jose Melendez-Perez stood and observed the first row of customs agents screening passengers seeking admittance to the United States. From afar it all seemed pretty routine: *Name, passport, nature of trip. Then give them a stamp and let them through.* But Melendez-Perez knew better. This job was far from routine.

He checked his watch, his eyeglasses slipping a little down his angular nose. He stroked his salt-and-pepper mustache and reflected on how his job was not unlike combat: moments of extreme intensity, followed by long periods of quiet during which even the best were challenged to maintain their focus and discipline.

Seventeen hundred hours, he whispered to himself. After two combat tours in Vietnam and twenty-six years in the U.S. Army, Melendez-Perez found no need to transition to "civilian time." His life was about protecting the United States of America—be it with a gun in some far-off land, or with a badge right here within shouting distance of one of the biggest tourist attractions in the world.

The muted television in the operations center was tuned to Fox News. The big stories of the day played out in a seemingly endless loop:

large protests at the G-8 Summit in Genoa; Robert Mueller confirmed as FBI director two days earlier; a small car bomb attack in London, perpetrated by the IRA. The biggest news seemed to be about President Bush's recent visit to Kosovo and NATO's commitment to send peace-keeping troops to Macedonia to quell a Muslim uprising in the former Yugoslav republic.

Melendez-Perez thought back to the recent security briefings. There had been a few warnings in the aftermath of the G-8 Summit, but nothing that warranted a state of heightened security.

Melendez-Perez's supervisor walked over and handed him a file. "Got a Saudi. No English. Incomplete I-94 and Customs Declaration. You got secondary."

Melendez-Perez nodded. "Roger," he said.

Incomplete arrival or departure forms and customs declarations were not unusual—especially among those who didn't speak much English.

Walking to the holding room, he rehearsed the usual process in his mind: question the traveler; check his credentials; determine his eligibility to be admitted into the United States. *Question, check, determine eligibility*. Routine, but important. Never one to be complacent, Melendez-Perez put on his game face and ran through his checklist of tasks.

First task: secure an interpreter. He looked up the on-call Arabic translator and saw that it was Dr. Shafik-Fouad. He called, explained the situation, and put him on standby. The next step was to review the subject's information. Melendez-Perez opened the file and scanned the important details.

Mohammed al Qahtani had departed Dubai for London, checking one bag, before arriving here in Miami on Virgin Atlantic Flight 15. Melendez-Perez knew that many Saudi nationals connected from Riyadh or Dubai through London in order to visit Disney World. *Nothing unusual here*, he thought, as he stepped into the small waiting room, quickly scanning the twelve faces to identify his subject.

"Mohammed al Qahtani," he called, staring directly at the man who was the best match for the picture in the file.

Melendez-Perez watched as Qahtani lifted his dead eyes from gazing at the floor and locked his black irises onto him. The subject wore a black, long-sleeved shirt, black pants, black shoes, and a black belt with a silver buckle. He had a wild black mane, thin facial hair, broad shoulders, and a scowl that could probably melt ice.

"Please follow me," Melendez-Perez said, indicating the way with his hand. He led Qahtani to a small room that resembled an interrogation cell, but he left the door open. *The illusion of free will*, he thought as he ushered the Saudi into the room.

Kandahar, Afghanistan
Three months earlier: May 11, 2001

Mohammed al Qahtani dug his foot into the sand like a bull about to charge a matador. His basic training instructor stood nearby with a stopwatch. Qahtani's heart raced with anticipation.

"Thalatha, ithnan, wahed . . ." Three, two, one . . .

Qahtani sprinted toward the mud pit covered in barbed wire— navigating it with ease, spitting grit as he charged forward to the rope climb. His powerful shoulders and long arms helped him scale the wall in record time as he flipped over the backside and high-stepped through a series of old tires.

Qahtani knew that he was on a record pace, and, if he finished that way, he would likely be chosen to go the front lines to fight the Northern Alliance. It would be a once-in-a-lifetime chance to demonstrate his personal courage and fervent dedication to Islam.

After that it would be up to his commanders to decide if he would be chosen for another mission—one that had been whispered about in tents and caves for a long time, but one that no one outside of senior leadership seemed to know much about. Qahtani didn't care about the details. If it was important to the cause, he wanted in.

Inshallah. God Willing.

Orlando International Airport
August 4, 2001

Melendez-Perez leaned across the small gray table and put Dr. Shafik-Fouad on speakerphone. At the sound of the interpreter's voice Qahtani smirked, as though a familiar accent implied he had an ally.

"On the phone is Dr. Shafik-Fouad. He is our interpreter. I am Officer Melendez-Perez of United States Immigration and I am empowered to ask questions of you so that we may determine whether you are able to be admitted to the United States."

Melendez-Perez waited while Shafik-Fouad translated. Qahtani's icy stare remained steady, as though he were a boxer attempting to intimidate his opponent.

"Why don't you have a return ticket?" Melendez-Perez asked.

Qahtani stood and pointed his finger at the immigration agent.

"I have no idea where I am going next. How can I buy return ticket when I don't know where I will be?"

As Dr. Shafik-Fouad interpreted, Melendez-Perez's eyes narrowed. He'd heard these kinds of responses before. In Vietnam, assassins were often not told of their final destination or target. This ensured that they would have no intelligence to share if they were compromised. While this Saudi in front of him was a long way from a Vietcong mercenary, Melendez-Perez felt the resonance of a familiar chord.

He pressed ahead.

"Who is picking you up at the airport?"

"A friend."

"What's his name?"

"He is arriving at a later date."

"Then how is he picking you up?"

"He arrives in three or four days."

"Then who is picking you up?"

"I am traveling for six days."

"Where are you staying?"

"A hotel."

"Which one?"

"I forget the name."

"If you don't speak English and don't have a hotel reservation, you will have difficulty getting around Orlando."

"There is someone waiting for me upstairs."

The rapid-fire questioning from Melendez-Perez, translated by Dr. Shafik-Fouad, had either confused Qahtani or trapped the Saudi in his own lies.

Not wanting to lose momentum, Melendez-Perez kept pushing.

"Who is waiting for you?"

"No one is waiting for me. I am to call him when I get to where I am going."

"What is his phone number?"

"You do not need to know these things! This is personal and you do not need to contact him."

Melendez-Perez stood. "I'll be back in a minute."

Panjshir Province, Afghanistan
Three months earlier: May 18, 2001

His obstacle course time the previous week had indeed impressed his superiors and Qahtani had been granted his wish to be sent to the front lines. Now he was running again, sprinting at full throttle, his wavy black hair tousled by the hot May winds of Afghanistan. Today the mud pit and old tires had been replaced by Northern Alliance troops—and they were not far behind.

As he scrambled downhill, the mountains north of Bagram, Afghanistan, cast large, black shadows against the gray twilight. Darting along the rocky goat trail with his AK-47 rifle, shale and pebbles skidded beneath his boots, falling over the cliff onto the rocks far below. While his instructors had warned him not to venture beyond the front lines, Qahtani knew that, to stand out, he'd have to do something extraordinary. That meant disobeying orders, but the upside was that, if he succeeded, his superiors would recognize his devotion to Allah and his willingness to sacrifice his own life for the cause. Never once did he consider that his self-centered foray into enemy territory might have consequences for that cause if he were captured.

Athletic and powerful, Qahtani widened the distance between him and his pursuers, but the narrow path soon turned into an open stretch of trail that led to a road. He wondered if they would pursue him beyond the entrance to the fabled Panjshir Valley, the place where "the Lion of Panjshir," Ahmad Shah Massoud, had destroyed the Soviet army thirteen years ago, in 1988.

Night had fallen and the darkness closed a tight fist around the looming mountain peaks. Qahtani leapt over a rock and was forced down into a narrow gorge with a well-maintained gravel road running through it. Looking over his shoulder, he saw a Hilux pickup truck rounding the hairpin turn he had just avoided.

Almost immediately rapid machine-gun fire came from the truck, growing more intense, and more accurate, as Qahtani raced toward the gatehouse. *How fast can I run fifty meters?*

He darted past the cantilevered metal arm that blocked vehicle access and dove onto the bank of the adjacent river, water raging loud enough to drown the sound of the approaching truck.

The pickup was close behind him. Bullets sparked off the metal trusses of the fence surrounding the gorge as Qahtani risked the current and slipped across the river, up the opposite bank, and onto a trail that led into the mountains.

He paused and took several deep breaths, trying to get as much oxygen to his starving lungs as possible. He had made it.

An odd squeaking noise disrupted his brief celebration. He looked back at the gate. The metal arm was lifting as the truck sat waiting patiently, like a panther about to leap—less than one hundred yards away. Men stood in the bed of the pickup, searching for him in the darkness. A large spotlight flicked on, silhouetting the .50-caliber machine gun mounted in the back.

Qahtani dove over the side of the trail into a shallow valley. His heart pounding through his chest, he slithered along the ground as far as he could. For the first time since his self-directed mission had begun, he sensed failure. As he crawled along the ground he thought back over his brief, insignificant life. In his teens he had drifted from job to job, never proving worthy enough to stick anywhere. He had no education to speak of and had little practical talent in anything other than athletics.

His last job before embracing this new path in life was as an ambulance driver in Riyadh, Saudi Arabia. By then, Qahtani had absorbed the radical sermons of his local mullah for so long that he'd finally approached him to ask how he could join in the fight against the infidels. His mullah sent him to Syria to study and train with like-minded Muslims. It was there that he'd become a true believer and realized that his calling was to join in the jihad against the West.

Now, as he hid from the searchlight mounted on the Northern Alliance truck in a rocky outcropping, that trip to Syria, and his subsequent stop in Iran, seemed like ages ago. He squeezed his eyes shut as he heard the truck engine rev and tires crunch off toward the valley. He opened his eyes and took a deep breath: *I have survived*. He prayed that his commanders would view his actions as courageous, rather than defiant.

Qahtani looked at the night sky with its tiny lights flickering brightly against the darkness. Perhaps, he thought, his life would be like that: a flickering light against the endless void of darkness.

Orlando International Airport
August 4, 2001

Melendez-Perez paced the halls, thinking through the situation, which was more delicate than it appeared. While his instincts screamed that something was wrong, he knew that denying entry to a legitimate Saudi national could have serious professional consequences.

But he also knew something else: His instincts were the only thing that had kept him alive in Vietnam. He trusted them implicitly.

Returning to the small room, Melendez-Perez began a different line of questioning, but Qahtani quickly lost control again. The Saudi was standing up, leaning forward, his hands on the table, leering, and shouting.

Melendez-Perez remained calm. "Sit down, please. I'm not finished. You have two thousand, eight hundred dollars in cash and a one-way ticket to Dubai will cost you two thousand, two hundred. How will you get money for both travel in the United States and your return?"

"Someone will bring me money."

"Why would someone bring you some money?"

"Because he is a friend."

"How long have you known this person?"

"Not too long."

Melendez-Perez stood and left the room again.

"I am placing you under oath. It is a serious offense to lie to an immigration officer."

Qahtani's eyes narrowed at the translation of what Melendez-Perez had just told him, but he agreed. After the swearing in was read, translated, and recited, the questioning continued.

"Who is picking you up?"

"I won't answer," Qahtani said.

Shafik-Fouad, whose sole purpose thus far had been to interpret and relay Melendez-Perez's words, spoke out of turn. "Something's not right here."

Melendez-Perez agreed and he saw a dark cloud of fear slide across Qahtani's eyes. For the third time in ninety minutes, he left the room.

His feet as cold as ice cubes, Melendez-Perez walked to the operations center and checked NAILS, the National Automated Index Lookout System. It came up empty—Qahtani had no countries interested in his arrest. *That would've been too easy*, he thought to himself.

Melendez-Perez reentered the interview room with several documents and a small container. Qahtani stared at him intently as he wrote on several different forms. "What is your occupation?"

"Car salesman," Qahtani said.

Melendez-Perez returned the Saudi's icy stare as he removed an inkpad and began to take Qahtani's fingerprints. He grasped his fingers one by one, placing them on the pad, rolling them back and forth, gathering ink, and then pressing them firmly into the hard, white stock paper.

Oddly, Melendez-Perez perceived a softening of Qahtani's demeanor. Perhaps the Saudi believed this to be a good sign. Maybe he was under the impression that the fingerprints were the final part of the admittance process.

The paperwork complete, Melendez-Perez stood again. "You do not appear to be admissible into the United States. I am offering you an opportunity to withdraw your application. I will escort you to the gate for the next departing flight to Dubai, where you will pay for your return ticket."

As the interpreter relayed Melendez-Perez's message, Qahtani looked from the phone to Melendez-Perez's face and shouted, "You cannot do this! Why do all of this paperwork? Why put me through this? You are harassing me! I will not pay!"

Melendez-Perez remained calm. "If you do not pay for your ticket, then we will detain you here in the United States until such time that you do."

Qahtani, looking defeated, reluctantly agreed. "I will pay," he muttered.

Standing at the entrance to the jetway, Qahtani turned back toward Melendez-Perez and spoke one final time—now using perfect English.

"I will be back."

Dania Beach, Florida
August 5, 2001

Ziad Jarrah jabbed tirelessly at the heavy bag until his instructor slowed him down.

"No need to destroy the bag, Ziad. What do you want to work on today?"

But Jarrah wasn't working on anything except venting his anger. He and a friend had made the long trip from Fort Lauderdale to Orlando International Airport yesterday, waiting for hours before finally giving up on their arriving passenger, who was apparently a no-show.

He continued to pummel the bag, ignoring his instructor and temporarily abandoning the perfection with which he had been playing his role as a moderate, westernized Muslim. Conflict stormed in Jarrah's mind as sweat streamed down his face. His oval wire-rimmed glasses were cocked oddly on his nose as his fists let loose their fury.

His life was a study in contradiction. On the one hand, he was smart, educated, and fluent in English, German, and Arabic. He had a beautiful girlfriend in Germany, whom he called nearly every day. He was living a life that many people only dreamed of. On the other hand, it was this life that also made him the perfect person to wage jihad against the West. No one ever saw him as a threat because there was no reason for him to be one.

Though raised as a Christian in the Bekaa Valley of Lebanon, Jarrah became friends with Muslims while at school in Germany. Under their tutelage, he had begun to believe in the extreme reaches of Islam.

For months he had been taking self-defense classes at this Florida gym. He had perfected sleeper holds, defensive maneuvers, and rapid-fire jabs. But, unbeknownst to most people, these weren't the only things for which Jarrah had been training. The previous December he'd begun training in a flight simulator, pursuing his childhood dream of becoming a pilot.

West Milford, New Jersey
September 10, 2001

Just south of the New York State border, in the Adirondack foothills of West Milford, New Jersey, Jeremy Glick slipped quietly into his backyard. As the predawn mist of an Indian summer morning began to clear, he closed his eyes and began running through the judo routine that had won him the college national championship eight years earlier. His breathing slowed, his eyes closed, and he visualized his beautiful wife, Lyzbeth, and his two-month-old daughter, Emerson—a name they'd chosen because of his fondness for the poet. Glick stepped forward as he practiced the Deashi Harai technique; his foot swept over and out and his muscles stretched taut on his six-foot-two, 220-pound frame.

Thirty minutes later, Glick stepped through the back door and into his home. It was dead quiet—no phones ringing, no babies screaming, no roar of commuter trains, honking of cabs, or growl of city buses— the kind of silence that only those who lead busy suburban lives can really appreciate.

Lyz and Emmy were still inside, the former undoubtedly trying to catch what little sleep she could after a long, restless night with their newborn. Jeremy had been up early packing for his flight to San Francisco. A couple of hours later, Lyz would be leaving to drive up to the Catskill Mountains with Emmy to visit her parents. Glick smiled. It took him a lot of years, but he finally understood what really mattered in life: family. And now he had one of his very own. He showered and dressed and quietly kissed Lyz and Emmy good-bye.

A few hours later—after first stopping to interview for a job that wouldn't require so much travel—Jeremy Glick arrived at Newark International Airport and moved quickly through the security checkpoint. He walked to a monitor to confirm his gate number and saw the one word that every traveler dreads: CANCELED. It was flashing red right next to his flight number: United 93 to San Francisco.

Confused, Glick approached the ticket counter. "I'm sorry sir," the agent said. "There's been a fire in the airport where we are doing some construction and all of our flights have been delayed or canceled. If you provide me with your boarding pass and ID, I'd be happy to rebook you for tomorrow's flight."

Glick was by no means immune to the same anger and frustration that all travelers feel when their plans are disrupted, but judo had taught him discipline and control. Maximum impact with minimum effort. Anger was the opposite. It took a lot of effort, and it resulted in nothing. So, instead of letting frustration overcome him, Glick let his mind drift back to the positive: his family. It was too late to stop their trip to the Catskills, but at least he'd be in his own bed for another night.

Newark International Airport
September 11, 2001
7:03 A.M.

Jeremy Glick learned his lesson and checked the flight monitor before clearing security: DELAYED. At least that was an improvement from the previous day.

After going through security he headed to Gate 17 and called his in-law's house, hoping to speak with his wife. Instead, his mother-in-law,

Jo Anne Makely, answered. "Emmy had a rough night," she told him. "I did what I could, but Lyz was up for most of it so she's trying to get a couple hours of sleep in now."

A pang of guilt stuck in his heart. He always helped with Emmy, especially on the challenging nights. "Tell Lyzzie I'm boarding the plane and I love her and I'll call her when I get to San Francisco."

7:42 A.M.

Ziad Jarrah boarded United Airlines Flight 93 and thought back on his now five-week-old argument with Mohammed Atta.

"We cannot do this without al Qahtani," he had told Atta, their car idling outside Orlando International Airport. "All of the other teams have five. We will only have four."

"We have waited for hours. Obviously he was turned away. There is no time for another. You must do this without him," Atta said as he stepped on the accelerator.

Now, as Jarrah took his seat in the first row of the first-class cabin, he sat back and watched the others on his team board. Closing his eyes, he silently said his supplications and recalled the note he wrote to his girlfriend the previous night: "I did what I was supposed to do. You ought to be very proud, because it is an honor and you will see the result and everyone will be very happy."

Still, the absence of Qahtani bothered him. Jarrah knew that he, and possibly one of the other men, could fly the aircraft. But with two people in the cockpit, that only left two to guard and defend the cockpit. They'd always planned and rehearsed with three.

Jarrah looked over his shoulder at the many empty seats behind him. That gave him some measure of comfort. Fewer passengers meant fewer opportunities to overpower his team.

A resolve came over him. It was time. He thought back to a video he'd made with Atta about eighteen months earlier. They'd both proclaimed their dedication to today's task but he'd laughed through most of the taping as he'd tried to read his part of the script. *Is this plan for real?* he'd thought. It was so audacious, so . . . ridiculous. Could he really go through with it?

As the captain's voice asked the flight attendants to prepare the cabin for takeoff, Jarrah realized that he would learn the answer to that question very soon.

Tarnak Farms Training Camp, Afghanistan
September 11, 2001

After his unexpected escort to the jetway in Orlando months earlier, Qahtani had returned to Dubai briefly, before flying to Kandahar to rejoin his comrades at the training camp near the airport.

Following three weeks of advanced infantry training, Qahtani was standing at the rope climb on the obstacle course when he heard a shout. He ran into the first room of the Habash Guesthouse and found dozens of cheering men huddled around a television set. On the screen was an image of the World Trade Center in New York City. One tower had a gaping hole in its side. Smoke and fire poured out as shards of glass and falling bodies rained down on the streets below.

As they watched, an airplane flew into the picture of the burning tower and struck the second tower, this time much lower than the first. The room erupted into another round of applause and celebration. Then, a new image: the Pentagon in Washington, D.C., up in flames. A third plane had struck.

Amid the cheering, Qahtani heard a voice.

"The next plane was yours, Qahtani. This is the most important symbol in Washington, D.C. Watch closely and you will be proud." Khalid Sheikh Mohammed, Al Qaeda's operations officer—the man who planned and coordinated the logistics of the attacks—was smiling as he spoke.

"This was my plan."

United Flight 93, 36,000 feet over Ohio
September 11, 2001
9:37 A.M.

Jeremy Glick watched the scene unfold before him as though he were watching a movie. The hijackers had stabbed the flight attendant, stormed the door of the cockpit, stabbed the pilots, and took control of the airplane. Meanwhile a man with a bomb strapped to his waist shouted at all of them to move away from the cockpit, toward the back of the plane.

Now seated in row twenty-seven, Glick picked up an air phone and called his wife in the Catskills. His father-in-law answered on the first ring.

"Jeremy, thank God. We're so worried."

Glick cut to the chase. "It's bad news. Can you put Lyz on, please?"

A moment passed and Glick struggled to maintain his composure. When Lyz picked up he cut right to the chase.

"These three Iranian-looking guys took over the plane. They've got red bandanas, knives, and one says he has a bomb. I need to know, have other planes attacked the World Trade Center? That's what some of the others are saying."

"Yes, Jer. Planes have crashed into both," Lyz said.

Glick was silent a moment, stifling a sob as he soaked in the full magnitude of what was happening.

"You need to be strong, Jer," Lyz said.

"I know." But at that moment Glick wasn't thinking about himself. "I just need you to be happy," he said. "I love you and Emmy so much."

They spoke quietly for a few more minutes, professing their love for one another. Then Glick said, "Whatever decisions you make in your life, no matter what, I will support you." It was the ultimate act of love: having the courage to see past his immediate danger and into his family's future.

"We're taking a vote to rush the hijackers," he said. "Do you think the bomb is real?"

"No. I think they're bluffing. I think you need to do it. You're strong. You're brave. I love you," Lyz said.

A long pause.

"I think we're going to do it. I'm going to put the phone down. I'm going to leave it here and come right back to it."

Glick and the other men who voted to overtake the hijackers huddled and introduced themselves to each other: Todd Beamer, Mark Bingham, and Tom Burnett.

Glick was listening for skill sets as the men spoke. Bingham played rugby, Burnett was a quarterback in college, and Beamer played baseball. *Good, four athletes*, he thought.

Glick saw Beamer go back to his seat and pick up the air phone he'd left hanging. He spoke into the receiver for a moment and then turned to Glick and the other two men. "You guys ready? Let's roll."

Kandahar, Afghanistan
September 11, 2001

Qahtani paced nervously. The television room in the guesthouse was still full of revelers rejoicing in Al Qaeda's successful attack on America.

Yet, there still had been no word on United Flight 93. And then, hours later—it finally came: a breaking report from Al Jazeera. An airliner had crashed in a farmer's field in someplace called Shanksville, Pennsylvania.

"The initial reports," the anchor said, "are that passengers of United Flight 93 overpowered the hijackers, preventing them from striking their intended target, which is believed to be either the White House or the U.S. Capitol."

Khalid Sheikh Mohammed turned toward Qahtani and said, "You stupid Bedouin."

As he lost control and began to sob, Qahtani ran from the guesthouse and hid inside one of the tunnels of the obstacle course. He hugged his knees to his chest, rocking back and forth inside the sweltering culvert. The encounter at the Orlando airport five weeks earlier kept running through his mind.

Nineteen others had made it. He had not. Bin Laden and Zawahiri had recruited him, selected him, and trusted him.

And he had failed.

Tora Bora Mountains, Afghanistan
Three months later: December 2001

After the reports of United Flight 93 reached the training camp, Qahtani thought he would be killed immediately to send a message to the other fighters. "Each plane with five men was successful," Khalid Sheikh Mohammed had said. "The one plane with four men—the one you should have been on—was not. So you tell me, Qahtani, what should be the price for your failure?"

He expected death, but what he got instead was a one-way ticket to Tora Bora to fight the Americans. Now, cowering with thirty others in a dark cave, he sat, waiting for the moment that an American daisy-cutter bomb would carry out the sentence he'd been spared just months earlier.

But the bomb never came.

A few days into his stay in the mountains, Qahtani's commander gathered the men. "Our position has been compromised," he said. "The Americans and Northern Alliance are just over the ridge. We must go." They left the cave in a rush and fled toward Pakistan.

Less than thirty minutes after their departure, Qahtani saw the explosion before he heard the sound. Their cave had taken a direct hit from an American bomb.

Hours later, as night fell, Qahtani heard machine-gun fire in the distance, followed by the thump of two mortars. The echoes of combat reverberated from the mountains onto the valley floor near Parachinar, Pakistan. The Americans were closing in from the north.

He pressed forward quickly through the narrow streambed. The other fighters followed behind him in single file, sometimes turning to spray random rifle fire at the advancing enemy.

With his senses deadened from lack of food and sleep, Qahtani at first missed the noise. By the time he realized that he was hearing engines idling, they were too close. And it was too late.

Automatic weapon fire began to ping overhead as armored vehicles closed in around them. Qahtani's first instinct was to flee. He ran toward a canyon about a hundred yards away. Reminded of his escape from Panjshir, he was encouraged. This was an opportunity for redemption directly from Allah. He may have failed in Orlando, but he would not fail here.

The thought was just beginning to take hold in his mind when he was tackled from behind and handcuffed by a group of Pakistani soldiers. He and his comrades were dragged along the ground and loaded onto the backs of several trucks.

The soldiers placed a burlap bag over his head and he was soon transferred to the Americans. He heard their voices. Crisp and authoritative. He felt someone with large hands grab his fingers. One by one they were pressed into something soft and cold and then rolled from side to side.

Camp X-Ray
Guantanamo Bay, Cuba
January 2002

Sergeant Raul Romeo watched the military C-17 Globemaster airplane taxi and then drop its ramp. Military personnel escorted the prisoner onto the hot tarmac. The man wore an orange jumpsuit, white shoes, black socks, earmuffs, and a black cloth over his eyes.

An experienced interrogator, Romeo was excited about the inbound package. He was a fresh capture and rumored to be a highly placed Al Qaeda operative. He waited with his hands clasped behind his back until the man was directly in front of him.

"This is prisoner number 063," the escort said. "Says he was in Afghanistan as a falconry expert."

Romeo smiled. "Falconry? That's what they all say."

The handler returned the grin. "He was captured with an AK-47 and twenty-nine of his best falconry buddies."

For all the details the handler seemed to know about this man, he still could not answer the most basic question: *What is his name?*

Camp X-Ray
Guantanamo Bay, Cuba
Ten months later: November 17, 2002

On a warm November morning, Sergeant Romeo's commander called him into his office. Romeo reported with a sharp salute. "Sergeant Romeo reporting as ordered, sir."

"Two things," the major said. "Look at this."

Romeo took the piece of paper from his commander and saw that he was looking at a fingerprint analysis between a set of prints taken on August 4, 2001, at Orlando International Airport and a set taken in December 2001 in Jalalabad, Afghanistan.

"Your guy was the twentieth hijacker," the major said.

Romeo read the report and looked up. He and his friends had heard all of the speculation about a missing hijacker, but it had just been rumor.

The major continued, "Detainee 063 is Mohammed al Qahtani. Nothing he has told us since he's been here is true."

Sergeant Romeo gathered himself. "You said there were two things."

"Right," the major replied, handing him another sheet of paper. "New interrogation techniques, hot off the press—and approved all the way up the food chain. How's that for timing?"

Romeo scanned the sheet. *Restraint on a swivel chair, deprivation of sleep, loud music, prohibition of praying, threats of rendition to countries that torture.*

His commander just shrugged. "Let's see what it gets us."

Camp X-Ray
Guantanamo Bay, Cuba
November 28, 2002

Sergeant Romeo called Sergeant Lisa Smith and said, "Get 063. It's been over a week. We're ready."

The interrogation room was musty. Romeo directed Smith to place the blindfolded prisoner in the swivel chair in the center of the empty room with the air conditioner set at maximum blast.

After fifteen minutes of silence, Romeo removed Qahtani's blindfold. "Take a look at these."

On the table Smith had laid out pictures of each of the hijackers. Qahtani looked down and then quickly looked away.

Romeo paced behind Qahtani. "Go ahead. Look at your successful brothers. You failed them, didn't you, Mohammed al Qahtani?"

Romeo watched as Qahtani visibly reacted to his name. *Now we're getting somewhere*, he thought. He exchanged glances with Smith, who was now stationed directly in front of Qahtani.

Smith pointed to the Arabic words she'd written on the chalkboard in front of Qahtani: *Liar, Coward, Failure*.

"This is you!" she shouted.

Qahtani closed his eyes and shook his head. "Na'am." *No.*

Romeo leaned in from behind him and shouted into his ears.

"Look at the pictures, Qahtani! You are the twentieth hijacker! Tell me about your training! Tell me about your commanders! Where is bin Laden?"

Qahtani jumped at Romeo's voice. He looked down at the pictures and began to quietly sob. Romeo knew he must be feeling guilty for not completing his mission. Guilt was something he could use.

"Who was your leader?"

"Osama bin Laden."

Romeo stopped. For the first time in nearly a year of captivity, prisoner 063 had provided a truthful answer.

"Why did you go to Orlando?"

"I wasn't told the mission."

"Who was meeting you?"

"I don't know."

Romeo spun around and slammed his hands on the table, the carefully spread photos bouncing into the air and landing askew, some skittering to the floor.

"Who was on the plane with you?"

"I was by myself."

"You're wasting my time!" he lied. The truth was that these answers were, for the first time, getting them somewhere.

"Give me one name! One name of someone who trained you!"

Qahtani looked up, tears streaming down his face.

"I have to use bathroom. Please."

"One name!"

"Abu Ahmed al-Kuwaiti. Taught me Internet."

"Internet? You're going to fly an airplane into the White House and you give me the name of your tech support guy?"

Romeo walked out of the room, calling over to Smith. "I'm done with him. Make him go to the bathroom in the bottle in front of you."

Returning to his cube, Sergeant Romeo quickly entered this new name, al-Kuwaiti, into the database: *063 claims Abu Ahmed al-Kuwaiti taught him how to use the Internet. Follow up with Defense and Central Intelligence Agencies.*

Islamabad, Pakistan
Seven years, nine months later: August 4, 2010

CIA paramilitary operative "Ron" listened intently to the voice on the intercept.

For years, Ron and his teammates had been trolling for any usable scrap of information—but, like the tip lines the police use after a serious crime, most of the information they'd received was only marginally useful at best. Ron was on the lookout for names of highly placed operatives or mentions of weapons of mass destruction. But long ago, when the hunt for bin Laden had first begun, they'd decided that messengers would help lead to the ultimate quarry.

"We've got someone talking about a courier!" Ron said to the small group huddled in the plywood-paneled communications room of the safe house.

"What's the name? We need a name!" the station chief answered.

"He's calling him Sheik al-Kuwaiti."

"That's *got* to be the same guy."

"I've got his number and recorded voice. We're triangulating his position right now," Ron confirmed, simultaneously relaying the information and coordinates to CIA headquarters in Langley, Virginia.

"Abbottabad, Pakistan," Ron reported. Quickly the satellite spun to the location on the outskirts of the capital of Islamabad. It was a large compound framed by a trapezoidal wall.

Looks fit for a sheikh, Ron thought to himself.

Abbottabad, Pakistan
May 2, 2011
2:00 A.M.

The point man from Navy SEAL Team Six's Red Team had rehearsed it a thousand times, but he was still shocked when he saw the unmistakable face of Osama bin Laden staring right back at him.

The SEAL fired his Heckler & Koch 416 carbine as bin Laden dove back into his bedroom. While the SEAL's index finger reflexively squeezed the trigger, he thought about Jeremy Glick and the brave passengers on Flight 93, all those who had perished in the 9/11 attacks, and all those who had come before him in the wars.

Stepping into the bedroom, he saw that bin Laden was on his back, two of his wives shouting at him. A teammate shot one of the women in the leg and pushed them away. Another pumped two more rounds into bin Laden's heart.

The point man made the call over his radio: "Geronimo, Geronimo, Geronimo!"

Osama bin Laden was finally dead. And while it may have been a Navy SEAL's bullet that struck the fatal blow, it was a long-ago airport encounter between a young Saudi extremist and Jose Melendez-Perez, a veteran who continued to serve his country, that first sealed his fate.

This story is dedicated to all of the American heroes who've fought in the War on Terror. Melendez-Perez is a perfect example of how an ordinary person can make an extraordinary difference, but he's not the only one. Each of us has the opportunity to prove that every single day.

About the Writing of This Book

This book comprises twelve stories that took place over a period of about 230 years. Not one person alive today was alive when even half of these events actually took place. That means we are left with history books, biographies, oral accounts and, in some cases, court transcripts and official reports to tell us what happened. Like anything that spans so much time and, in some cases, is so controversial, these accounts often conflict with each other. It is up to all of us to read all of the evidence and discern what is fully true, what is exaggerated, and what is a lie.

This section is meant to help you better understand the research and writing process for each story, including any key decisions we made regarding major facts, characters or scenes. A chapter-by-chapter accounting is below, but there are also a few things that apply to the entire book that I want to point out.

1. We sometimes modified quotations for clarity. This mainly applies to quotes from the revolutionary period, but we occasionally modified more modern quotes as well if we felt that they left the reader confused. We tried to be as delicate as possible and we *never* changed the meaning of any direct quotations.
2. In some cases we imagined characters or scenes. Whenever we did this we were careful to ensure that nothing we created contradicted anything that we knew to be true from the historical record.
3. Dialogue and character thoughts were often imagined based on the historical record. None of this dialogue contradicts anything about the characters or story that we know to be true.

Chapter 1: Jack Jouett: The Ride That Saved America
Most of the facts used to create this story came from the following sources:

"Charles S. Yordy, III: The Pennsylvania Line Mutiny, its Origins and Patriotism." *Unearthing the Past: Student Research on Pennsylvania History*, Pennsylvania

State University. http://www.libraries.psu.edu/psul/digital/pahistory/folder_2
.html.

Crews, Ed. *Captain Jack Jouett's Ride to the Rescue*. Colonial Williamsburg. http://
www.history.org/Foundation/journal/Summer06/ride.cfm.

Jack Jouett: Louisa County's Revolutionary Hero. Louisa County, Virginia. http://
www.louisacounty.com/LCliving/jouett.htm.

"Jack Jouett of Virginia: The 'Other Ride.' " *Valley Compatriot*. February 1984.
Donal Norman Moran, ed. http://americanrevolution.org/jouett.html.

Jack Jouett's Ride. History Happens: Stories from American History on Music
Video. http://www.ushistory.com/story_jack.htm.

Jack Jouett's Ride. Thomas Jefferson Encyclopedia. http://www.monticello.org
/site/research-and-collections/jack-jouetts-ride.

Lieutenant Colonel Banastre Tarleton. National Park Service. http://www.nps.gov
/cowp/historyculture/lieutenant-colonel-banastre-tarleton.htm.

The George Washington Papers at the Library of Congress: 1781. http://memory.loc
.gov/ammem/gwhtml/1781.html.

Timeline of the Revolutionary War. Ushistory.org. http://www.ushistory.org
/declaration/revwartimeline.htm.

Visit the Home of the "Paul Revere of the South." Jack Jouett House Historic Site.
http://www.jouetthouse.org.

Notes on specific scenes and characters:

The scene in which Jouett overhears a conversation in the tavern is factual, but some of the dialogue is imagined to provide historical context.

The scene with Tarleton and a young, unnamed soldier at the campfire is imagined, though all of the information conveyed in the scene is factual.

The scene in which Jouett arrives at Monticello is factual, but the dialogue is fictional. There is no record of what he actually said to Jefferson, but the imagined dialogue is supported by reports of how Jefferson reacted.

The scene in which the Dragoons arrive in Monticello is based on the records that we believe are most authentic. That said, there are varying accounts of how Jefferson responded to Jouett's news (some have him eating breakfast before heading out) and where he rode to first (one account says that he rode up the mountain and hid in the hollowed-out shell of an oak tree).

The scene at the end with Jouett and Stevens is factual, but the dialogue is imagined.

Chapter 2 : Shays' Rebellion: A Loud and Solemn Lesson

Most of the facts used to create this story came from the following sources:

Acts and Resolves of Massachusetts Passed by the General Court: 1786–87. http://
archive.org/details/actsresolvespass178687mass.

Allen, Herbert S. *John Hancock: Patriot in Purple*. Beechhurst Press, 1953.

Barry, John Stetson. *The History of Massachusetts*. Ulan Press, 2012.

Buckley, Kerry W. *A Place Called Paradise: Culture and Community in Northampton, Massachusetts, 1654–2004*. University of Massachusetts Press, 2004.

Clogston, William, and Moses King. *King's Handbook of Springfield, Massachusetts: A Series of Monographs, Historical and Descriptive*. Ulan Press, 2012.

Copeland, Alfred Minott. *"Our County and Its People": A History of Hampden County, Massachusetts*. Vol. 1. Ulan Press, 2012.

Cushing, Thomas. *History of Berkshire County, Massachusetts: With Biographical Sketches of Its Prominent Men*. Vol. 1. J. B. Beers, 1885.

Danver, Steven L., ed. *Revolts, Protests, Demonstrations, and Rebellions in American History: An Encyclopedia*. Vol. 1. ABC-CLIO, 2010.

Davis, Kenneth C. *America's Hidden History: Untold Tales of the First Pilgrims, Fighting Women, and Forgotten Founders Who Shaped a Nation*. Harper Perennial, 2009.

Everts, Louis H. *History of the Connecticut Valley, with Illustrations and Biographical Sketches of Some of Its Prominent Men and Pioneers*. Louis H. Everts, 1879.

Feer, Robert A. *Shays' Rebellion*. Garland, 1988.

Field, David Dudley. *A History of the County of Berkshire, Massachusetts, in Two Parts: The First Being a General View of the County: the Second, an Account of the Several Towns*. Ulan Press, 2012.

Fiske, John. *The Critical Period of American History, 1783 to 1789*. Kessinger, 2010.

"Friday December 1st. 1786." National Archives. http://founders.archives.gov/documents/Adams/03-02-02-0001-0011-0001.

Harlow, Ralph Volney. *Samuel Adams, Promoter of the American Revolution*. Henry Holt, 1923.

Hart, Albert Bushnell, ed. *American History Told by Contemporaries*. Vol. 3. University of Michigan Library, 1917.

Herrick, William Dodge. *History of the Town of Gardner, Worcester County, Massachusetts from the Incorporation, June 27, 1785, to the Present Time*. Ulan Press, 2012.

Holland, Josiah Gilbert. *History of Western Massachusetts: The Counties of Hampden, Hampshire, Franklin, and Berkshire, Embracing an Outline, or General History, of the Section, an Account of its Scientific Aspects and Leading Interests, and Separate Histories of its One Hundred Towns*. Repressed, 2012.

Kaufman, Martin, ed. *Shays' Rebellion: Selected Essays*. Institute for Massachusetts Studies, 1987.

Leibiger, Stuart. *Founding Friendship: George Washington, James Madison, and the Creation of the American Republic*. University of Virginia Press, 2001.

Lockwood, John Hoyt. *Westfield and Its Historic Influences, 1669–1919: The Life of an Early Town, with a Survey of Events in New England and Bordering Regions to which it was Related in Colonial and Revolutionary Times*. Vol. 2. Nabu Press, 2012.

Masur, Louis P. *Rites of Execution: Capital Punishment and the Transformation of American Culture, 1776–1865*. Oxford University Press, 1991.

Minot, George Richards. *The History of the Insurrections, in Massachusetts, in the Year 1786 and the Rebellion Consequent Thereon*. British Library, 2010.

Munroe, James Phinney. *The New England Conscience: With Typical Examples*. Richard G. Badger, 1915.

Richards, Leonard L. *Shays' Rebellion: The American Revolution's Final Battle*. University of Pennsylvania Press, 2003.

Sears, Lorenzo. *John Hancock: The Picturesque Patriot*. Gerbert Press, 2008.

Starkey, Marion L. *A Little Rebellion*. Knopf, 1955.

Stewart, David O. *The Summer of 1787: The Men Who Invented the Constitution*. Simon & Schuster, 2008.

Szatmary, David P. *Shays' Rebellion: The Making of an Agrarian Insurrection*. University of Massachusetts Press, 1984.

Thompson, Francis McGee. *History of Greenfield: Shire of Franklin County, Massachusetts*. Ulan Press, 2012.

Trumbull, James Russell. *History of Northampton Massachusetts from Its Settlement in 1654*. Forgotten Books, 2012.

Willard, David. *Willard's History of Greenfield*. Kneeland & Eastman, 1838.

Most of the dialogue in this chapter was imagined, but the following quotations were taken in whole or in part from the historical record:

"We are either a united people, or we are not": Stan V. Henkels, *Washington-Madison Papers Collected and Preserved by James Madison, Estate of J. C. McGuire*. 1892, p. 25.

"Tell 'em we can't afford to pay neither debts nor taxes": Fiske, 179.

"Gentlemen: By information from the General Court": Holland, 250.

"They say Captain Shattuck has perished in his prison cell": Richards, 21.

"The men of property": Hart, 191–93.

"You know it. Your very manner tells me you know it": Starkey, 130.

"If the matter isn't settled by sunset": Starkey, 131.

"If you advance": Lockwood, 109.

Luke Day's letter: Lockwood, 107–8.

"Barracks and stores": Herrick, 95.

"That's all we want, by God!": Feer, 367.

"Take the hill": Szatmary, p. 102.

"Fire o'er the rascals's heads!": Elizabeth Cobbs Hoffman, Edward J. Blum, and Jon Gjerde, eds., *Major Problems in American History*, vol. 1, Cengage Learning, 2011, p. 141.

"March on! March on!": Stewart, 13.

"Another volley—this time waist height": Minot, 111.

"I'm afraid I've only four": Copeland, 97.

"Whether you are convinced or not of your error": Charles Oscar Parmenter, *History of Pelham, Mass. From 1738 to 1898, Including the Early History of Prescott*, Ulan Press, 2012, p. 379.

"My boys, you are going to fight for liberty": Everts, 77.

"Sir: However unjustifiable the measures": Holland, 268–69.

"I must have a word with you": Richards, 31.

"And discipline breaking down": Richards, 31.

"In monarchies, the crime of treason": Ira Stoll, *Samuel Adams: A Life*, Free Press, 2008, p. 224.

"What country can preserve its liberties": *North American Review, January–April 1830*, p. 524.

"As you have set yourselves against": Caleb Smith, *The Oracle and the Curse: A Poetics of Justice from the Revolution to the Civil War*, Harvard University Press, 2013, p. 76.

"Our fate is a loud and solemn lesson": Smith, 75.

Chapter 3 : The Virginia Convention: Compromising for the Constitution

Most of the facts used to create this story came from the following sources:

Bailyn, Bernard, ed. *The Debate on the Constitution: Federalist and Antifederalist Speeches, Articles, and Letters During the Struggle over Ratification, Part Two: January to August 1788*. Library of America, 1993.

Beeman, Richard R. *Patrick Henry: A Biography*. McGraw-Hill, 1974.

Beveridge, Albert J. *The Life of John Marshall*. Vol. 1. Cosimo Classics, 2013.

Broadwater, Jeff. *George Mason, Forgotten Founder*. University of North Carolina Press, 2006.

Brookhiser, Richard. *James Madison*. Basic Books, 2011.

DeRose, Chris. *Founding Rivals: Madison vs. Monroe: The Bill of Rights, and the Election That Saved a Nation*. Regnery History, 2011.

Grigsby, Hugh Blair. *The History of the Virginia Federal Convention of 1788, with Some Account of Eminent Virginians Who Were Members of that Body*, Vol. 1. Forgotten Books, 2012.

Gay, Sydney Howard. *James Madison*. Ulan Press, 2012.

Gutzman, Kevin R. *James Madison and the Making of America*. St. Martin's Griffin, 2013.

Hunt, Gaillard. *The Life of James Madison*. Ulan Press, 2012.

Ketcham, Ralph. *James Madison: A Biography*. University of Virginia Press, 1990.

Kidd, Thomas S. *Patrick Henry: First Among Patriots*. Basic Books, 2011.

Maier, Pauline. *Ratification: The People Debate the Constitution, 1787–1788*. Simon & Schuster, 2011.

Mayer, Henry. *A Son of Thunder: Patrick Henry and the American Republic*. Grove Press, 2001.

Mayo, Bernard. *Myths and Men: Patrick Henry, George Washington, Thomas Jefferson*. University of Georgia Press, 2010.

Meade, Robert Douthat. *Patrick Henry: Practical Revolutionary*. Lippincott, 1969.

Robertson, David. *Debates and Other Proceedings of the Convention of Virginia, Convened at Richmond . . . June 1788: For the Purpose of Deliberating on the Constitution*. Ulan Press, 2012.

Rowland, Kate Mason. *Life of George Mason, 1725–1792*. Ulan Press, 2012.

Smith, Jean Edward. *John Marshall: Definer of a Nation*. Holt Paperbacks, 1998.

Tyler, Moses Coit. *Patrick Henry*. Echo Library, 2009.

Unger, Harlow Giles. *Lion of Liberty: Patrick Henry and the Call to a New Nation*. Da Capo Press, 2010.

Willison, George F. *Patrick Henry and His World*. Doubleday, 1969.

Writ, William. *Sketches of the Life and Character of Patrick Henry*. University Press of the Pacific, 2004.

Most of the dialogue in this chapter was imagined, but the following quotations were taken in whole or in part from the historical record:

"Caesar had his Brutus": Writ, 83.

"a scarecrow with a wig": Unger, 162.

"The people gave them no power to use their name": Mayer, 402.

"The government is for the people": Mayer, 402–3.

"I am a friend of the Union": Beveridge, 377.

"Randolph has thrown himself fully into our scale. Mason and Henry take different and awkward ground, and we are in the best spirits": Gutzman, 207.

"Worthy friend": Robertson, 36.

"The former is the shield and protector of the latter": Robertson, 37.

"Don't ask how trade may be increased": Robertson, 43.

"What are the checks of exposing accounts?": Meade, 356.

"This illustrious citizen advises you to reject this government": Robertson, 152–53.

"I beg the honorable gentleman to pardon me": Robertson, 187–88.

"Our progress is low": Gay, 114.

"Nothing has excited more admiration in the world": Gutzman, 232.

"His proposed amendments could be subsequently recommended": Gutzman, 233.

"Madison tells you of the important blessings": Robertson, 625.
"Virtue will slumber": Robertson, 165.

Note that some scenes in this chapter were imagined or expanded beyond what we know from the historical record. This includes, for example, the scene at the end of the story in which James Madison thinks about Patrick Henry's warnings and ultimately decides that they have no merit.

Chapter 4 : The Barbary War: A Steep Price for Peace
Most of the facts used to create this story came from the following sources:

"Battle of Derna, 27 April 1805: Selected Naval Documents." http://www.history
.navy.mil/library/online/barbary_derna.htm.
Baepler, Paul, ed. *White Slaves, African Masters: An Anthology of American Barbary Captivity Narratives.* University of Chicago Press, 1999.
Fremont-Barnes, Gregory. *Wars of the Barbary Pirates: To the Shores of Tripoli: The Rise of U.S. Navy and Marines.* Osprey, 2006.
Lambert, Frank. *The Barbary Wars: American Independence in the Atlantic World.* Hill & Wang, 2007.
London, Joshua E. *Victory in Tripoli: How America's War with the Barbary Pirates Established the U.S. Navy and Shaped a Nation.* Wiley, 2005.
Oren, Michael B. *Power Faith and Fantasy: America in the Middle East: 1776 to the Present.* Norton, 2008.
Ray, William. *Horrors of Slavery: Or, the American Tars in Tripoli.* Rutgers University Press, 2008.
Thomas Jefferson's First Inaugural Address. March 4, 1801. http://avalon.law
.yale.edu/19th_century/jefinau1.asp.
Whipple, A. B. C. *To the Shores of Tripoli: The Birth of the U.S. Navy and the Marines.* Bluejacket Books, 2001.
Zacks, Richard. *The Pirate Coast: Thomas Jefferson, the First Marines, and the Secret Mission of 1805.* Hyperion, 2006.

Most of the dialogue in this chapter was imagined, but the following quotations were taken in whole or in part from the historical record:

"No man will hereafter love you as I do—but I prefer the field of Mars to the bower of Venus": Oren, 63.
"We are all Republicans, we are all Federalists": Jefferson's First Inaugural Address.
"Nothing but a formidable force will effect an honorable peace with Tripoli": London, 146.

"I sincerely wish you could empower": London, 145.

". . . that I might never experience the horrors of another morning": William Ray Diary, December 22, 1803.

"We are now about to embark on an expedition": Oren, 59.

"A fleet of Quaker meetinghouses would have done just as well!": Zacks, 7.

". . . limit to the avarice of the Barbary princes": Zacks, 39.

"Stop! I will cut off the head of any man who dares to fire a shot!": Whipple, 199.

"We have marched a distance of two hundred miles": Whipple, 202.

". . . for the purpose of obtaining a peace with my brother": Whipple, 214.

". . . more favorable and—separately considered—more honorable": Lambert, 153.

"I firmly believe we would have entered Tripoli": Whipple, 256.

". . . settled policy of America, that as peace": Oren, 74.

"The United States, while they wish": Oren, 74.

Some scenes in this chapter were imagined or expanded beyond the basic historical record, including:

The May 15, 1801, scene in Tunis is imagined. The attack in Tripoli on the U.S. consulate it describes was real, although it is unclear to what degree the people in the consulate would have felt they were in danger, as the Tripolitans' main act of aggression was cutting down a flagpole outside.

The July 1, 1803, scene is imagined. While Jefferson did make the decision to send the USS *Philadelphia* to Tripoli, it is unclear exactly when he came to this decision.

The May 1, 1804, scene is imagined. Ray kept a diary, and he did not mention this incident in it. The scene's focus is on the beating of an American prisoner. The Tripolitans were famous for abuse of their slave prisoners.

The battle of Derna had more fronts than the one described in the April 27, 1805, entry. Eaton divided his army, and this scene tells the story from Eaton's point of view, focusing on his bayonet charge. Eaton kept a diary, but most of the battle details are imagined (for example, Eaton plunging his bayonet into an enemy soldier), as is the dialogue. (Eaton getting shot is real.)

Chapter 5: Edison vs. Westinghouse: An Epic Struggle for Power

Most of the facts used to create this story came from the following sources:

A Warning from the Edison Electric Light Company. Edison Electric Light Company, 1887. https://play.google.com/store/books/details?id=RylRAAAAYAAJ&rdid.

Bellis, Mary. "Death, Money, and the History of the Electric Chair: The History of the Electric Chair and Death by Execution." *About.com*. http://inventors .about.com/od/hstartinventions/a/Electric_Chair.htm.

Daly, Michael. "Topsy: New Book Tells how Thomas Edison Electrocuted an Innocent Elephant at Coney Island." *New York Daily News*, June 29. 2013. http://www.nydailynews.com/new-york/topsy-elephant-slain-thomas -edison-article-1.1385182#commentpostform.

"Edison Electrocuting a 28 year old Elephant named Topsy." http://www.you tube.com/watch?v=ow-CwEdwktg.

"Electric Light Companies—Domestic: Edison Electric Light Co (1887–1889)." http://edison.rutgers.edu/NamesSearch/glocpage.php3?gloc=CA019&.

"The Great Barrington Electrification, 1886." Edison Tech Center, 2010. http:// edisontechcenter.org/GreatBarrington.html.

"The History of the Electric Chair." Canadian Coalition Against the Death Penalty. http://www.ccadp.org/electricchair.htm.

Jonnes, Jill. *Empires of Light: Edison, Tesla, Westinghouse, and the Race to Electrify the World*. Random House, 2003.

King, Gilbert. "Edison vs. Westinghouse: A Shocking Rivalry." *Smithsonian .com*, October 11, 2011. http://blogs.smithsonianmag.com/history/2011/10/ edison-vs-westinghouse-a-shocking-rivalry/.

Kosanovic, Bogdan R. "Nikola Tesla." University of Pittsburgh, December 29, 2000. http://www.neuronet.pitt.edu/~bogdan/tesla/.

Prout, Henry G. *A Life of George Westinghouse*. American Society of Mechanical Engineers, 1921. http://books.google.com/books?id=NglTzPG3-18C&pg.

"Seat of Power." *Snopes.com*. July 21, 2007. http://www.snopes.com/science/ edison.asp.

"Tesla: Life and Legacy: War of the Currents." PBS.org, http://www.pbs.org/ tesla/ll/ll_warcur.html.

"Thomas Edison and the Electric Chair." Free Enterprise Land, 2005. http:// www.freeenterpriseland.com/EDISON.html.

Most of the dialogue in this chapter was imagined, but the following quotations were taken in whole or in part from the historical record:

"The most effective of these, are known as 'alternating machines'": Mark Essig, *Edison and the Electric Chair: A Story of Light and Death*. Walker, 2003.

"I believe there has been a systemic attempt": Jonnes, 167.

"The only excuse for the use of the fatal alternating current": *The Electrical Engineer: A Monthly Review of Theoretical and Applied Science*, August 1888, p. 360.

"In your judgment, can alternating electric": Liz Sonneborn, *The Electric Light: Thomas Edison's Illuminating Invention*, Infobase, 2007.

Chapter 6 : The Battle of Wounded Knee : Medals of Dishonor
Most of the facts used to create this story came from the following sources:

"Battle of Wounded Knee." *Record Union,* February 13, 1891. http://chronicling america.loc.gov/lccn/sn82015104/1891-02-13/ed-1/seq-1.pdf.

Beyer, Walter F., and Oscar F. Keydel. *Deeds of Valor: How America's Heroes Won the Medal of Honor.* Detroit: Perrien-Keydel, 1901.

Carroll, John M. *The Arrest and Killing of Sitting Bull: A Documentary.* Glendale, CA: A. H. Clark, 1986.

Coleman, William. *Voices of Wounded Knee.* University of Nebraska Press, 2000.

"Col. Forsyth Exonerated: His Action at Wounded Knee Justified." *New York Times,* 13 February 1891. http://query.nytimes.com/mem/archive-free/ pdf?_r=2&res=9A03E7DA1F3BE533A25750C1A9649C94609ED7CF& oref=slogin&oref=slogin.

Congressional Medal of Honor Society. "John Lafferty." *CMOHS.org.* http:// www.cmohs.org/recipient-detail/778/lafferty-john.php.

Eastman, Elaine Goodale, and Kay Graber. *Sister to the Sioux: The Memoirs of Elaine Goodale Eastman, 1885–91.* University of Nebraska Press, 1978.

Ewing, Charles B. "The Wounded of the Wounded Knee Battlefield, with Re- marks on Wounds Produced by Small and Large Calibre Bullets." *Boston Medical and Surgical Journal* 126 (1892): 463.

"Fields of Fire: Massacre at Wounded Knee." *Oneofmanyfeathers.com,* January 14, 2013. http://www.oneofmanyfeathers.com/massacre_at_wounded_knee .html.

Green, Jerry. "The Medals of Wounded Knee." *Nebraska History* 75 (1994): 200–8.

Huntzicker, William E. "The Sioux Outbreak in the Illustrated Press." South Dakota State Historical Society. Vol. 20, No. 4, 1990. http://www.sdshs press.com/index.php?id=279&action=950.

"Indian Fighter Quits Army." *New York Times,* January 15, 1911. http://query .nytimes.com/mem/archive-free/pdf?_r=1&res=9A06E3D81731E233A25 756C1A9679C946096D6CF.

"Indian Police." *Encyclopedia of the Great Plains.* http://plainshumanities.unl.edu/ encyclopedia/doc/egp.law.022.

"Indian Wars Campaigns." U.S. Army Center of Military History. http://www .history.army.mil/html/reference/army_flag/iw.html.

Kelley, William Fitch. *Pine Ridge 1890: An Eye Witness Account of the Events Sur- rounding the Fighting at Wounded Knee.* Pierre Bovis, 1971.?

Lindberg, Christer, ed. "Foreigners in Action at Wounded Knee." *Nebraska His- tory* 71 (1990): 170–81.

"Massacre at Wounded Knee, 1890." *Eyewitnesstohistory.com*, 1998. http://www
.eyewitnesstohistory.com/knee.htm.

Mauer, Lauren. "Rank and File: The Rocky History of Compulsory Military
Training at MIT." *MIT Technology Review*, February 21, 2012. http://www
.technologyreview.com/article/426941/rank-and-file/.

McLaughlin, James. "An Account of Sitting Bull's Death." *PBS.org*, 1891. http://
www.pbs.org/weta/thewest/resources/archives/eight/sbarrest.htm.

"Native American Sioux Dance 1894." http://www.youtube.com/watch?v=HQ
GW5a0q51w.

9th Memorial Cavalry. "William Othello Wilson." *9thcavalry.com*, 2013. http://
www.9thcavalry.com/history/wilson.htm.

Ostler, Jeffery. *The Plains Sioux and U.S. Colonialism from Lewis and Clark to
Wounded Knee*. Cambridge University Press, 2004.

Richardson, Heather Cox. *Wounded Knee: Party Politics and the Road to an American
Massacre*. Basic Books, 2010.

*Selfless Service: The Cavalry Career of Brigadier General Samuel M. Whitside from
1858 to 1902*. Thesis presented to the Faculty of the U.S. Army Command
and General Staff College by Samuel L Russell, Maj, USA, B.S., Virginia
Military Institute, 1988, Fort Leavenworth, Kansas, 2002.

Senate Joint Resolution 14, 111th Cong., 1st session. April 30, 2009.

Shackel, Paul A. "Wounded Knee Memorialization." In *Myths, Memory, and
the Making of the American Landscape*. University Press of Florida, 2001,
pp. 112–15.

Spotted Elk, Calvin. "No Medals for Massacre." *Avaaz.org*. www.avaaz.org/en/
petition/No_Medals_for_Massacre_Justice_for_Wounded_ Knee/.

Viola, Herman. *Trail to Wounded Knee: The Last Stand of the Plains Indians*. National Geographic Society, 2003.

"Wounded Knee Massacre: Battle of Wounded Knee: Sioux Campaign of
1890–91: United States Army Reports." http://www.paperlessarchives
.com/wounded-knee-army-reports.html.

*Most of the dialogue in this chapter was imagined, but the following quotations were
taken in whole or in part from the historical record:*

"the assassin of the brave Custer": Huntzicker.

"In the annals of American history, there cannot be found a battle": Huntzicker.

"Troops were not disposed to deliver its fire": *New York Times*.

"The interests of military service do not, in my judgment": *New York Times*.

"Mr. President, what happened at Wounded Knee was not worthy": Letter to
the White House from Calvin Spotted Elk, https://m.facebook.com/note
.php?note_id=10151398571283035&p=10&_rdr.

Most of the scenes in this chapter were developed based on facts from the historical record. However, while Nelson Miles was at the massacre site on January 1, 1891, it was a few days later that the arguments presented in our story were used to convince the Sioux to return to the reservation. In addition, while a Sioux named White Lance was at Wounded Knee and did visit the massacre site on January 1, the rest of the White Lance story is imagined.

Chapter 7 : Easy Eddie & the Hard Road to Redemption
Most of the facts used to create this story came from the following sources:

Cantwell, Robert. "Run, Rabbit, Run." *Sports Illustrated*, August 27, 1973. http://sportsillustrated.cnn.com/vault/article/magazine/MAG1087714/4/index.htm.

Ewing, Steve and John B. Lundstrom. *Fateful Rendezvous: The Life of Butch O'Hare*. Naval Institute Press, 1997.

"Lt. Butch O'Hare: Navy's First Flying Ace." National WWII Museum. February 20, 2012. http://www.nww2m.com/2012/02/lt-butch-ohare/.

Offner, Larry. "The Butch O'Hare Story." *St Louis Magazine*, July 2005. http://www.stlmag.com/St-Louis-Magazine/July-2005/The-Butch-OHare-Story/.

Sherman, Stephen. "Grumman F4F Wildcat: 7860 Planes Produced, Starting in December, 1940." *Acepilots.com*. May 2002. http://acepilots.com/planes/f4f_wildcat.html.

Sherman, Stephen. "Lt. Cdr. Edward "Butch" O'Hare: First U.S. Navy Ace, Medal of Honor Recipient." *Acepilots.com*. June 1999. acepilots.com/usn_ohare.html.

"USS *Lexington* (CV-2)." *Wikipedia*. https://en.wikipedia.org/wiki/USS_Lexington_%28CV-2%29.

There are a few imagined characters and sequences in this chapter that are worth pointing out: Eddie's girlfriend at the speakeasy is not a specific, real-life person. The scene when Eddie first meets Al Capone is fictionalized; we do not know specifically when they met each other for the first time. It's not known specifically when and how the first contact was made between Eddie and the authorities, or when Eddie first made his decision to turn on Capone.

Chapter 8 : The Saboteurs: In a Time of War, the Laws Are Silent
Most facts used to craft this story were taken from a terrific book by Michael Dobbs, Saboteurs: The Nazi Raid on America, *published by Vintage in 2005.*
    Other sources used:

Fisher, Louis. *Nazi Saboteurs on Trial: A Military Tribunal and American Law*. University Press of Kansas, 2005.

Goldsmith, Jack. *The Terror Presidency: Law and Judgment Inside the Bush Administration*. Norton, 2009.

Transcript from *260: The Facts Don't Matter*. Originally aired on March 12, 2004. http://www.thisamericanlife.org/radio-archives/episode/260/transcript.

Williams, Nathan. "What Happened to the 8 Germans Tried by a Military Court in World War II?" George Mason University's History News Network. July 8, 2002. http://hnn.us/articles/431.html.

Most of the dialogue in this chapter was imagined, but the following quotations were taken in whole or in part from the historical record:

"If you fellas are ready to ship out tonight, we will take you. If not, leave now.": Dobbs, 90.

Most of the dialogue between John Cullen and George Dasch during their Long Island encounter was taken from Dobbs, pp. 92–94.

"I have a lot to talk to you about": Dobbs, 115–16.

"I know what you are going to tell me. I am quite sure that our intentions are very similar": Dobbs, 116.

"I want the truth, nothing else—regardless of what it is": Dobbs, 119.

"I never intended to carry out the orders": Dobbs, 122.

"Can you spell that, sir": Dobbs, 125.

"I, Franz Daniel Pastorius": Dobbs, 126.

"a statement of military as well as political value": Dobbs, 140.

"Did New York tell you I was on my way?": Dobbs, 141.

"Got safely into town last night and contacted the responsible parties": Dobbs, 142.

"I have a long story to tell but I want to tell it my own way": Dobbs, 143.

"Is there any way you can get in touch": "This American Life," *WBEZ*, March 4, 2004, http://www.thisamericanlife.org/radio-archives/episode/260/transcript.

"Ammonia! I passed the handkerchief": Dobbs, 166.

"My mind is all upside down": Dobbs, 181.

"apprehended all members of the group which landed on Long Island": Dobbs, 166–67.

"Urinated at 11:40 P.M. Appears a little depressed": Dobbs, 182.

"I have a very important statement to make": Dobbs, 193.

"Before the men could begin carrying out their orders": Dobbs, 194.

"Not enough, Francis. Let's make real money out of them": Dobbs, 195.

"Realism calls for a stone wall and a firing squad": Goldsmith, 51–52.

"Shoot them": Dobbs, 222.

"Americans want to hear": Williams, History News Network.

"The Eight Nazi Spies Should Die": "This American Life."

"six who I take it are German citizens": Dobbs, 195.

"the roar of rifles in the hands of a firing squad": Williams, History News Network.

"Here again it is my inclination": Dobbs, 195.

"I want one thing clearly understood, Francis": Dobbs, 196.

"There go the spies": Dobbs, 209.

"invalid and unconstitutional . . . open in the territory in which we are now located": Dobbs, 211.

"The commission does not sustain": Dobbs, 212.

"Not guilty": Dobbs, 213.

"What should be done with them? Should they be shot or hanged?": Dobbs, 223.

"The United States and the German Reich are now at war": Dobbs, 242–43.

"damned scoundrels . . . low-down, ordinary, enemy spies": Dobbs, 241.

"Yes, sir": Dobbs, 259.

Letter from Herbie Haupt to his Parents: Dobbs, 250.

"Inter Arma Silent Leges": Dobbs, 270.

"I certainly hope the military": Dobbs, 268.

"The opinion was not good literature": Dobbs, 269.

"an obsessive, compulsive, neurotic personality type": Dobbs, 270–71.

Notes on specific scenes and characters:

In the Supreme Court courtroom scene, we quote from a memo that Frankfurter wrote to his colleagues. As currently written, it's clear that Frankfurter is not saying the quote live during the oral argument, but it is ambiguous in our story when Frankfurter actually wrote it. According to the record, he actually wrote it a few months later, as the Court was trying to write the opinion.

Peter Burger actually did send Hoover a Christmas card annually after his release. The scene in December 1971 where Hoover is going through Christmas cards is, however, imagined.

The epilogue tells the story of Yasir Hamdi. We have told the story as if Hamdi and his family were credible sources, although, of course, they had an incentive to whitewash his actions in Afghanistan.

In addition, the Hamdi decision is a complicated and controversial decision, and any interpretation of it is likely to generate disagreement. There is ongoing debate about what the decision means and we used the case merely to prove the point that the saboteurs' decision continues to influence important cases.

Chapter 9 : Who Is Tokyo Rose?

Most of the facts used to create this story came from the following sources:

Close, Frederick P. *Tokyo Rose/An American Patriot: A Dual Biography*. Scarecrow Press, 2009.

Duus, Masayo. *Tokyo Rose: Orphan of the Pacific*. Kodansha America, 1979.

Gunn, Rex B. *They Called Her Tokyo Rose*. Expanded 2nd ed. Brent Bateman, 2008.

Howe, Russell Warren. *The Hunt for "Tokyo Rose."* Madison Books, 1989.

Kawashima, Yasuhide. *The Tokyo Rose Case: Treason on Trial*. University Press of Kansas, 2013.

" 'Tokyo Rose' Vindicated Before Her Death." *Human Events*, September 27, 2006. http://www.humanevents.com/2006/09/27/tokyo-rose-vindicated -before-her-death/.

Most of the dialogue in this chapter was imagined, but the following quotations were taken in whole or in part from the historical record:

"We will show that in one broadcast after the Battle of Leyte Gulf": Gunn, 189.

"The men often tune in on Radio Tokyo to hear the cultured, accentless English": Close, 199.

" 'homesicky' . . . This is an Imperial Order . . . The only women we can trust, Iva": Gunn, 81.

"This is crazy! I can't do this! I'm no good at it": Kawashima, 32.

"Until we've defeated Japan": Howe, 26.

"Who is Tokyo Rose? Tokyo Rose delivers": Close, 199–200.

"Greetings, everybody!": Gunn, 115.

"No one knows for sure who Tokyo Rose really is": Close, 200.

"Want to make a deal?": Kawashima, 38.

"You are Tokyo Rose? . . . I am just one of them": Duus, 21.

"You worked at Radio Tokyo . . . You announced": Duus, 21–22.

"she will do": Duus, 22.

"The one and original Tokyo Rose": Duus, 22.

"TRAITOR'S PAY: TOKYO ROSE GOT 100 YEN A MONTH . . . $6.60 . . . In an exclusive interview with this correspondent": Duus, 25.

"Good evening, Mr. and Mrs. America, and all the ships at sea!": Duus, 111.

"Emperor-lovers and friends of the Zaibatsu": Duus, 117.

"There is insufficient evidence to make out a prima facie case": Gunn, 168.

"The government witnesses, almost to a man": Gunn, 169.

"The government's evidence likewise will show": Gunn, 169.

"Any other Japanese bring you food besides": Gunn, 219.

"Did you do anything whatsoever . . . Never": Duus, 208.

"Has the jury arrived at a verdict? . . . Guilty": Kawashima, 1.

"Throughout an ordeal that has lasted decades, Iva Toguri": "Tokyo Rose Vindicated Before Her Death," *Human Events*, September 26, 2006, http://www .humanevents.com/2006/09/27/tokyo-rose-vindicated-before-her-death/.

"I'm proud of you, girl. You didn't change your stripes": Duus, 130.

Notes on specific scenes and characters:

Some details in the July 4, 1946, scene are imagined, including the exact date. What's known is that around that time a group of peeping-tom congressmen watched her get out of the shower in prison.

One year before Iva Toguri's trial, Thomas DeWolfe wrote a memo in which he said that the charges against her should not be brought and could not be proven. However, we do not know for certain that he believed her to be innocent at the time of the trial.

The description of the government's case against Iva is told from Iva's point of view. Undoubtedly, if told from the government's point of view, the case against her would appear stronger. In addition, we say that Harry Brundidge suborned perjury from Mitsushio and Oki. Brundidge did actually go to Japan and suborn perjury from some potential witnesses, but we don't know whether Mitsushio's and Oki's perjury was directly suborned by Brundidge or by someone else.

Chapter 10 : The Battle of Athens: Repeated Petitions, Repeated Injuries

Most of the facts used to create this story came from the following sources:

"The Battle of Athens: 2 August 1946." http://www.constitution.org/mil/tn/batathen.htm.

"The Battle of Athens, Tennessee." *Guns and Ammo* (October 1995): 50–51. http://jpfo.org/filegen-a-m/athens.htm.

Byrum, C. Stephen. *The Battle of Athens, Tennessee.* Tapestry Press, 1996.

Gibson, Kelly. "Ex-GIs Battle for the Ballot." *VFW Magazine*, August 2012.

Martin, Ralph G. *The GI War, 1941–1945.* Little, Brown, 1967.

Pierce, Charles P. "The Battle of Athens Revisited." *Esquire*, December 18, 2012. http://www.esquire.com/blogs/politics/larry-pratt-gun-owners-action-league-on-battle-of-athens-121812.

Seiber, Lones. "The Battle of Athens." *American Heritage*, February/March 1985.

"Tennessee: Battle of the Ballots." *Time*, August 12, 1946.

University of Tennessee Knoxville, An Interview with Bill White for the Veteran's Oral History Project, 2000. Note: Bill White's oral history was given fifty-four years after the events and some of his recollections are inconsistent with the recollections of others who were present. For these reasons, we do not consider White's oral history to be entirely reliable, and we consequently were not bound by it.

White, Theodore H. "The Battle of Athens, Tennessee." *Harper's Monthly* (January 1947): 54–60.

Most of the dialogue in this chapter was imagined, but the following quotations were taken in whole or in part from the historical record:

"My God, there ain't none of them gonna get in here": Bill White Oral History, 12.

"Jesus is Coming Soon!" and "Prepare to Meet God!": White, "The Battle of Athens, Tennessee."

"Got some big huntin' to do—some *big* huntin'": Byrum, 121.

"You can't vote . . . You can't vote here today!": Byrum, 129.

"bravest of the brave . . . best of the best": Bill White Oral History, 39.

"That government, being instituted for the common benefit": Martin, 490.

"We're going to have to get some charges up there on the building": Bill White Oral History, 22.

Notes on specific scenes and characters:

The August 3, 1936, scene is imagined, as are many of the details. We don't know much about what Bill White's parents did for a living, but we do know that Bill grew up relatively poor (the part about not having a lot of shoes is from his oral history). We also know he liked westerns, though we don't know specifically whether he listened to the Lone Ranger.

The December 8, 1941, scene is imagined, though it is based on known facts about the characters present, such as Windy Wise.

The November 16, 1945, scene is imagined but was inspired by the fact that many GIs were beaten up, arrested, and fined. The record is not clear about specific names.

The March 24, 1946, scene is imagined, though it was inspired by the fact that there was a secret meeting before this date that Bill White was not at.

The July 3, 1946, scene is imagined. There were threatening phone calls made, but it's unclear whether Bill White received one.

Much of the July 4, 1946, scene is imagined. There was a rally that day, but we don't know whether or not Bill White spoke at it. White's speech does, however, use some of the epithets that were used by others throughout the campaign to criticize Cantrell's machine, like "Gestapo thugs."

In the July 25, 1946, scene, the wording of the letter is imagined. The record merely says there was a letter requesting FBI observers be present on election day.

The conversation in the August 1, 8:20 A.M. scene between Bill White and the delivery man is imagined, though the record is clear that the delivery man had been making a lot of deliveries in recent days as people in the county stocked up on ammo. White's actions in this scene are also imagined.

In the August 1, 3:00 P.M., scene, several reports say that Wise actually used the n-word (we have him saying "Boy.")

The dialogue in the August 1, 7:00 P.M., scene is imagined. Some of it was said by White earlier in the day, and the scene imagines him saying it again to the crowd here. It is not clear that White was at this specific gathering.

Many of the details in the August 1, 9:00 P.M., scene are imagined or composited based on several differing accounts.

The August 2, 1:15 A.M., scene, in which Wise and Cantrell debate whether help from the governor is coming, is imagined.

Many of the details and the dialogue in the 2:45 A.M. scene are imagined. There are contradictory versions of exactly what happened with the dynamite.

The August 2, 5:45 A.M., scene is imagined, though the major facts relayed in it are true.

As a general matter, the record of these events in Athens is fairly sparse. The few accounts that do exist often contradict other accounts. The result is that we took some license when telling this story—so long as that license did not contradict a fact we knew to be true.

Chapter 11: The My Lai Massacre: A Light in the Darkness
Most of the facts used to create this story came from the following sources:

"Biography: Selected Men Involved with My Lai." *PBS.org*. http://www.pbs.org/wgbh/americanexperience/features/biography/mylai-biographies/.

Bock, Paula. "The Choices Made: Lessons from My Lai on Drawing the Line." *Pacific Northwest*, 2002. http://seattletimes.com/pacificnw/2002/0310/cover.html.

Mackey, Robert. "An Apology for My Lai, Four Decades Later." *New York Times*, August 24, 2009. http://thelede.blogs.nytimes.com/2009/08/24/an-apology-for-my-lai-four-decades-later/?_r=0.

"Nov 12, 1969: Seymour Hersh Breaks My Lai Story." *History.com*. http://www.history.com/this-day-in-history/seymour-hersh-breaks-my-lai-story.

"Timeline: Charlie Company and the Massacre at My Lai." *PBS.org*. http://www.pbs.org/wgbh/americanexperience/features/timeline/mylai-massacre/.

"Transcript: Complete Program Transcript: *My Lai*." *Pbs.org*. http://www.pbs.org/wgbh/americanexperience/features/transcript/mylai-transcript/.

Vietnam Magazine. "Interview—Larry Colburn: Why My Lai, Hugh Thompson Matter." *Historynet.com*. February 7, 2011. http://www.historynet.com/interview-larry-colburn-why-my-lai-hugh-thompson-matter.htm.

Note: Several key elements of this chapter were imagined in order to tell the My Lai story properly. Tuttle-Woods convalescent home, Morgan Campbell (the old man recounting the events at My Lai), Everly Davison (the security guard), and Julia Geller (the reporter who interviews Campbell about the massacre), are all fictional or composited based on real places or people.

Chapter 12 : The Missing 9/11 Terrorist : The Power of Everyday Heroes

Most of the facts used to create this story came from the following sources:

Glick, Lyz, and Dan Zegart. *Your Father's Voice*: Reprint ed. St. Martin's Griffin, 2005.

Interrogation Log, Detainee 063, *Time*, March 3, 2006.

Longman, Jere. *Among the Heroes: United Flight 93 and the Passengers and Crew Who Fought Back*: HarperCollins E-Books, January 2010.

Melendez-Perez, Jose. Testimony before National Commission of Terrorist Attacks Upon the People of the United States, January 26, 2004. http://govinfo.library.unt.edu/911/hearings/hearing7/witness_melendez.htm.

"Mohammed al Qahtani." *Wikipedia*. http://en.wikipedia.org/wiki/Mohammed_al-Qahtani.

Pauley, Jane. "Lyz Glick's Courage." NBC News, August 20, 2002.

Rumsfeld, Donald. *Known and Unknown: A Memoir*. Sentinel, 2011.

Smerconish, Michael. *Instinct: The Man Who Stopped the 20th Hijacker*: Lyons Press, 2009.

"Ziad Jarrah." *Wikipedia*. http://en.wikipedia.org/wiki/Ziad_Jarrah.

Notes on specific scenes and characters:

The conversation that Melendez-Perez has with Qahtani is taken from Melendez-Perez's testimony: http://govinfo.library.unt.edu/911/hearings/hearing7/witness_melendez.htm.

The May 11, 2001, scene is imagined. While we know that Qahtani visited the Taliban front lines north of Kabul, we do not know if he was ever in the Panjshir Valley or if Northern Alliance soldiers chased him.

Ziad Jarrah is not known to have been at Orlando International Airport but Mohammed Atta and "another accomplice" were there. Jarrah was living in Fort Lauderdale at the time and was a known associate of Atta and was the leader of the cell Qahtani was assigned to.

The conversations between Khalid Sheik Mohammed and Qahtani are known to have occurred, but we obviously don't know precisely what was said.

Sergeant Romeo and Lisa Smith are fictional characters. While Qahtani was interrogated at Guantanamo Bay, we do not know who his interrogators were. During these interrogations, Qahtani did provide Kuwaiti's name (the courier).

The scene with CIA agent Ron intercepting Kuwaiti's phone call is real, but the record on it is classified so everything has been sterilized, including names.

Our Fading History

I am growing increasingly fearful that our history is being lost to time.

It's actually kind of ironic that in this age of Google and the Internet and hard drives capable of holding a century's worth of information we are still losing sight of our past—but it's happening.

And it's getting worse.

As time goes by and new generations come through our public schools, history will continue to fade. It just doesn't seem to be a priority anymore. Most schools teach kids only to memorize dates and places and names. *In 1492 Columbus sailed the ocean blue.* We no longer take the time to understand the *why or how* of anything because of the exaggerated importance placed on the *where and when*.

That is one reason why I chose to write this book in a narrative style. I want people to read these stories and feel as if they were there beside the characters. I don't want people to just read about Tokyo Rose in a textbook, I want them to understand who she really was and why she made the decisions she did. Only once you have that context can you judge whether history has treated her properly.

The same goes for most of the other people found in the stories in this book. Even if you've heard of the Battle of Wounded Knee, for example, you may not have really understood the roles that people like General Miles and Colonel Whitside played. And what about Thomas Edison? Are all sides of his complex life talked about or do most people only know him as a gentle genius inventor?

Americans weren't always so ill educated. We used to know our past. We used to understand the Constitution and unapologetically teach our children that it was the greatest and most enlightened system of government ever created.

In 1828, Arthur J. Stansbury, a Presbyterian minister from New York, wrote the "Elementary Catechism on the Constitution of the United States." This work consists of 322 questions and answers on the Constitution and the

functioning of our federal government. It was written with the explicit intention of being a concise and simple guide for use in public schools.

I found this catechism so fascinating and eye-opening that I wanted to in-
clude a small excerpt of it here. I think it's a sad statement on our priorities as a
nation that the answers found in it demonstrate a far greater understanding of
the Constitution and history than the vast majority of adult Americans have—
let alone our children.

Preface

That a people living under a free government which they have themselves orig-
inated should be well acquainted with the instrument which contains it, needs
not to be proved. Were the system, indeed, very cumbrous and extensive, running into minute detail, and hard to be retained in the memory, even this would
be no good reason why pains should not be taken to understand and to imprint
it upon the mind but when its principles are simple, its features plain and obvious, and its brevity surpassing all example, it is certainly a most reprehensible
negligence to remain in ignorance of it.—Yet how small a portion of the citizens of this Republic have even a tolerable acquaintance with their own Constitution? It has appeared to the author of the following sheets that this culpable
want of acquaintance with what is of such deep interest to us all, is to be traced
to the omission of an important part of what ought to be an American education, viz. the study of the civil institutions of our country.—We prize them, it is
true, and are quite enough in the habit of boasting about them: would it not be
well to teach their elements to those whose best inheritance they are?

The following work has been prepared with a view to such an experiment. It
is written expressly for the use of boys, and it has been the aim and effort of the
writer to bring down the subject completely to a level with their capacity to understand it. Whether he has succeeded the trial must show. He has purposely
avoided all abstruse questions, and has confined himself to a simple, common-
sense explanation of each article.

[...]

Q31. What was the change produced by the Revolution?

A. The different Colonies became each a free STATE, having power to govern
itself in any way it should think proper.

Q32. Had not one state any power over the other?

A. None at all—and the several states might have remained entirely distinct
countries, as much as France and Spain.

Q33. Did they?

A. No. Having been led to unite together to help each other in the war,
they soon began to find that it would be much better for each of them that
they should all continue united in its farther prosecution, and accordingly

they entered into an agreement (which was called a *Confederation*) in which they made some laws which they all agreed to obey; but after their independence was obtained, finding the defects of this plan, they called a Convention in which they laid a complete plan for uniting all the states under one GENERAL GOVERNMENT—this plan is called THE FEDERAL CONSTITUTION. On this great plan, or Constitution the safety and happiness of the United States does, under Almighty God, mainly depend: all our laws are made by its direction or authority; whoever goes contrary to it injures and betrays his country, injures you, injures me, betrays us all, and is deserving of the heaviest punishment. Whoever, on the contrary, loves and keeps it sacred, is his country's friend, secures his own safety, and farthers the happiness of all around him. Let every American learn, from his earliest years, to love, cherish and obey the Constitution. Without this he can neither be a great or a good citizen; without this his name will never be engraved with honor in the pages of our history, nor transmitted, like that of Washington, with praises and blessings to a late posterity.

[...]

Q99. Is not this a better way of making the laws of a Country, than either of those we first considered?

A. It is hard to conceive how greater care could be taken that no wicked, unjust, oppressive, hasty, or unwise Law should pass. There is full time to consider whatever is proposed; such fair opportunity to oppose it, if wrong, and improve it, if imperfect; so many persons, and from so wide a space of country must agree in approving it, that it is scarcely possible any thing very injurious can be enacted; or, at least, if it is, that a different form of Government would have prevented it.

Q100. Are there not some evils which attend this mode?

A. Nothing of human contrivance is wholly free from some defect or other; and, in time of war, when the public danger is great, and it is needful that Government should act, not only wisely, but rapidly; some disadvantage may be found to arise from so deliberate a method of passing every Law. But it is far better to put up with this, than to lose the precious blessing of so free and safe a mode of Legislation.

Q101. You have said that no Laws can be made for the United States, but by Congress; may Congress make any Laws they please?

A. No. Their power is limited by the Constitution; that is, they have no power, but what the Constitution says they have. It must always be remembered, that the States, when they united to form the General Government, had full power to govern themselves; and that they gave up only a *part of their power*, for the general welfare. Whatever power, therefore, is not given by the Constitution, to the General Government, still belongs either to the State Governments, or to the people of the United States.

[...]

Q150. Suppose any American citizen is seized and put in prison, may he be kept there as long as those who seized him think fit?

A. No; he may get a *writ of Habeus Corpus*.

Q151. What is that?

A. It is a command from Court, by which the jailor is forced to allow the prisoner to be brought up before a Judge, that the cause of his being put in prison may be examined into; in order, that if there is no law to keep him there, he may immediately be set at liberty.

Q152. Must this command be given whenever it is applied for?

A. Yes, except at certain times, when this privilege is *suspended*; (that is, interrupted for a time, but not taken away).

Q153. When may this right of having a writ of Habeus Corpus, which belongs by the Constitution to every citizen, be suspended?

A. Only in cases of rebellion by our own citizens, or invasion of the country by an enemy; when the public danger is so great as to require persons to be kept in prison, who might otherwise be set at liberty. As soon as this extreme danger is past, the right of *Habeus Corpus* must be immediately restored.

Q154. Is this a very great and important privilege, and ought all Americans to guard it with the greatest care?

A. It is one of the greatest rights of a freeman—and Americans must never surrender it, under any pretext, if they value and would preserve their liberty.

Q155. May a man's children be punished by law for his offence?

A. In some countries, where a man has been guilty of treason, (that is making war against the Government) a law is passed called a *bill of attainder*, by which his children are prevented from being heirs to him or to any other person; and, if he belonged to what in those countries is called the nobility, and his children would have belonged to it too, they are prevented; nor can they nor their children, nor their children's children, recover this privilege, till an act is passed for that purpose. No such law can be made in this country; it is expressly forbidden by the Constitution.

[...]

Q181. Who *executes* the laws which Congress have made, that is, who takes care that every body shall obey the laws?

A. The President of the United States.

Q182. Can he make the law?

A. Not at all. These two powers, of *making* law, and *executing* law, are kept by the Constitution, entirely separate; the power that makes the law cannot execute it, and the power that executes the law cannot make it. (The one of these powers is called the *Legislative*, and the other is called the *Executive* power.)

Q183. Is there any advantage in this?

A. Certainly; it is the great safeguard of freedom; because, if the one makes *oppressive laws*, the other may refuse to execute them; or, if the one wishes to do *tyrannical acts*, the other may refuse to make a law for them.

[...]

Q210. Does the President take any oath before he enters upon his office?

A. Yes.

Q211. What is an oath?

A. It is a solemn calling upon God, who knows the hearts of all men, and will call every man to account for his conduct in this world, to bear witness that what a man says is true, or that what he promises he means to perform.

Q212. What is the President's oath of office?

A. It is in these words—"I do solemnly swear, that I will faithfully execute the office of President of the United States; and will, to the best of my ability, preserve, protect, and defend the Constitution of the United States."

[...]

Q231. Does he know what is the state of the nation better than the Members of Congress?

A. Yes; his office is such that he has a better opportunity of knowing it. Each Member of Congress resides only in one State, but the President resides at a spot in the middle of them all. It is the duty of all officers below him, to send reports of the various affairs in which they are employed, to one or other of the Heads of Departments, and these lay all the knowledge they thus obtain, before the President for his direction and assistance in the many and great duties he has to perform. He is, therefore, of all persons, best acquainted with the general concerns of this nation.

Q232. When does he lay this information before Congress.

A. He makes a very full statement of it when they first meet, in what is usually called the *President's Speech*; and from time to time, while the two Houses are met, he sends to each of them *messages*, in which he gives more particular statements than he could do in his first general speech.

Q233. Suppose Congress wish to know from the President something which he has not told them in his speech or messages, may they call upon him to communicate it?

A. Yes, and if he does not think that the public good requires it to be kept secret, he always answers the call, and gives them the knowledge they desired, if he can do so.

Q234. Does he do more than communicate information to the Congress?

A. Yes; his duty is also to recommend to them such things as he thinks will be for the advantage of the country.

Q235. Are they obliged to do as he advises?

A. No. They pay respectful attention to what he says to them, and listen to the reasons he gives in favor of the measures he recommends, but they are at full liberty to follow their own judgments in all cases.

Q236. Is it to be desired that Congress should always comply with the advice of the President?

A. No; for then his advice would, in time, come to have the authority of a command; it would be the President and not Congress who made the laws; and the liberty of the country would be in the greatest danger. There is no more dangerous despot than one who can make his will obeyed, and yet preserve the forms of a free government. August Caesar ruled the whole Roman Empire with absolute sway, yet did every thing by resolves of the Senate, as if Rome was free.

[...]

Q245. What do you understand by a Court?

A. A place where a Judge sits to hear and determine causes according to law.

Q246. Are Courts necessary?

A. Certainly. Wherever laws are made there must be some way of determining when they have been disobeyed, and of causing those who disobey them to be punished. This is the use of a Court and of a Judge. When one person believes that another has broken the laws, to his injury, or to the injury of the public, he may cause that person to appear before a Judge and have it determined by witnesses, whether he has broken the laws or not; and if he has, he is forced to suffer such a punishment as the law directs.

[...]

Q264. How are the Judges of the Courts of the United States appointed?

A. By the President, with the advice and consent of the Senate.

Q265. How long do they remain in office?

A. During good behavior; that is, until they resign their office or are turned out of it for some great offence.

Q266. Why are not Judges elected from time to time, like Members of the House of Representatives and Senators? and why may they not be removed from their offices unless they are proved to be guilty of great offences?

A. If Judges held their places at the mere good pleasure of the people, they would be greatly tempted to act in a partial and improper manner in order to please those who chose them to office, and to keep their favor; but when they know that no man or number of men can turn them out of office so long as they do their duty, they administer justice without fear and with an equal regard to all who ask it.

Q267. **Why then should not Legislators hold their office in the same way?**

A. Because they make the laws, while Judges only explain and apply them; it would be very dangerous to liberty to give our law *makers* power for life; they require restraint lest they should become our tyrants;—therefore their time of office is made short, so that if the people thought them unwise or unfaithful they may refuse to give them the office again.

Q268. **You said that the use of Courts was to determine when the laws have been disobeyed, and causing those who have disobeyed them to be punished. How do Courts answer this end?**

A. When a person is charged with having done something to his neighbor, or to the State, which is forbidden by law, the fact is judged of by a *Jury.*

Q269. **What do you mean by a Jury?**

A. A company of citizens, chosen by lot, and who have no interest in the matter, who listen to the proofs brought against the person accused, and who then agree among themselves whether the accusation has been proved or not. When they declare this agreement in opinion, it is called their *verdict*; and according to this, the cause is decided.

Q270. **Is this a wise regulation?**

A. Certainly. The trial by jury, is a most precious privilege—as it secures to every man a fair hearing, and is the best safe-guard of his liberty, property, and life; all which might be taken from him by a partial or corrupt Judge, if that officer alone had to decide on the guilt or innocence of those who are tried before him.

[...]

Q296. **The majority of the people of any State may certainly alter its laws, provided they do not violate the Constitution: but may the Constitution itself be altered?**

A. Yes. The Constitution being nothing more than an expression of the will of the people of the United States, is at all times within their own power, and they may change it as they like, but it ought not to be changed till it is very clearly shown to be the wish of the people.

Q297. **How is this to be found out?**

A. When two thirds of the members both of the Senate and the House of Representatives shall agree in opinion that an alteration would be proper, they may state such alteration and propose it to be considered by the people of all the States. The alteration must then be considered by the Legislature of each of the States, or by a Convention in each State, (which is a meeting of persons chosen by the people for this particular purpose); and if three fourths of the States agree to the amendment, it then becomes a part of the Constitution.

Q298. **But if three fourths of the States should thus agree to an amendment which would deprive the remaining States against their will of their equal vote in the Senate, would such amendment be binding?**

A. No. This case is provided against in the Constitution, and one other (in relation to slaves) which could only happen previous to the year 1808; but as that year is now past, no farther notice need be taken of it.

Q299. **What is the supreme law of the United States?**

A. The Constitution itself is supreme; and all laws and treaties made by Congress and the President, in conformity with it, are superior to any law made by one of the States, so that if the law of a State contradicts a law of Congress, the State law is no force, and the United States law alone must be obeyed.

Q300. **What security have we that the Constitution will be observed?**

A. The President, the Members of Congress, the Members of all the State Legislatures, and all public officers of the United States, and of each one of the States, takes an oath, when they enter upon their several offices, to obey the Constitution. But the great security for its observance lies in the wisdom and excellence of the Constitution itself, and the conviction of the whole people of the United States, that it is for their true interest to observe it inviolate. It has been tried for fifty years, and has done more to render this nation peaceable, powerful and happy than any form of government that ever existed among men.

Q301. **You said that the Constitution, however wise or good, might nevertheless be amended if the people of the United States choose?**

A. Yes; the Constitution says so expressly.

Q302. **Has it ever been amended?**

A. Yes, several times.

Q303. **What was the subject of the first amendment?**

A. The subject of religious freedom.

Q304. **What do you mean by that?**

A. I mean the right every man has to worship God in such way as he thinks fit, without being called to account for his opinions, or punished for them.

Q305. **Is this a sacred right, which ought to be guarded with the greatest care?**

A. Certainly. God alone is the Judge of our religious belief and service, and no man has a right to interfere with it, so long as it does not lead us to injure or disturb our neighbor. A great part of the misery and oppression which has existed in the world, began with forcing men to do what their conscience disapproved.

Q306. **What amendment was made in the Constitution on this subject?**

A. Congress was forbidden to make any law respecting an *establishment* of religion; that is, giving the preference to any one form of religion above another, and making laws to support it; or making laws to prevent men from freely holding or observing any particular form of religious belief and practice.

Q307. Was any other subject introduced into the same amendment?

A. Yes; the freedom of speech and the freedom of the press.

Q308. What do you understand by these expressions?

A. In a free country like ours, every citizen has a right to express his opinion of the character and conduct of our rulers, and of the laws they make for our government; to forbid this, or punish it, would be highly dangerous to our liberty. If those chosen by their fellow citizens to rule the State, rule in a foolish or wicked manner, it ought to be known, that they may be speedily turned out of office; but if nobody might find fault with them without danger of punishment, their bad conduct would never be exposed, and they might continue in power to the great injury of us all. The right to *speak* our opinions is the freedom of speech; and the right to *print* them, that they may be read by others, is the freedom of the press.

[...]

Q330. Because the Constitution only speaks of certain rights belonging to citizens of the United States, does it follow that the citizens have no rights but these?

A. By no means.

Q331. Has the United States Government any power but such as is contained in the Constitution?

A. No.

Q332. Have the different States of the Union all the powers which rightfully belong to a State, except those which are denied to them by the Constitution?

A. Yes. When the States united to form a constitution for their General Government, they agreed to give up to that government some of the powers they had before, and they set down in the Constitution what these powers were. All other powers they keep. The same thing is true respecting the people. All the powers they have not given up to the State Governments or to the General Government, they keep in their own hands.

Conclusion

In the first place, consider how happy and how highly favored is our country, in having a system of government so wisely calculated to secure the life, liberty, and happiness of all its citizens. Had you lived or travelled in other parts of the world, you would be much more sensible of this, than you can possibly be without such an opportunity of comparing our lot with that of others. But, as your reading increases, particularly in history and in travels, you will be able to form a more just estimate of what you enjoy. When you read of the oppression which has been, and still is exercised, I do not say in Africa and Asia, whose inhabitants are but partially civilized—but even in the most enlightened countries of Europe; under absolute monarchs, a proud and haughty nobility—a worldly, selfish, and ambitious priesthood—a vast and rapacious standing army, and a host of greedy officers of government; and then turn your eyes on your own happy home, a land where none of these evils has any place—where the people first make the laws and then obey them—where they can be oppressed by none, but where every man's person, property, and privileges are surrounded by the law, and sacred from every thing but justice and the public good; how can you be sufficiently grateful to a beneficent Providence, which has thus endowed our country with blessings equally rich and rare?

In the next place, remember that this precious Constitution, thus wise, thus just, is your birth-right. It has been earned for you by your fathers, who counselled much, labored long, and shed their dearest blood, to win it for their children. To them, it was the fruit of toil and danger—to you, it is a gift. Do not slight it on that account, but prize it as you ought. It is yours, no human power can deprive you of it, but your own folly and wickedness. To undervalue, is one of the surest ways to lose it. Take pains to know what the Constitution is—the more you study, the higher you will esteem it. The better you understand your own rights, the more likely you will be to preserve and guard them.

And, in the last place, my beloved young countrymen, your country's hope, her treasure, and one day to be her pride and her defence; remember that a constitution which gives to the people so much freedom, and entrusts them with so much power, rests for its permanency, on their knowledge and virtue. An ignorant people are easily betrayed, and a wicked people can never be ruled by the mild influence of their own laws. If you would be free—if you would see your country grow in all that constitutes true greatness—cultivate knowledge—flee from vice. The virtuous citizen is the true noble. He who enlightens his understanding—controls his passions—feels for his country's honor—rejoices in her prosperity—steps forth to aid her in the hour of danger—devotes to her advancement the fruits of his mind, and consecrates to her cause, his time, his property, and his noblest powers, such a man is one of God's nobility; he needs neither riband, nor star; his country knows and remembers his name; nor could any title add to its honor, or to his reward. We have seen such men among us; we hope to see many more. And though the glory of giving to their country such a Constitution as this, is what none but they have been so blessed as to enjoy, yet you succeed to a task, but one degree removed from it, that of preserving what they have committed to your virtue, unsullied and unimpaired.